TALES
THE BOOTH

AN AURAL ANTHOLOGY OF DJ
AND DANCEFLOOR CULTURE

THE THIRD BOOK THAT'S NOT IN THE TRILOGY
OF TALES FROM THE SECRET DJ

VELOCITY
PRESS

First published by Velocity Press 2022

velocitypress.uk

Copyright © The Secret DJ, 2022

Printed and bound in Great Britain by Clays Ltd, Elcograf S.p.A.

Editor
Duncan Dick

Contributing editors
Manu Ekanayake, Dave Jenkins, Tracy Kawalik, Joe Roberts, Nicolas
Stecher, Duncan Dick and the Secret DJ.

Cover illustration
El Zeorge

Cover design
Hayden Russell

Typesetting
Paul Baillie-Lane
pblpublishing.co.uk

ISBN: 9781913231132

CONTENTS

INTRODUCTION
THE SECRET DJ

I didn't write this finely-crafted opus you currently hold in your hands. Not entirely. In fact, this is a book of stories from many DJs, of all stripes and persuasions, from all over the world. The voices here are truly diverse. Large and small, short or wide, every creed, angle and colour of the rainbow is within. The Secret DJ project has always been about pulling a veil over things. The live shows have us performing behind a screen, so no one knows who is playing. Freedom from musical expectation, with skill and taste highlighted over blunt celebrity. So we took that theory and applied it to this book. The Secret DJ is not a person; it's always been an idea. Since the start, we've been trying to surgically remove the ego from dance music. We use anonymity as the instrument. It is a 'we'. Yes, I 'am' the Secret DJ writing this intro, but there is a team of three of us behind it and even more involved in this particular book. I don't do anything without them unilaterally. OK, sometimes I do. But I get very much told off for it.

In fact, this book is one of the most collective efforts we've done so far. It was started during the great lockdown of 2020, when COVID hit hard across the music industry, not just hammering DJs and performers but also some massively talented fellow music journalists who found themselves with few opportunities to do what they do best. We rounded up some of them to join our quest. Hats aloft to Tracy, Joe, Manu, Nicolas, Dave and Duncan! Each with a very different contact book and a different insight into this global scene. Off they went, like literary Indiana Joneses, searching all over the planet to interview what ended up as nearly 80 DJs, producers and industry staff.

Some of these tales are pure gold. Some are a little obscure and strange. Some are funny. Others are deadly serious. It's not down to me this time: once again, these are real stories by real DJs. If some jar and there is no narrative to join them together, then that is the nature of an anthology. Reality is not always well-packaged and smooth-flowing. In my previous books, I had the luxury of being able to jiggle around the chronology of my own adventures. We don't get to do that here. Here's an advisory note for anyone expecting 'Book 3' of the Secret DJ's memoirs: sorry, not this time. I have contributed a few, but this is a different beast. You could perhaps subtitle it '*not* the third book in a trilogy'.

However, as well as reflecting the ideas behind our live shows, this book is arranged a little like a mix. I sometimes plan DJ mixes using a loose interpretation of 'The Hero's Journey' by Joseph Campbell with a clear beginning, middle and end with the odd twist thrown in. A mix is a musical journey of sorts, after all. Being presented with a wildly eclectic catalogue of different styles and stories, I thought: why not return that literary theory I borrowed for music and bring it full circle and implement it in a book, through the prism of a mix? I treated each story like a tune. So here we attempt to start strong, follow up purposefully over a three-act structure and come to a rousing finale. There's also a loose historical journey through club culture in the book, a chronology from the early rave days to contemporary times.

Ever since the first book, other DJs have been saying how they wished they had the freedom to tell their truth behind a veil of secrecy. 'Tales From The Booth' is our response. We got lots of great stories, but many of them had to be cut; for legal reasons, for space, or simply because we were unable to fit them in a way that made sense. Tragically, some people felt afraid of reprisals and decided to back out. I apologise personally and effusively if your contribution did not make the cut and thank you sincerely. It really isn't personal. I don't even know who many of the stories are from. Really. I can make a jolly good guess for one or two! But it is truly an anonymous project. Conversely, it's fine if you contributed and want to tell everyone! We cannot thank you enough. That call is yours; we will never reveal who's behind what. In many cases, we also had to take identifying details out, like names and places. The gratitude for your efforts is sincere and this extends particularly to the journalists who facilitated anonymity and even translations for some contributors.

I see this book more as a document or an archive than a narrative story. A snapshot of the biggest global youth movement in history. A verbal record of music and musicians. An account of certain times and places. These voices stretch across 40 years and further into time. Some arrived in this industry almost yesterday. Some long ago. All are united in being participants, observers, commentators and players in the game. Truly a spectrum. Broad not just in age and diversity but geographically too. Here we have tales from Japan, Britain, America, Uganda, Portugal, Spain, Singapore, Russia, Hong Kong, Seoul, Paris and indeed anywhere loud repetitive music is played in darkened rooms or bright fields.

Try to remember there are all sorts of DJs. All of them are allowed to speak. Some do weddings and corporate. Some are international megastars, some never leave their hometown. Some are super cool. Some are not. All are entirely relative positions. Naturally, we have continued to address the things that very much need talking about. If ever there was a clear example of the continuing discrimination in the industry, it is in the fact that so many of the stories we got from women and 'minority' DJs were about how terribly they have been treated, while the majority of the stories from straight white men were about what a jolly wheeze everything is. Very telling right there. It has been an honour and privilege to give everyone a safe forum to speak, and we salute especially those DJs who told stories that must have been painful to recall.

In contrast, we literally could have done a whole book on DJs shitting themselves. Seriously, we got sent about 20. There's something there that Freud would have a field day with. Look out for 'Tales From the Porcelain Bus' coming 2023 on Velocity Press. So let's not close our eyes to DJing's seamy or ridiculous side, but balance it along with the fact that since the Acid House days, this industry has given opportunities to people from all different backgrounds to express themselves, and sometimes even make a living. And we are *definitely* here for all those moments of pure joy behind the decks that make it all worthwhile.

Finally… Yes, this business does have a drug problem. Dur. Obviously, that's reflected in a lot of these tales. We're hoping that they won't glorify it but might actually help people, DJs or not, to reconnect with what's important in life.

Anyone can be a Secret DJ. That was always the point of this thing. Welcome.

EDITOR'S NOTE

Many, many thanks to all the DJs from around the world who contributed to this book with nothing 'in it' for them personally but the chance to tell some tall tales (and in some cases, harsh truths) while we waited for the music to start again.

DD

BILLY IDLE

I've always wanted to confess why I chose DJing. It's got nothing to do with fame or fortune, and honestly, if we're 'fessing up, not a lot to do with music either. I mean, listen, don't get me wrong. I'm *totally* in love with it. Married to music. I have been since I was a kid. But even at an early age, when I was learning music at school, it was what we called 'a doss'. A dodge. I always found it easy; I came from a very musical home. Doesn't everything begin and end there? The fulcrum moment was when I got a special pass at school for 'early dinners', as most of my music lessons were during the lunch break. Music was 'extra' at my school, sadly and as far as I can see, it's not gotten any better or more respected in the education system since. In fact, I was the only pupil for some of the peripatetic teachers that came in to teach an instrument.

School lunch worked on a simple principle; it wasn't bad as long as you got there first. It was like Mad Max when the bell rang for lunch. Bedlam. Over a thousand kids all launching themselves at the entrance to the canteen, forming a massive queue that had its own politics about 'saving places', pushing-in, trading spots and generally vying for supremacy. It was heavily policed too, with a teacher every couple of yards along this huge snake of tattered blazers, pencil ties and crackers hair. Basically, there was some choice on what was on offer at the front half of it, and naturally, anything edible went fast. The further towards the back you got, the fewer choices there were. Around the rear third of it, you could pretty much bet your lunch would be properly horrible, congealed muck-in-a-tin. If anything stopped you from getting in with the first wave, you often didn't even bother and went to the shop for crisps, if indeed you could afford any.

My music lessons meant that I got lunch first, along with a handful of others who had a pass for other reasons. In fact, we got to go in, choose and eat before they even let anyone else into the hall. 'Early lunch' was everything. Nirvana. A sign of the blessed. There were kids in my school who *only* ate at school. We weren't just poor; we were in the middle of the legendary miners' strike. Local dads lost their entire income, and some of the kids used to man the picket lines with their dad and only came to school for an hour to eat. The school sort of went along with it, but it was never mentioned... anyway! Sorry. Losing my place. For me, music was a very large escape. An escape from 'the system', reality and concern, as well as being 'rewarded' by early lunch. Thing is, I had a flair for it. It was a doddle. Which also meant I totally coasted. All the teachers would always say in reports that if I just tried a bit instead of messing around, I'd be really good at things. I never tried. I was a born underachiever. Still am, maybe. This was to set the pattern for the rest of my life.

It feels good to confess. I've never said this to a living soul, but I became a DJ because I am bone idle. Truly a very, *very* lazy person. I hate the rat race. I loathe 'normality' or whatever that is. I have for as long as I can remember. I see imported American TV and films showing people who never sleep and stab each other in the back and charge around carrying coffee and talking fast and witty and utterly bereft of morals, and I just look at it like they are fish in a tank. It's beyond me why anyone would want to be that way. In what universe is any of that attractive?

The closest I ever came to that nonsense was when I'd do a paper round at stupid o'clock before school, and I'd resolutely be *knackered* by the afternoons. I'd just put my head on a desk at the back and sleep. Rest of the time, I'd be in the library. This is when still bestowed with the energy of a 12-year-old. I never fitted in with any of the other kids.

I still don't. All I ever wanted was to be left alone. So what could be better for someone like that than only working for two hours at weekends? I'm not great at maths, but that puts my leisure time at around 90%. At the peak of my career around 2005, I was, to be fair, pretty busy at weekends – but during the week, I'd literally not know what to do with myself. I'd be in arcades playing video games like a kid or going to museums like a big tourist. I'd watch three or four films a day. I could go into a cinema complex before lunch and still be in there at midnight. When take-aways started to regularly deliver (for a long time, it was pizza or nothing), I'd not leave the house all week. Could easily spend two or three weekdays in a row in bed if the previous weekend was particularly harsh. Don't get me wrong, I knew I was an awful, *terrible* person. I never glamourised myself as some sort of Parisian poet, all sickly, pale, interesting and artistic. I just didn't care. DJing was the target of my ambitions, but it was purely to facilitate a lifestyle I'd always dreamed of. Total and utter irresponsibility. A perma-child who still read comics and got excited by sci-fi despite allegedly being an adult.

Being outside of society is a position I've been in for as long as I can remember. Imagine this if you can, since that paper round I've never once in my life woken up at a specified time. To this day, I wake up when I wake up. It might be 5am, it might be the crack of lunchtime or just in time for tea. I sometimes rationalise it to myself that we are the first generation to truly understand the futility of existence, but really I probably just properly love being in bed. In my heyday, I was an Olympian. I could arrive back from a weekend of gigs and sleep for two days and nights quite easily. No assistance needed at all from any pills or potions. I could sleep standing up, in a speaker or inside a helicopter. All which I did. I always complete what needs to be done in full, but that's it. I never strive beyond that. I have almost zero ambition. All my intelligence, what there is of it, is focused on doing as little as possible at all times. As I've gotten older, I've gotten *really* good at it. As you would naturally expect from doing it for so long. I don't feel any guilt at all. Not a shred of it. As I say, I am fully aware of the awfulness, but that judgement comes from a world that I simply do not inhabit. In my defence, I put a lot of time and thought into getting to this point. I've paid a boatload of tax and put a lot back into the system and not asked much in return other than to be left to it. I'm very OK with it. I see it as pure victory.

Thinking about it, I'm *petrified* of normality. A headshrinker would have a field day with me, I reckon. I spend nearly all my time alone and have done so for a really long time. Relationships just cannot survive. Coming into my life must feel like being thrown out of an airlock into space. A vacuum few living things can exist in. A total absence of normal. I mean, I read and look at screens a *lot*. All the time. People don't like playing second fiddle to those sorts of obsessions. They want to be the thing looked at and obsessed over, and it's just something I can never manage for them. People who want that attention seem insane to me. Like they are shamelessly proclaiming that they are more interesting than the greatest writers who ever lived, more engaging than this science magazine, more beautiful than that painting or more lyrical than those poets. People are alright, I suppose, in small doses. But ultimately, they are part of and represent normality. My sworn lifetime enemy.

Give me some credit, though. Like the lunchtime dodge thing, I am doing stuff while everyone else is comprehensively *not*. I never got to play football or socialise with the other kids at school, and since then, I've literally never had a weekend off, ever. I've worked every weekend for so long I often have little or no clue what day it is. They totally merge into each other. When you aren't in step with everyone else, it is not a shared experience. The weekend is important not just because you get time off the giant hamster wheel; it is also a ritual you all do together. That means something. This is why I am chosen to help you celebrate the ritual. A sort of daft priest, cheerleader or shaman of nonsense. But when you are buzzing for TFI Friday, I'm rolling my sleeves up for starting work. And when it is all over, Monday is like my Saturday, but it's just me alone. Tuesday is my solitary Sunday. The fun things you do on the weekend are often closed midweek to me. I don't get to go out. I don't get to party. Not really. Not in the way you do. I might be there at your party, but I'm not really a participant; I'm attending in a professional role. Not really there. Much like I am absent from society as a whole. A sort of ghost.

Listen, I'm not looking for pity. That would be obscene. I also very much understand my privilege. I didn't just choose this life; I engineered it extremely carefully. I guess I am just saying, "think about it for a minute". How different this life is. Being truly outside. Divorced from reality. Several steps out of the door and hanging around in the garden, looking in your window like a cat left out in the rain. And like a cat, much more capable and at-home than you think. Just a different species. I am deeply proud of being an idler. I stand by it. I think much of modern life is deeply diseased. Greedy and insane. I'm with the louche and dry. The sarcastic and slow. The dreamers, thinkers and dancers. I think our 'thing' is important in its own little way. It's a valve. Discos are an essential release, and I am also deeply proud to help you out with that. So I am OK with my choice. You might hate me for it; you might thank me for it. Either way, it is what it is. There is a purity to it. It's real. It separates me from the current generation of Patrick Bateman-type DJs who are all about what DJing can do for them and their oily ambitions. I only do it when I want to these days; I don't charge much and live very modestly. After all, all that running about the world, going to the gym and taking pictures of yourself seems like an awful lot of gruesome effort. And who the hell wants to *work* for a living?

LAST NIGHT A DJ
CAREER SAVED MY LIFE

Now, I've been in this game a long time. I think I was 16 or 17 when I first started DJing, and I'm 54 now, so you figure it out. And I really think so much of it is about being in the right place and the right time. Probably more so now as there are so many more people who want to be DJs. It definitely wasn't like this when I started out in the late 80s. Back then, working in a record shop got me my start as a DJ, as in someone who could play records for money. But things could have gone very differently for me. I was a very angry young man, and if dance music didn't come along, I might have gone down a very different path.

You see, I lost my mum very young, and that really affected me. She'd been an alcoholic and died in a terrible car wreck. I was separated from my brother, who also ended up dying very young. This was when I was about nine, so I moved in with my aunt and uncle. Now, this is where music first became a big thing for me. My uncle was a member of the Bonzo Dog Doo-Dah Band, so music was a massive part of their lives. They were 60s Mods, basically, with all the cool clothes and loads of Tamla Motown records, all the Rolling Stones and Beatles stuff, of course. Records that, in mint condition, now go for hundreds of pounds but that I totally ruined as a kid. Scratched 'em to fuck and coloured-in the bloody covers. The usual kids' stuff.

Soon I was starting to go off the rails. It started off with detentions at school, and then it was fights. Also trying to bring girls back to the house. I wasn't even a teenager. I thought I was Jimmy from

Quadrophenia, basically! Even down to robbing a chemist where I worked after school. My mate and I lifted all the blues (speed) and valium, and then, of course, I decided I would be an 'entrepreneur' and started selling them at school. Obviously, we got caught right away and expelled. Obviously, then we ran away. Well, we couldn't go home now, could we?

We bunked into an empty army barracks just by putting our skinny arms through the letterbox. And we were sniffing around in there, as you do, and we ended up finding a thousand pounds in cash. Totally out of the blue. Must have been wages or something but bear in mind this was the early 80s, so a thousand quid was a LOT of money. Especially to us two kids. So we did what you do at that age, spent it quick as you like down Carnaby Street! 'Jam' shoes like the band used to wear, nice pair of Sta-prest trousers, boating jackets, got our hair cut.

That's what we were wearing when we got collared in the street by Old Bill: "right, you're nicked, we know exactly who you are and exactly what you've been up to!" We'd not even been putting the lights on in the barracks in case someone saw us, but someone must have reported us for spending all that money. Not that they could get it back... but still, we both got two years on remand for that. Not nice, especially as I wasn't even a teenager.

So after that, I lived in a Dr Barnado's children's home as my aunt and uncle wouldn't have me back. Next, I met these two black guys who introduced me to jazz-funk and fusion, which added to my other musical habits of soul, funk and 60s and 70s rock. I was bunking out of Barnardo's to go and listen to that, plus northern soul at the Richmond clubs like Cheeky Pete's and Brollies. How I got in, I don't know. I was only 14 or so, but I do remember some of the tunes. Eloise Laws' 'Love Factory'. 'On My Way' by Dean Parrish and 'There's a Ghost In My House' by R. Dean Taylor will always take me back to those days.

Eventually, my aunt and uncle let me move back in, and though I hadn't liked it at the time, Dr Barnado's really helped me. They taught me that bottling up my feelings was why they were coming out as anger, and it explained why I was getting myself in trouble. Because I was *angry*. I mean, I'd be smashing up shop front windows with my bare hands. How I didn't chop my fucking hands off, I have no idea, to be honest. But ever since those days, I've always been open about how I've felt. It's better that way, and I should know; I've tried it the other way, believe me. But more people, especially men, are feeling more open that way nowadays and I'm glad for that at least.

But anyway, when I turned 16, my aunt sent me out to get a job. So I got myself a job as a welder, which I *hated*. Burned my hands to pieces. It was horrible. But then I joined Bentalls as a mover, and when we were doing house clearances, I'd always help myself to a few records. It was always "Go on, take a few for yourself, they won't fucking know" from the boss back then. Soon I was spending all my money in a record shop in South London buying records for myself: Punk, Mod, The Kinks, Small Faces, all that stuff. And one of the guys in the record shop one day asked me, "mate, what do you actually do?"

"I'm a removal man, and I fucking hate it!" I said. I can remember that so clearly. He laughed and then invited me out for a drink with him and his partner in the shop, and they took me on as a tea boy. This was 1986, and I stayed for 19 years, going from tea boy to assistant manager, to manager to owner, before eventually selling it. And that's where I met all the DJs you know and love that I'd end up being mates with. Now we were not in the West End, but we still got the big imports from 'Record Corner', that area of Soho with all the shops (there are sadly far fewer now, which is bad for all of us really). But anyway, we got all these imports like 'R-Tyme' on Transmat and' 'Keep Moving' by Mike Peras, so I ended up meeting all these amazing people when I was working. All the best DJs passed through, and I got to meet them all. But it was being in the shop that got me DJ gigs in the first place. I mean, I got to do three mini-tours of the USA around 1990 just from meeting someone in the shop and getting on with them. I wasn't even 25! Right place, right time. I hope those lucky chances are still there for kids like me today.

SHOWING OUT

It was an interesting process learning how to DJ when there was no 'scene' to speak of. No one owned much tech. There were no mixers or decks at home. Who could afford one turntable of that quality? Never mind *two*. Everyone learned on the job. Or the people I know did anyway. Not that you could call it a job as none of us got paid. We started out doing 'discos'. They were not cool places. Not then. I first got into it as a dancer, believe it or not. I think, you know, if you really want to get involved in something in life, any sort of career, you need to get *involved*. You can't do it from home or standing on the sidelines. I used to go out every single night, and while there wasn't much happening where I am from that you might call 'cool', there were a couple of righteous spots. So you'd become a regular there. A *face*.

Being a face is everything in a scene. I suppose it was the pre-internet version of Instagram. You'd dress up to get noticed, but it was a lot more about personality. Sure, you'd stand out if you wore something outrageous, but people soon sussed if you were fake and vanilla inside. Anyone can buy and wear clothes, *anyone*. But can you really *wear* them? If you know what I mean? It was about attitude. Anyone can hold a sword, but can you wield it? 'Shy wallflowers need not apply' was the code. Although ironically, many of the quietest ones went on to do a lot of the backroom biz and ended up running the show.

So yeah, I was a dancer. There was a sort of dancefloor politics. A hierarchy based on where in town you were from, which crowd you ran with, whereabouts in the club you hung out and how often and, most of all, where you showed out. 'Showing out' was all about being seen. If there was a stage, you'd be at the front and centre. If there was a dance-off, you'd be in the circle. If there was a podium, you'd try to be the focus. No one cared about the DJ. It really was all about the music and very communal. So showing out was about being elevated for a short time to sort of belle of the ball. It wasn't a battle or anything. Some folks were happy in a dark corner. Some liked being in the spotlight. I didn't feel particularly full of myself at the time; it was more that sort of dense unawareness you have as a kid. Too inexperienced to even realise what you were. I can see now looking back I was an extrovert, but I honestly didn't even know what the word was at the time. It was all very natural, as kids tend to be. I wasn't outgoing the rest of the time. I only came out of my shell in the disco. I guess maybe that is what it's for.

So as a regular at the disco, you soon became a music fan, if you weren't already one. And fans want to know stuff. You wanted information about what the records were and who made them, and where could you go to hear them in the cold light of day? This is the first stage, if you like, the bit that separates you from the pack. Other people are just happy to have fun, look good, cop off, get fizzy, whatever. You know. Footsoldier types. When you come up through the ranks, as it were, you get promoted. Some get jobs in the disco. You might do flyers. Good dancers might get a free drink.

I mean, we were poor. Dirt poor. Everything was a sham, a front. Spent everything on clothes and tapes. Every penny you had was on 'the look'. You'd walk home something like five miles after the dance because the taxi money was the difference between leaving early because you couldn't afford to stay or going to the last record like a pro. We even ranked ourselves. 'Bitter Enders' was our gang. Only Enders had what it takes: still there when the lights came on. We were the dancefloor professionals. That effort got you noticed. By the venue and the promoter. Although a lot of the time, the DJ was the promoter too. The idea of the two being separate was still new. Most of all, because in theory anyone at all could DJ then. Mixing didn't exist. You needed knowledge, though, and records were not cheap.

So yeah, I won a dancing contest. Sounds cheesy, but it was totally normal at that time to have fun and do contests and such. It didn't get all moody until much later. I had these 'magic dancing shoes' that I found in a vintage gaff that had a mad heel on them, but they were like *proper* dancing shoes and seemed to be completely frictionless. Like you could skate with them on. Just slide about, no kidding. Northern soul folks will know what I am talking about. This was also a time when you had actual dancefloors. Designed in the olden days for real dancing. Sprung like a gymnastic floor. Polished and cherished and looked after like a top-flight football pitch. I wasn't trained in dance at all, just enthusiastic as hell. The shoes gave me a real edge, though. Could spin and slide and jink like no one else, thanks to them.

I was wearing them on the 'fateful night', that crucial point in the timeline where everything changed. I was in the dance circle, which was where those of us who took it quite seriously would form a little arena of bodies. The DJ or promoters or whoever would walk around and tap people out. If you got tapped on the shoulder, you had to move out of the circle. Eventually, there'd be three, then two, and finally the winner. For the first time (and I think maybe the last), I won. I did some sort of silly move as a sort of grand finale in the middle of the dance circle (the dance circle was everything, you'd know if you were there!), and one of the magic shoes shot off my foot like I meant to do it. And in-time with the music too. It was like "ta-daaah!" and I was standing there on one heel like a drunk flamingo, sweating and heaving with everyone clapping... Yeah, we clapped then. American-style whooping and whistling was unheard of! Bad form what-what! All I could think about was *where's my fucking magic shoe!?* And trying to style it out with one leg about six inches shorter than the other. Not really paying full attention to my triumph, more scuttling about looking for my footwear, which meant a lot to me; when the lights came on, and it was all over. I barely noticed because I was under the stools, searching. This is when the DJ finds me, arse-first.

So the DJ has been trying to give my rear-end this prize, something dead cheesy like a bottle of Babycham and a plastic bum crown, and no one could find me as I had disappeared under the furniture. Never found the fucker either. Gutted. But then suddenly I'm chatting in the disco to someone in the white 'working light' with no noise, like being 'backstage' for the first time. The DJ says they (there were two of them) had noticed how keen I was and how often I was coming, and that if I came every week and danced they'd pay me. I mean, let me be clear it was something like ten pounds, which wasn't to be sniffed at, and maybe some drinks were thrown in. I forget. But I was INSIDE now. In the game, instead of a punter looking in. Of course, I didn't see it like that at all at the time. Life was just unfolding as life does. But only a few weeks passed, and I was inside the DJ booth. Again, different time.

The DJ booth couldn't be seen clearly. Was absolutely *not* the focus. It wasn't important to the dancers or to the venue… or to anyone really. It was to me, though! For the first time, I saw the kit. It would look nasty now. Held together with tape and shitty as hell. To me, it was like the cockpit of a 747. And the DJ did the lights then too. I think that's a lost art. The same person knowing what was going to happen and adjusting the lights to fit the mood or drama… yeah. It's just a theory, but I think before mixing was important and people didn't care about who was playing the tunes, just the tunes mattered …maybe the DJ was more involved? Generally? You had time to think about lights and what to play and where to take it all. Mixing sort of killed that luxury off a bit. It was less of a performance and more of a caretaker's job. Maybe.

Yeah, it seems funny now, but at the start of this thing, you'd often find that DJs got the job basically because they had the records, and that was it. A good weekly wage was about £150, the dole was about £20. If a record was about a fiver, you work it out. A large record collection was simply not something many could afford. There was a Revox reel-to-reel in our booth not because it was cool but because tape was cheap and re-usable. We'd play cassettes too. I started DJing using someone else's records. The DJ duo at my club who took me under their wing had a sort of 'working crate', and it was always crates 'cos you could get cases for 7"s then but proper carrying cases for 12"s didn't exist… Yeah, the working crate was communal. There was no reverence either, not like these collectors today. I mean, a record was just a record. You took 'x' amount of care with it, although not all did. No one thought *ooo, must use white gloves 'cos in the future this will be worth money!* Nah. The sleeves were mashed up. The vinyl was well worn and scratched. Some you used often, and you knew when the scratch was coming and would very gently press the needle down for a mo to pass over the bump. No one booed at the format. You'd get a boo for a bad scratch tho, one that looped. But yeah, the records were battered! The records were not things you worshipped any more than a window washer would worship their bucket. Also, this was a time when you'd play the same records every week. New releases were rare! You'd 'break' a record too. Make the crowd like something oddball or very new by forcing it on them. 'New' didn't mean newly released either, often just something you didn't hear in discos. Or just new to your crowd. The crowd wanted to hear familiar stuff then. Familiarity was welcomed, and the unfamiliar was treated with hostility. You had to do a balancing act of the two.

A lot of DJs just played the same thing in almost the same order every time they played. I certainly wasn't up for that; straight away, for me, there seemed to be an immediacy there about matching the vibe. I was fresh from the floor myself and I played records like I was on the podium or in the dance circle, for the people. Match the vibe. But early on, yeah, it was definitely a crate that rarely had newcomers in it. So that familiarity really helps you learn the basics. It seems funny now, but just a few knobs and faders looked like sci-fi. I liken it to learning to drive. It is infuriating teaching the basics to someone else as it seems so intuitive and simple, but remember when you first sat at the wheel? How dangerous it seemed and how jerky and clumsy you were? I mean, just remembering not to have the fader up on the mixer when you pulled the needle off was very major. Seems funny now looking back. It was something that could blow the entire sound system up, though. That could *cost*.

Then as you progressed, you'd almost, out of boredom, sometimes try a new trick. Some records just very obviously synced with others. They had almost the same breaks on the outro or intro. You know, like, say 'Jive Talking' and 'Superstition' have almost the same beat, to use a couple of obvious examples. It wasn't obvious at all then. No one blended records! I mean, first and foremost, no one asked you to. There was no demand for it. If anything, people would sometimes complain. We didn't talk on the mic by this point; that was naff. Wrong. The music was everything, so 'showboating', which was what we called doing any kind of trick on any kind of stage, was considered by many to be out of order. Like a bit gimmicky. If I did a 'mix', although the word then was strictly a studio word for a studio recording process, it was sometimes booed.

At this point, anything that overlapped the music was verboten. Like an annoying radio DJ chatting over your favourite hits. It was OK to maybe miss out boring intros unless of course, that intro was powerful and well known. The idea generally was to keep the energy levels up. Without mixing, it's much easier to lose a crowd. So you became more adept at finding a cue point and cutting into the previous track at an appropriate point. There was pretty much only one rule: don't lose the vibe. But like I say, demand was different. No one expected more than tunes that made them happy and made them dance.

Learning on the job was gladiator school. I say folks weren't demanding, but if you dropped a clanger, you'd get pelted with bottles in some places. By 'learning on the job', I mean that literally, the first time you put your hands on a turntable and mixer was in front of hundreds of people pissed out of their minds. I figure that's why, in my circle anyway, it was nearly always some sort of musician who became a DJ. I was. I wasn't by any means blasé about it, but playing records was nothing compared to standing on a stage and playing a guitar or singing. In terms of pressure and technique. For me anyway. That isn't to say I wasn't fucking petrified the first time I DJ'd. Or the tenth or twentieth time either! It's LOUD, you see. And you are green around the gills, so you do things like find the cue point on the record, and then you hold it for ages and you cramp up and your hand starts to wobble and maybe a fader is still up a bit, so you can hear this bass rumble which is actually the sound of you physically shaking with fear. All very analogue. Mechanical. Very connected to your body via your hands. The record is an object you handle, and the devices are more about levers and dials than buttons.

To begin with, everything you are being asked to do is the polar opposite of everything you've been taught. Hi-fi rules meant never touching a record except by the edges as if it's made of feathers and wishes. To put the needle on very reverently using a lever that lowers it gently. To never touch the needle until the tune is over.

Disco rules were the opposite, the stuff of heretics! Speeding up and slowing down!? Madness! Unheard of. Chucking records about and spinning them back and forth and putting your filthy hands on the precious vinyl!? You had to unlearn all that precious nonsense. But there was a far greater reverence for music and records then. You could hear about records coming out like it was an event like a blockbuster film is now. You'd be buzzed up for weeks before and mark the date. You'd get a bus into town, and by far, the coolest, most oppressive and important place in the universe was the record shop. If you were lucky and early enough, you'd hand over what was sometimes every penny you had, and the thing was *valuable*! I mean, you hugged it and sniffed it and pored over the details of the sleeve on the bus home. It's hard to describe. How so very important it all was. Maybe it still is to some people, a clue perhaps that you are one of us. But that *zone* you get into with music. I mean, in our house, having the giant headphones on was literally the only time you got any privacy. Another world. A place to escape to. Maybe it is all about escape. Discos are escape pods to another world.

So yeah, the act of the needle on the record was almost ritualistic. A sacred thing. You used to crouch over and look at it as if inspecting it through a magnifying glass to start with. Learning how to DJ kind of took that away a little. Made it workmanlike until eventually, you were flinging discs about like frisbees and not even looking when you took the needle off. Eventually, you became so adept you could do mad shit like roughly tell what genre a record was just by looking at the grooves. That was a long way off, though. The L plate days seem funny now. I mean, my 'mentors' didn't exactly give me rigorous training. There was nothing to learn on; the kit was in the club. I think the first time I ever got close to the equipment was about 10 minutes before the doors opened.

One of them basically said, "do this, don't do this, and this does that" (which totally went in one ear and out the other) and then stood next to me for about an hour and would slap my hand if it went towards the wrong fader and laugh uproariously whenever I cocked-up, which was more than once. Lately, there's this weird thing where everyone has to be praised all the time. I honestly think there is no stronger learning process than being shamed and bullied. I'm only half-joking there too. Can you imagine anyone now just being pushed blinking into the lasers and performing, having never done it once before? And fairly soon doing it every night afterwards? Back then, there were no guest DJs. Each venue had its own DJs, and that was it. You'd start at 9pm, and finish at 2am and do it every single night except Sundays.

So you learned pretty fast. I didn't really have time to think about it at all. Big factor, though, was the difference in expectation. No one was staring at me. No one was judging. Even in the fairly low-rent disco we worked in, every night felt like a party. It wasn't an art gallery or a concert. It had a vibe of people letting off steam and getting loose. To be fair, life was way more brutal then. Harsh. Discos weren't totally new, but there was a sort of thing where there were 'pubs and clubs' and 'clubs' were like Phoenix Nights. Chicken in a basket and someone's Dad impersonating Jim Reeves. Pubs were pubs. For a while, discos were all about the music. They went cheesy pretty fast, granted. The same sort of blokes from the working men's clubs would get some records from the charts and a mic, and that was the end of it. But by then, we'd moved on to warehouses and such.

Then one day, after my mates had got to grips with a sequencer, they had a hit record. Everything changed. Mostly that meant me getting 'promoted' and DJing and running events a lot more for our crew. Suddenly it almost made money. You could stop the brutal physical labour jobs on the side that you had to do to pay the rent. The bands you played in got fewer and fewer bookings, but for some reason, DJs seemed to be popping up everywhere. You start to get fancy with the 'blends' and can afford new records. You get bored of the same tunes, and when the crowd doesn't like the new stuff, you decide they are wrong, and you are right. Eventually, you force them to agree. All of a sudden, you are doing a version of your night in the next town. Then another. Then suddenly, you seem to always be on the motorway. Then one day they say they can't run the London flagship event anymore as they are too busy and can you take it over? Which means moving there, basically. Then you go to Clink Street, and everything changes forever...

KNIGHTS OF THE RAVE

The thing is, it's hard to remember dates and places now. I can tell you about being at the very beginning of this whole thing, though. Before house music kicked off, I used to go to rare groove parties. Back then, my nickname was Kebab. It's a long story to do with the kebab knife, not the meat lolly. One night one of my mates came back from this acid rave. We were all laughing because he was buzzing his chops off; we didn't have a clue what was happening. "You wait," he said. "I'll take you to this club next week, and it'll totally change your life," all of that. How right he was.

He took me to Spectrum at Heaven under Charing Cross Station. We actually paid to get in the club next door, then bunged the bouncer to let us through the side door to get into Spectrum. What gave us away, in the end, was that we were black. There weren't any black people in the club. We soon realised they just weren't letting any black folks in at all.

There were about five of us that night, and after we got the E's, man, it *changed* me. It was the best night of my life. There was a spaceship hanging down from the high ceiling that would light up. I was underneath that, watching people hanging off the walls and with their heads in the speaker boxes just going for it.

After that, I found out where you can buy all the clobber, the Converse, the printed t-shirts. This white guy who ran the shop said to me, 'I know you'. He'd seen me in the club. Because I was black, it was that easy to remember me. Next time he told me to come straight to the door and said I could bring my girlfriend along. We felt like royalty walking to the front, and from there, we all got membership cards for a fiver.

Once my brother got involved, we started promoting our own parties, and he launched his label, which is still putting out jungle today. After that, I really wanted to DJ. I was working in a record shop and getting the latest tunes every week, so I joined up with the guy I'd been doing rare groove dances with, and we met the other member of our crew in Spectrum.

We were only doing little clubs in London. Then one night in Astoria, Grooverider came in and said, "you guys need to get up-country". The following week at Spectrum, we met a promoter from Amnesia House, a party in Coventry. We gave them a tape, they called the next week, and that was it. That was our break. That first gig they put us on at 10pm. We played two records, then they pulled us off to play themselves when it was full.

We got gigs everywhere after that. It was a crazy time; we didn't come back to London for years. The north made our name.

And by about '91, nothing could stop the party. I once saw a police superintendent tied up because he wanted to shut down a rave. I think that was at Perception over on the east side of the country on a speedway track, Kings-Lynn. They bundled him into the boot of a car. True story. We were playing an early set that night; we had other jobs to do later. When the crowd outside heard my voice, they tore down the entrance to get in. What a buzz. That whole era was complete, uncontrolled madness.

DJ GOALS

I used to do a lot of festivals, but back in the early 90s, dance music wasn't a big feature at the mainstream rock fests; indeed, we were not at all welcome. There was either no dance music at all or a tiny tent at the bottom of the bill for the first time. So I used to work a lot in the hospitality areas. I didn't invent it, but it was very much part of a thing that changed backstage at festivals from some sad folding tables with ageing fruit and nasty crackers to an area that was inviting, looked good and was a party in itself for the acts and staff. For good or ill.

Reading. The aroma of fires made by people who had no idea how to make a fire and the plastic cups they'd chuck onto the poorly burning pallets like tiny eggshell heretics. If I smell burning plastic, I am always transported back to the Reading Festival. Awake for days on budget whizz and that bad gas forever in the nostrils. We (I say 'we', I was a promoter of sorts as well as the DJ) managed to get a very major beer brand to sponsor these new backstage areas. They'd just invented a brewing technique that produced a new beer that wasn't very tasty but seemed to have almost no hangover. 'Cold Press' brewing, they called it. It didn't last long, no idea why, as beer with no hangover seems like a truly great idea and the peak of human achievement to me. Anyway, I mention this as they had a new product to push and for us, that meant absolutely *totally* unlimited free beer. A beer with no discernible bad side. Basically, we started drinking on the Thursday we arrived and were permanently drunk and awake until Tuesday. 'Celebrities' came into the main backstage tent, saw the party and didn't leave for the entire weekend. Some acts missed their sets. It was great!

The non-stop party in the 'VIP' (it was only just starting to be called that, by the terminally naff) would always tail-off a bit around lunchtime as those who didn't have vast amounts of MDMA and/or amphetamines inside them would be passed out or stagger off from the previous night. There was food served, and it was the only time I didn't play records. For about an hour twice a day, I could leave the tent whilst, ironically, they served up. I got banned from playing while the food was out because on the first day, Paul Weller came in, started queuing with his plate, and I saw an opportunity and mixed 'Start' by The Jam with the Beatles' Tax-man'. A musical piss-take that didn't go down well at all. It was raining as usual, and I started a chant of "Weller, Weller, lend us yer umbrella!" and the beer people quietly lobbied thereafter for a period of calm during lunch and dinner. Yeah, it was the 90s. Sorry and all that.

So I was wandering about in one of these breaks, and it was, for a change, a beautiful day. I was young enough to be absolutely ham-mered but still maintain functionality. There was 'celebrity 5-a-side' that year with a compere on the mic, probably from Loaded magazine, as they were the 'brains' behind it. As I ambled (French for 'staggered') over, I heard them ask for players as they were a bit short. I ran back to the VIP, grabbed four 'celebs' that were up for it, and we entered the contest. I should point out at this point that this was Reading, so no one was particularly famous. Either musicians or the very lower end of the spectrum that could manage to be in ankle-deep mud for days and not cry and call their agent. Essentially well-known people who didn't really consider themselves as famous. Still normal enough to have a laugh with. I like those ones. We started playing football.

What was really weird was we kept winning. We were paralytic, but it seemed that indie bands were generally really unfit and shit at football. We ran rings around Ned's Atomic Dustbin, goaded Massive Attack mercilessly ("Massive Attack?? TINY Attack! No attack at all! etc.") into a rage and generally seemed to luck our way through by force of not caring at all. I dunno. Looking back, I think class had something to do with it. Dance music was a working-class thing, and we could drink *and* play football. The wider 'music biz' is deeply middle class, even when it is pretending very hard that it isn't. It's one of the reasons they had to destroy us. Sorry, liddlebiddapollodigs there.

So. Younger readers will have to Google this and be amazed, but for the next game, we were drawn against Frank Sidebottom's Timperley Bigshorts.

The coin was tossed by the sarcastic lads' mag compere. Frank won the kickoff and honked a highly nasal "FANTASTIC!" and hoofed the ball into space and then ran in completely the wrong direction.

The rest of his team were tiny cardboard Franks. Frank couldn't see at all due to his enormous papier-mâché head. It was boiling hot and noisy, but that didn't stop him one bit. He'd fall over his own tiny teammates and shout "BRILLIANT!" and get up and launch himself at nothing at all. Shout "GOAL!" without having ever touched the ball. We were laughing so much we could hardly move.

We somehow managed to win. A miracle victory over a single opponent who was deaf and blind.

The Gods of the festival had their revenge on us for beating the Bigshorts. As the tournament progressed (it wasn't very serious, 15 minutes a game), we ended up playing The Guardian, who had two sportswriters who were former professionals, and they soundly beat us 12-0. But it was just one of those days that was impossibly awesome. We got to go back to a tent that was like Willy Wonkaland but with endless beer and food and play records again, forever. We got to play the Timperley Bigshorts. I've since done all sorts all over, but I always go back to that sunny day and utterly deranged festival and think, well, THAT weekend was a DJ gig. Yes, sir. We did. You know we did. We really did.

ARTHUR

The heroes of acid house weren't all DJs and promoters, or even the dancers or pure ravers. This is a shout out to Arthur, who in the heyday of it all kindly allowed London's Pulse 90.6 FM, the main hardcore station of the time, to broadcast from his tiny spare room in Hackney Wick. It was a time when the area was *really* run down. There were loads of industrial estates and warehouses where parties were happening and an old, dilapidated dog racing track.

Back then, the DTI (Department of Trade & Industry, responsible for policing the airwaves) were constantly trying to track down and bust pirate stations. To stay one step ahead, the station used a microwave link. You'd have your studio in one tower block, then your transmitter, which you broadcast from, on another. Then these were connected by a microwave beam. It meant if the DTI tracked down your signal, they'd only get the transmitter setup and not find your actual studio. Basically, the decks and the aerial were split between totally separate buildings.

The problem was that someone kept snipping the cable to Pulse's transmitter, which at that time was on top of a tower block on the Trowbridge Estate. It could have been the DTI trying to shut us down, but this seemed unlikely. The alternative was a rival pirate station, of which there were a lot around Hackney at this time, trying to claim the spot for themselves. The whole pirate game is unsurprisingly very territorial. After replacing the cable a few times, the station manager kept a lookout and eventually caught this middle-aged, slightly shabby-looking man completely red-handed. That's how we met Arthur.

He was an odd character. In his forties, possibly even older, he looked a bit like Norman Wisdom and was a recluse who lived alone, keeping himself very much to himself. He had a three-bedroom flat on the top floor immediately below the roof and thought that our pirate transmitter directly above his place was some kind of surveillance device from the council, so he kept trying to disable it. In hindsight, it's entirely possible he was 'on the spectrum'.

Our station came to an agreement to rent one of his spare rooms. Arthur was happy, as he was getting some money, and we had somewhere relatively safe. Most of the DJs thought he was weird, so didn't talk to him or even let him come into the studio. I thought he was odd too, but I quite liked him, so I would let him come in during my shows. He was obviously very interested in what we were up to, although he didn't know anything at all about the music. He said he didn't even know what a record was.

Because of this, I was probably one of the only people he gave a tour of the rest of his house, which very much added to the strangeness. One room was completely full of doors, literally just loads and loads of doors leaning up against one another like that scene from 'Monsters Inc' cartoon. The other room was packed with cookers. He was an extreme hoarder, although it turned out there was some logic to it.

The doors were there because he was really into locks and picking them. Even weirder was the fact that he wasn't even about trying to break in anywhere. He just had a very deep fascination with discovering how they worked, so that was his kind of workshop. I never did work out what the cookers were about.

In the end, we moved the studio, which was wise to do every so often because otherwise, the authorities would get wind of where you were. The next spot was in Barking, and I actually got caught by the DTI whilst on-air. They burst in with a few police officers and confiscated all the gear and all my records. I got taken to court and slapped with a massive fine. I was still a student at the time, so I had to negotiate to pay the authorities a little bit at a time.

I did once bump into Arthur again a couple of years later at Dalston market. He was standing next to a shop selling locks. Locks were obviously *very* much Arthur's thing.

I'LL HOUSE YOU

That first time as a DJ you play a house music party in Chicago, it is everything. What you do in the context of being in that town at that moment is steeped in dance floor history. No matter how much you've developed your own take on the music, no matter how much credibility you have, you are returning to the source. There is pressure, and there should be pressure. But there is pride too. So you can imagine how excited I was to play in a fine uptown establishment about which, apparently, around the city, there was a definite buzz in the air.

I arrived early, well before the venue opened. Tunes were all thought-out in my head, so I spent the time before the doors opened pacing nervously around the venue. Eventually, I settled down with a few choice margaritas and as people started filing in, I slowly got the party started; I was playing all night. Within an hour of the doors opening, there is definitely a vibe. People are on the floor, on podiums, on tables all friggin' their funky stuff. I am slowly, but nicely, settling into my stride. A few hours in and the place is rammed to the hilt. It's getting sweaty and pumping, just the way we all like it.

Then I start to notice someone shouting every time I cue in another track and fade it into the next. At first, I can't make it out. I think maybe it's just enthusiasm from the crowd. Then it gets louder and louder as the night goes on. And it is starting to sound like someone is shouting, "FUUUUUCK YOOOOU!" every so often at the very top of their voice. They must be getting closer to the booth too because as the night goes on, I hear it clearer and clearer.

Yup, it's 100% "FUCK YOU!" to every track. And now I can tell where it's coming from. The bartender pops in, asking if I want another margarita. The stress of this constant heckle is getting to me, and I tell him, "Yeah line them up!" and ask him, "Do you know who the guy is over there? The guy who keeps shouting at every mix?"

"Oh yeah, of course. That's Ralphi Rosario," he explains, and disappears to get my drink.

It's something of a bombshell.

I am in Chicago, and one of the forefathers of house music, a man behind the legendary 'Hot Mix 5' and classic records like 'You Used To Hold Me', and he is basically barracking me every time I line up a track. Suddenly I do not want to be in Chicago in a club playing house music. Look, the place is *jumping*, but I'd literally rather be anywhere else. Maybe even involved in a different career altogether. I want the ground to open and swallow me up. The last few hours of the night go on, and the random "FUUUUCK YOOOOU!" persists from the side of the dance floor.

I end my set. The lights go up, and people start leaving. A few are coming up to say they enjoyed the music and shake hands. But out the side of my eye, I see Ralphi Rosario slowly wandering over. *Oh shit*, I think. Right now, I really don't need this.

He comes up and grabs me, and gives me a big hug.

"That was so good my man," he says.

Eh?!

"WHAT?! You were shouting 'fuck you' to every record I basically played!"

He starts laughing." Oh... no. That's a 'fuck-you-for-having-that-track'! I was throwing compliments at you all night!"

From that moment on, myself and the legendary Mr Rosario became pretty good friends, which you can imagine is pretty cool. And every year at about the same time, we text each other a message. A sort of anniversary. A warm 'FUCK YOU'.

THE XXX FILES

There's a very dark underbelly to London, and this happened a long time ago when I was new to town. Like completely fresh off the boat. I was working as a resident at a disco and was mates with all the staff and also, not being from London, friends with most of the regulars fairly quickly. I mean, for example, my new flatmate did not know *any* of the neighbours, and he'd been there many years. I was mates with every single person within about half a mile radius within a couple of weeks of arriving. It's quite a cold town when you are from a warm climate. I also guess that because I was new to the city, being friends with the clubbers was due to having so few options. I was a co-promoter, too, not just playing records, so for half the night, I'd be standing on the door. So I was mates with the security most of all, I'd say. I used to do the doors a bit myself, so I never see them as meatheads. One of them was a Swede who spoke four languages, Joachim.

We had all sorts used to come. A funny one was a breakfast TV morning workout type star. Shows you how long ago this was. Quite an odd fish. Always insisted on paying, which was fine, but it was more like 'I'm rich, so I must pay', and they would make this huge point that they absolutely were *not* there to have a good time; it was *strictly* a workout. And then be there in the crowd with a day-glo leotard on and legwarmers. Funny. The B-52s often came, or one of the lady singers did. Which was odd as I thought they were American. The Brand New Heavies became regulars. Also, a fella who used to arrive in loads of scarves and do a super camp but highly amateur 'dance of the seven veils'. Yeah, lots of oddballs used to come. I can't name the venue, but it was my co-creation and it was also the first time I really got to know other gay people and my first contact with trans people.

So two of my friends who came regularly were called Vida and Ludwig. Ludwig was a giant and very German and glam. Vida was mid-operative and Ludwig's partner but the more 'fem' of the pair, clearly, as she had colossal new knockers. Preferred pronouns were not really discussed then in the mainstream, but we knew the correct form instinctively. They were very brave and open for the late 80s, and I never gave it any thought at the time, but I guess perhaps it was a mark of a good club I was running if people like them felt safe. I'm proud now, but back then, it all seemed like 'this is London'. I had nothing to compare it to. I didn't understand until much later how far on the fringes of society we were. This was also a little before 'clubbing' was a global phenomenon. Anything open after the British pubs was considered the freak zone. We came out only at night. I was totally a nightbird back then, as were many of my friends.

I use the word 'freak' carefully. We were proud to be freaky then. We identified as freakish and did not hide. I just sort of assumed that London was the centre of the universe and everyone in it was a weirdo, just like me. Yes, of course, we brushed up against the daytime sorts now and then, but really? Not much. It was all very Andy Warhol in the 80s and early 90s. For me anyway.

So you could say Joachim was one of the most 'international' people I knew and maybe the toughest. Former Scandi army, huge but also very travelled and educated. Ludwig and Vida were, forgive me, the most unusual people I'd ever met and I don't mean their orientation. They were highly artistic, cosmopolitan and interesting too. I think people like them understand immediately when someone like me is a newbie and in need of 'protection' as they were just like me once. Fresh meat that needed a wing to cower under. They became quite protective of me. I mean, a capital city is a magnet. I can't think of any people in our freak zone who were actually from London. None of the clubbers I knew were, and at the venue, not even the staff or owners were born in London. Everyone was an oddball fleeing something, seeking sanctuary. Safety. Hiding from Londoners too! They could be very hostile. Not all of them, obviously! I could pass for' normal' at a pinch. It was dangerous in those days, but for people as standout as Vida and Ludwig it was a hostile environment everywhere they went, every day and every night.

Then one night, we are chatting and Joachim is talking about working the door at the weirdest job he has ever done. He's currently working security at 'a thing' that just has to be seen to be believed. Back then, I used to go out every single night of the week, either working or not. I was always curious about other clubs. I went to a different one almost nightly just to check them out. He told me when and where, and I should ask for him personally; otherwise, I would not get anywhere near it. Got to say I was very intrigued. He was not forthcoming other than it was unbelievable and had to be seen. He said he'd signed a document (we didn't have the term 'NDA' back then) which meant he couldn't talk about it, but it didn't say anything about letting mates in, which amused him greatly. He said due to his thick accent and deep voice, they assumed he was an idiot and couldn't read. He had a law degree. I guess everyone can get stereotyped, right?

I went to the place at the designated time. It was a cobbled, old-school dirty London alleyway. I saw in the murk ahead was a big queue. Everyone had an overcoat on, and some even had cloaks, which for someone who often worked a cloakroom, made me smile. There's a sort of rule that maybe hasn't survived to this day, but if you work in the industry, you don't pay, and everyone is part of a community even if you don't know them or haven't met before. It used to spread right across the nighttime industries. Like we were good friends with a late-night cinema, local strippers and cab drivers. I think now everyone thinks they are special and expect to get in free, but this was about

'89 or '90, I think. Small industry. Very short lists on the door. So I go straight to the front, and already it is unusual; the doors are closed. I check the time, maybe very late opening? Then a sort of shutter at head height slides open and asks what I want, and I see it is Joachim's eyes, so I laugh and say, "Here I am, I've come to see this miracle". He laughs and opens the door. The place is a very fucked-up old warehouse, and I did not know at the time, but it would become a legit club. It did not look legit at all. Looked like a factory. I can hear throbbing sounds from above. Joachim points to the staircase: "up there". I get about one flight up and tottering downstairs, each on their killer heels, are none other than Vida and Ludwig. Vida looks ashen and clearly upset, and Ludwig is half carrying, half comforting her. I'm pleased to see them, it's been a long while, and they barely register me as they hustle past with Ludwig muttering "disgraceful!" or some such. Here were, without doubt, the two freakiest people I knew and the first thing I saw was them leaving in disgust! Whoa! I *have* to see this.

Eventually, I get up to the main event. It's pretty grubby, very much 'warehouse' more than disco. There's a main room and well… it wasn't so much like a fetish ball, it was too varied for that. And it wasn't particularly sexual, although many were there for their highly specialised peccadilloes. No, it was more like a mini-festival of the extreme. I mean, I've seen events where everyone is basically S&M, and in their highly specialised way, can be quite conservative. Those places have quite strict rules. This didn't. It was 'anything goes'. And you know what? That doesn't necessarily mean sinister, dark or wrong. Some people are just different and feel more comfortable with *any* kind of difference. Maybe there were just fewer people around back then, so you tended to band together across the party lines? I didn't want to be a massive tourist, so I told myself I'd have one drink and leave. I hated gawkers in my own club and weeded them out mercilessly. A safe space is entirely about being free. As you tend to get with these things, as well as milling about and mingling, some extroverts were there to do their 'set piece'. Others are quiet and don't want to be bothered. There were people spreadeagled on apparatus, not sure what for if not display purposes. It sure had a shop window sort of vibe sometimes. Some were dressed as wasps for some un-discernible reason. Some on shoes so high they may as well have been short stilts. Like I said, not all 'dark' at all. Some were dressed as fluffy toys, and others were merely slightly bewildered Goths. There were so many too. Close to a thousand throughout the whole place. It always amuses me when I watch films trying to recreate clubs, especially Hollywood. It's literally like no one involved has ever been to one in their life. I mean, I must have been to every significant club in the world at some point or another, but none of them look like films... BUT, this one came the closest to the cartoon-esque 'film' idea of a club where everyone in it is a special creature. What they always get wrong is how different everyone looks. How varied they are. They make out like everyone is skinny and perfect and in flawless latex, but the reality is far, FAR more interesting.

The music was, as perhaps expected, the most grinding industrial techno of the day. Which I personally found a bit much. I quite like it on a pill in a throng, dancing. But this was more like the opening of a gallery, really. Few danced or indeed moved much at all. I'd like to describe more, but it was all a blur. I didn't want to stare in a safe space, so I feigned nonchalance. Went to get a drink for courage, although I wasn't scared so much as just massively out of place. An interloper, really. Which was new for me as I ran clubs for weirdos for a living. This place was next level. I guess what I am saying is that no matter how cool or freaky or underground you think you are, there is always another level above or below. *Always*. I looked for the toilet and ended up in a room where a live crucifixion was taking place. I mean actual real nails-through-hands sort of 'live'. That definitely wasn't the bathroom. I found it eventually and nervously approached the urinals just as a little old man scuttled over with an empty ornamental tankard ('scuttling' is something you hear about but so rarely see done properly). Naked and wrinkly as a pink prune, he held his baroque receptacle out and, with a pleading look, asked, "you wouldn't be so kind as to do me the honour would you?" He was so unassuming and polite I almost considered it as a reflex.

The only thing that bothered me at all was that the music didn't seem to matter much. That was the thing I took away, ironically. The event went on to become quite well subscribed and notorious, I understand, but these were its early days. I'm glad I got to see them, although very briefly. It energised me, kind of legitimised what I was doing and gave me a boost to encourage even more diversity at my place. I think it's important to really get involved and see all aspects of what it is you choose to do in life. To self-educate is to never stagnate. I'd certainly rather go back there weekly than go to any EDM-type thing in Vegas just once, for example. Definitely! However, I don't think things like that special night happen quite so much anymore, though I'm certain they exist. Perhaps it's just me and being so green back then, but it felt like a different era entirely. So much more risqué and glamorous. Less plastic and commercial. It was *dangerous*. Things now seem much, *much* tamer. Mainly perhaps because it is all about money now. Money doesn't like risk. For me, the whole thing is, and always will be, entirely about risk. We need to find that edge again. It's like a missing ingredient. I've seen versions of it in Berlin, but that risky vibe used to be almost everywhere. And since that night, I've had a new threshold for what I consider pushing the boundaries in clubland. I like to ask myself, are you even on the edge of things unless someone is getting genuinely crucified?

CANAL-RENTENTIVE

Back in 1991, the organisation I was part of put on a two-night mega-rave for five thousand people in a Scottish new town. It was in a rural sports centre surrounded by countryside. A month before we'd discovered that if you put a TV advert on after midnight, it only cost £50. We'd made the most low budget advert of all time, and because we'd reached all the people still up getting stoned, we'd completely sold out the tickets. The first night was heaven, everything that could go right did. The second night was *hell*, with endless problems. But it was me personally who made it into the newspaper, a clipping of which a friend still carries around to this day.

I'd been DJing since before the acid house explosion but was relatively straight-edge at this point. I wasn't big into ecstasy, but I did like mushrooms and had done quite a bit of acid over the years. Meaning I was a fairly experienced tripper. Well travelled, you could say. So when an old friend turned up on day two, he immediately handed me a homemade mushroom brew. Normally this was quite a mild concoction, so as he was saying hello to someone else, I took a huge swig. When he turned back and saw this, though, I knew something was wrong.

"Oh fuck, I meant to tell you it's super-concentrated!" was his too-late warning. "You've just had the equivalent of about a thousand mushrooms."

Since I was supposed to DJ in half an hour, I tried making myself sick. It felt like I must have got most of it out of my system, so I started playing. It was full-on rave mania. The crowd was going absolutely mental. Then about another thirty minutes into my set, it all kicked-in. All I remember is standing there looking at the label of one of the records, entranced by whatever was on it. Then came the thought: 'I don't really want to be here'. The music ran out, this sea of faces staring at me. Then I just ran away clean out of the place, mid-set, grabbing my coat and rushing out of the nearby fire escape.

I suddenly had this insane febrile energy, so I was bounding through the countryside away from everything and everyone. My concerned friends, meanwhile, knowing what I'd taken, had sent off a panicked search party. They roved around looking for me in a car as I had disappeared so far off into the night. They also scrambled to find a replacement DJ.

Oblivious to all this, I'd now run a couple of miles and had never felt so liberated and free. I was completely out of my mind and just having the best time *ever*. When I came to a slope, I just kept going down, down, down and straight into the canal at the bottom. The puffy jacket I was wearing just filled up with air, so now I was floating on water which felt even more amazing.

My perception of time was completely distorted; I was just completely blissed out. However, it must have been near dawn because a guy walking his dog passed by and saw what looked like a body floating in the water. He rushed home to call the police, and they found me at around the same time as my friends did. I was enjoying the canal so much and so intently that when a friend tried to pull me out, I began punching him for interrupting my reverie. The police, having no idea how to deal with my complete and utter gibberish, put me in their van and took me to hospital.

By the time we got there, the intensity of the high was wearing off a little. I could tell the staff what year it was, so I was coming back down to earth. But when they put me in an old people's ward to rest, I was convinced I was in a celestial waiting room about to go to heaven. Two hours later, I was definitely aware I was in hospital and was completely embarrassed. Back home, most of my highly traumatised friends never wanted to talk about it ever again.

The next day, though, there was a story in the local newspaper about a DJ being fished out of the water. One of my mates cut it out and shows me every single time we meet up. I've since learned there are more straightforward ways to get press coverage. Thank God there wasn't an interview.

TAKEN

Often, when I'm on holiday, sitting on a beach and doing nothing, my memories come flooding back. There's so much that's been suppressed because it's just way too traumatising. I've been in some pretty sticky situations. Some of it is funny too. Looking back with the comfort of distance. I mean, how many DJs get held for ransom?

I was booked to play a big festival in the Balkans, my second time. When I came through arrivals in the airport, I saw a driver holding a sign with my name. I tried verbally checking if he was the man on my itinerary, but he told me he didn't speak very good English. I had a look around for other festival signs, but there weren't any, so off we went.

It's an hour-long drive to the one hotel, and I'd been there before. It's like the Grand Budapest, preserved from another era and really beautiful. So as the journey went on, I had a sense something was wrong. Then a short while into the journey, I got a call from another guy telling me he was the actual driver meant to pick me up. I tapped the guy currently driving on the shoulder. When he started reaching over to the glovebox, my heart leapt into my throat.

He grabbed my phone and started shouting in the local lingo that was quite naturally completely beyond my comprehension. Then he stopped the car, got out and handed my phone back to me. The man on the other end tried to keep me calm because I was absolutely *terrified*, obviously. They explained that the person I was now with wanted money to give me back. Apparently, it was a scheme being "run by a gang of gypsies", and I wasn't the first DJ to disappear this way.

In the back seat, I had a full-blown panic attack, thinking I was going to get raped or murdered. We were driving through cornfields, vast open countryside with no sign of anyone else around at all. He had my phone. This was in the days before smartphones anyway. So no GPS or no social media to alert anyone to my predicament. At one point, I steeled myself to fight and go out in a blaze of glory. Then a weird calm descended. I somehow just knew it wasn't my time to die.

After about three hours, we got to an area with people, and he threw my phone back to me. Then he got out of the car and dumped me, my suitcase and my records on the pavement. As he sped off, I burst into tears of relief. Then nearby, I heard the voice that had been on my phone calling my name. It was all sketchy as fuck.

After that trauma, I immediately got annihilated on the local liquor, which is like moonshine. It was too much for me to deal with there and then. When I got home, though, I completely flipped out. The emails that I sent regarding this were, shall we just say, *severe*."

A couple of years later, I was playing at a festival in Montenegro. The artist liaison there was like, "Do you remember me? I was the head person at that festival. Because of that incident with you, the government implemented a new law about unlicensed drivers picking up people. It was part of a new Terrorism Act." Not a claim to fame I ever wanted, to be quite honest.

REQUIEM FOR A RESIDENT

The resident DJ sees *everything*. Trust me, I am one. And over the years, I've seen it all; the egos, the arrogance, the idiots, the greediness and all the other antics you can imagine. I could tell you many stories about DJs sending us out on 3am cocaine missions, desperate requests for escorts, once we had an arrest, and there's even been a dirty protest in the green room, a brown mystery we've still yet to unravel. But there's one story that sticks with me. One that captures the tragic behaviour of a headline DJ when they let fame get to their head. One that makes me think I'll never make it further than where I am in this game because, quite simply, I'm not a gigantic asshole.

This is a story of pure stupidity and arrogance. It's one so simple in its plot and so easily avoided it's infuriating. And I am pretty sure I'm not the only person to see this. Let me set the scene. I am French. I play for and help promote and organise a techno night in a city in France. It's 2016, and it's one of our bigger nights that we do every season. A bigger venue and budget, usually with two or three big international names down to play while myself and another resident friend take turns to either warm-up and play the final 'graveyard' set. It's a pretty standard procedure for promoters the world over, and it works very well. It's something we've been doing for a few years, and the parties, I am proud to tell you, are a success.

But these parties are not without their problems. I don't mean technical ones necessarily; in fact, they rarely happen at all. We do soundchecks, we know our club's system, there is a sound technician present in the club. This is never a problem. No. The biggest problem is not the tech; it is always the headliners. It seems the bigger the DJ, the more likely we are to have some type of issue. Nothing is ever quite right for certain DJs. Of course, not all. I've met and played alongside some fabulous legends and pioneers. But it's people like this particular fool who really give superstar DJs a bad rep. He was playing at our summer event as the main slot from 2-4am. I was opening; another well-known act, a duo, played after me, then it was him before my friend closed the show. I remember it specifically because of the set-ups. The guests after me were playing a hybrid performance style set, so they were using the CDJs as controllers via its HID mode. This other guest was playing his music off USBs, so I just had to remind him to flick the turntables to 'CDJ mode', and that would all be fine. If you've never used CDJs before, then perhaps that sounds technical, but it's literally just pressing a button on each deck. It's not rocket science.

Or so I thought. This DJ, British I think it's safe to add, arrives around 20 minutes before his set (as he'd requested), and we can tell he's fully charged already. He is wavy. He's in that fierce state that only alcohol and cocaine can get you, and he starts to throw his weight around the moment he arrives. He says the hotel is shitty, and the car was late. Where was his rider? Who's got the drugs? And so on. I try to placate him a little. We'd already met quite a few years before playing together at a party in Paris. Back then, he was fairly reasonable, humble and friendly, but he's showing no recognition or effort to even try to recollect the situation. He just continues to moan about everything as I lead him and his 'friend' (who may-or-may-not be a tour manager) to the green room. I then fetch his rider and attempt to chill with him as we wait for his set time, but he's not up for any type of conversation or chilling at all. He turns his back on me, talks to his friend and chops up two substantial lines. I can't help but feel he was making a point out of not doing one for me, but I don't care. I just want to do my job and get him on stage in a few minutes.

As I take him to the stage, I lean to shout in his ear that he will need to turn on the CDJ mode, but he physically shrugs me off and tells me he knows what he's doing. Okay, I shrug and go through to the main room. It's about 1000 capacity and very busy. The last act finishes, and he goes to play, but nothing happens. It goes dead silent. I can see that this is totally a ticking time-bomb situation. With every second that passes that he can't get the music to play, he's going to get more and more irate. This is not what we paid our €4000 for. I run around and try to get on the stage but his friend physically stops me.

"Fuck off, this is *my* stage. I know what I'm doing!" shouts the DJ.

"I just want to ask if you have turned the CDJ to CDJ mode?"

"Of course I fucking have!"

I don't believe a word of it so I go to move further onto the stage to try and help but the friend (still not sure if it was his manager or wannabe manager) stands in my way. He literally pushes me back and tells me that it's best to leave him to sort out the situation. I argue that it's probably not, and as one of the team who puts on the night, it's *my* responsibility.

By now there's a curiosity from the crowd, and the silence from the speakers is excruciating. No full club at 2am should ever have silent speakers. But the DJ's behaviour is so outrageous most people just stopped to watch. They don't protest, they don't leave (well, some do, but not many). They get a drink, smoke a cigarette or just sit and watch as this well-known name in house and techno goes into full-on rage mode right there on stage. I look around for the sound technician, but he's nowhere to be seen. This does not help the situation at all.

"Amateurs!" spits the DJ. "No fucking sound technician! This is so fucking embarrassing. I've got to do everything myself!"

He is behaving like Gordon Ramsey in a kitchen tantrum. For the crowd, this is pure entertainment. For me, it is by far the most frustrating experience I've had in my career. There is just no telling him.

If he'd actually listen to me, the situation could be resolved instantly, literally at the push of a button. I stand there at the side of the stage shouting and two other friends involved in promoting the night also try to argue, but none of us can even get on stage at our own party. It is farcical. We ask the head of security, but he won't intervene. He reasons that no violence or trouble is being caused and that it is, in fact, quite funny.

By quarter-past two we have all had enough. We've watched this DJ press every button, take his USBs in and out of the machines and check all the connections so many times it was painful. He has cursed us in every English swear word I know and a few I'd never heard before. He was right; it was embarrassing. Not for us, however. For him. He'd created a situation that should *never* happen at a techno party, or indeed at any party. A whole quarter of an hour of musical silence at the peak time of a rave is unheard-of. On paper, this was a promoter's nightmare, but in reality, it was plain surreal. The crowd, like us, had never experienced anything like this before. They looked on curiously, chuckling as this red-faced Englishman got more and more infuriated with the situation. But a joke can only be taken so far, and just as we decided the only thing we can do is rush the stage and push his friend over, the sound technician miraculously appears out of nowhere. It seems he'd taken his mandatory break at the worst possible time and had been outside smoking.

"I thought it was a bit quiet in here," he says to us redundantly and leaps up the steps.

"What did I just say to you lot? He's sorting it!" says the DJ's friend and heroic protector.

"I'm the sound technician."

"Took your fucking time, didn't you?" shouts the DJ. By now, you can plainly hear laughter from the crowd. They came for a party and are experiencing that great British art form, the pantomime.

"You just need to change the CDJ to CDJ mode, look...."

Et voila. In seconds the sound technician does what we'd been trying to do for over 15 highly stressful minutes. The DJ shows absolutely no shame whatsoever. He just nods his head in the slightest of gestures and starts making up for lost time. His friend hovered around behind him, looking awkward. No longer a self-appointed bodyguard, he was surplus to requirements, and I suspect he knew he wouldn't be welcome in the green room anymore.

But here's the most galling thing of all. His friend might have had a bit of a reality check, but the DJ didn't. The crowd who'd waited for him to play thoroughly dug his music and gave him the biggest cheer of the night. I have to be honest, he did play an incredible set (I wondered if perhaps that was him actually showing some kind of professionalism?) and no matter how much of a total penis he looked and felt, he decided to carry on and deliver the set we'd paid for. I thought maybe it was the tension of those 15 minutes of silence that exploded when he started playing made it somehow feel special. But as he finished, he proved both of those theories wrong; he refused to let the last DJ, my fellow resident in arms, onto the stage until he'd finished and taken his USBs out. Causing another deafening silence between DJs. However, this silence wasn't awkward at all because it was so full of people cheering. He waves at them like the Queen and asks me where his driver is. Absolutely no reference to the shittiness he'd displayed two hours before. There and then I developed a new and final theory; he's just a complete egotistical bully of a tool who's had far too much done for him and thinks he knows best ...but also happens to be a damn fine DJ.

Of course, this wasn't an epiphany. I'd seen elements of this behaviour so many times but never quite the grotesqueness of this situation. His extreme lack of self-awareness or ability to listen was idiocy on a whole new level. And the last time I'd met him, he'd seemed like a pretty regular, appreciative human. I wondered what he'd be like in years to come? Or, worse still, when he loses his edge and doesn't play so well? What becomes of souls like that? It hasn't happened yet, though. In fact, he's even bigger. Three years after our cursed booking, he was back in town again. This time for another promoter in an even bigger venue. On all accounts, it was a sell-out, but I couldn't help but wonder how many people turned up in the hope they'd see another piece of scarlet-faced, furious British DJ theatre....

FROG'S LEGS

New Year's Eve on my first American tour. This was it! The big one. Prime-time party central with your boy right here headlining at the stroke of 12. The Miami club I was booked to play looked a lot more upmarket than most other breakbeat shows you'd traditionally find in the USA in the early 2000s, and the hotel didn't look too shabby either. I just knew this was going to go down in history as the best NYE I'd had in my career so far.

The first indication that this might *not* be the case occurred to me when we arrived at the airport. I was flying from Boston; my friend was flying in from New York. We arrived at a similar time and proceeded to wait. And *wait*. And then wait a little more. Even at this red flag-festooned stage, I hadn't even begun to suspect that this still might not be an incredible gig. Sure, I was standard-issue worried, but people can be late. It's life on the road. Things don't always go quite the way you'd like them to. But then we saw the pair of them, and I knew we were up for something a little more off-piste.

"Sorry we're late bro, we've had a few hiccups...."

Two dopey looking young guys shamble up to us. One is shuffling a little more slowly than the other because he is wearing massive fluffy Kermit The Frog slippers on his feet. Those monstrosities you might have worn as a kid. Strictly for home cosiness. Not for outdoors, *definitely* not for airports and 100% categorically not for promoters picking up their headline DJ. His silent associate appears to be wearing a dressing gown, and the pair of them look like they've been awake for a week.

Okay, I think to myself. Kermit is a noob promoter. A passionate fan who's come into some money and wants to put on a party. Now that part is great, it's how most promoters start, and I totally applaud that and encourage that behaviour. But there is something about this guy that suggests he isn't going to hit the big league. Sure enough, it becomes clear that his only experience of events is getting completely off his tits at them, not actually running any. He was a total space cadet, plain and simple. A stark, raving space cadet in a stupidly over-sized Sega Megadrive sweater and those infuriatingly ridiculous slippers. What had I got myself into? Some type of druggy slumber party? And what are these hiccups he speaks of? My friend and I share a slightly worried glance and follow them out to the car where, once again, I'm faced with another clue that tonight might not be the biggest gig of my career. Hang on:

"What the hell is up with your wheels!?"

The car itself is pretty decent. A Lexus of some sort and certainly not the type of executive whip you'd expect these kids to be driving. But there are huge wads of grass stuck up and around the car's wheel arches, and the rest of it looks like it's just done daily doughnuts in the Pyramid Field of a particularly soggy Glastonbury.

"Well, that was one of the hiccups bro, we got lost finding the venue and got the car stuck on a field for a while."

How could you lose a venue that's slap bang in the centre of downtown Miami? What *fields*? There are absolutely no fields in downtown Miami. I hazard a question, "Has there perhaps been a change of venue?"

"Yeah, like… errrr. Sorry dude. Right now, we haven't got one."

"Excuse me?"

It's currently around 3pm on NYE. The night I had put every hope on being the sparkly jewel in my USA tour crown, the type of show I'd come home and tell mates about for months or maybe even years to come …and there isn't even a *venue*. The club they had originally booked the party into had learnt it was an upbeat drum' n' bass affair and immediately cancelled the booking in favour of something slightly more lucrative for their biggest night of the year. These well-meaning but totally clueless young men had spent the morning driving around making crop circles trying to find another venue. I felt for them, these things happen, and venues can be totally ruthless. But, mostly, I didn't feel for them at all because, *dammit*, this was meant to be a legendary night and let's be clear; Kermit and The Dressing Gown were obviously rank amateurs with little or no signs of real gumption.

However, as we pull up to the hotel, a decent five-star joint with a pool, a gym and a reputable restaurant, I start to think that at least the hotel booking was legit. Bzzz! No.

"Sorry, sir, there's some type of mistake here. You are *not* booked in our flagship residence, you're booked in our travel motel located on the other side of Fort Lauderdale."

'Travel motel location' eh? By now, I am fully aware that this will not be the billy-big-baller gig I'd hoped it would be. In fact, I am beginning to worry about whether I'll get paid at all. These days tours are booked much more professionally, and an artist is paid upfront. Back then, you'd often be paid a small deposit and the rest in cash on the night. I think I'd received the paltry sum of $50 in advance. Even for an artist of my level, that was feeble. As we made our way to the real hotel/motel (I would've killed for a Holiday Inn), I realised that if these guys were going to pay me, I had to help them. Pull their socks up a bit. Whilst ignoring the slippers, ideally.

"So which venues have you tried?"

"All the ones we know. They're fully booked."

"Well, have you tried looking in the Yellow Pages?"

Before the internet, this was all we had. If someone needed advice on local goods or services, they looked in a big book of ads and phone numbers and rang around. I didn't know anyone good to recommend. I had never had to say any of this to any promoter before. Mind you,

I'd never dealt with a promoter with Kermit slippers on during the day, either. I find a Yellow Pages, and I head to the hotel room to freshen up and marvel at how this situation has so quickly and bizarrely gone south. A shower, a coffee and some anodyne US TV later, there's a knock on the door and a tiny ray of hope.

"Bro! We've found a venue! We're gonna rally up the troops and come back to pick you up later."

Well, there we go. Life on the road, eh? Things don't always go the way you plan, but sometimes things suddenly get better, too. The mood is lightened. We take a stroll, have a meal and get ready for the gig. Sure, so the hotel is basic, and we're kinda out in the sticks a bit. The promoter has dubious footwear and he's just found an emergency venue on New Year's Eve in the Yellow bloody Pages, but hey! Miracles happen around this time of year, don't they?

No. No, they don't. Again, the clues come thick, fast and clear the minute we drive north from the hotel. And keep driving. And keep driving. Further and further away from the glitz of Miami and deep into the Florida boondocks. We pull up at an industrial estate; warehouses, factories, gas stations, very seedy looking strippery / brothelly-looking places and one dive bar right in the corner; in fact it is our venue for the night. But hey, a booking is a booking. I hold my head high and walk in.

"Well, howdy there, strangers, I guess you're the music man for the night," the toothless barman drawls. I can't tell if he's being folksy or sarcastic. "There's all the equipment you need; we hired some extra lights for y'all."

In the corner is a classic 80s school disco traffic light set-up. The decks are the really basic tray-opening CD units, and the mixer is covered in a thick layer of unclassified sticky stuff. I still can't tell if the barman is being sarcastic.

"A whole load of people are coming now, trust me, bro; it's going to be sick!"

The promoter has thankfully changed his footwear to a pair of non-descript trainers, and I can't fault him at all for his positive outlook, but something tells me it won't be great. I'm not sure if it's the number of pool tables here, the grumpy looking truckers loitering around the bar fingering their beer bottles like they're itching to lob them at us, or the simple fact that we are in the middle of buttfuck nowhere, but there's just something about the vibe that tells me this could actually be the worst NYE gig I'd played during my five-year career so far. So my friend and I enjoy a beer and talk to the promoter. We decline about a thousand offers of weed and acid and various other cosmic oddities and watch as the venue fills up with approximately 10 people. I realise this is as good as it's going to get.

I have to say, the set itself was pretty good. I'm a DJ; I love DJing in any scenario and, despite the challenges, I had a lot of fun and even did the countdown at midnight. The promoter and his friends finally amounted to about 15 people, so it wasn't the emptiest dancefloor I'd ever played to and, as long as I avoided eye contact with the scary truckers at the bar who were plainly becoming increasingly uncomfortable at my pacey and noisy selection, I felt reasonably satisfied under the circumstances. This wasn't the job I had expected, but it's the job I've come to do and I take great pride in smashing it.

"SICK set, bro!"

The promoter seemed a lot happier than I'd expected when I finished my set. Usually, in these instances, when shows spectacularly flop like this, the promoter is nowhere to be seen. They've either locked themselves in their office or hot-shoed home before anyone who needs paying can notice they've disappeared. But they're all still dancing away, heads in the clouds, grinning like idiots.

"Thanks," I reply. "Can I get my money, please?"

I don't like asking this question. No DJ likes having to ask for their money. But needs must in a scenario like this. It's clear no tickets have been sold, there have been fuck-ups with the venue, and this guy has lost some serious money. I feel bad for him but, most importantly, I'm not a charity for nightwear-sporting stoners, and US tours for low-level underground artists barely break even anyway.

"Oh yeah, sure, just ask that guy…."

He and his friends stand aside and, for the first time that night, I see a very fucked looking guy half asleep / half dying on a pool table. He looks *terrible*.

"Just give him a prod, he'll wake up."

As if this booking can't be any weirder, I now find myself prodding a complete stranger with a very unhealthy pallor to ask him for my money. This is awkward. Thankfully he seems amenable enough, sits up and reaches for his wallet. It's predictably empty, so he takes a deep breath and hauls himself off the pool table in the way a dog might get up on a hot day and gestures to the ATM in the corner of the bar. He stumbles over and silently takes the cash out, shakes my hand (very clammy), pays me, thanks me for coming and goes back to his pool table 'bed' and lays down. We order a cab and get the hell out of there.

There was just one last dark twist in the tale before we took flight. It happened when they picked us up the following morning to take us to the airport. We get in the car with the grass and mud crust still stuck inhabiting the wheel arches. We see that the guy who'd paid me is in the back of the car. He still looks very unwell and is still apparently in some type of semi-coma, which I assume is drug-related.

"So… er… who's this dude? We never got introduced properly. He just paid me and kinda went back to sleep."

"Ah, he does that," laughs the promoter. "He's our investor, actually. Great guy."

"Yeah, life and soul of the party. Is he okay? He doesn't look very well…."

"That's a funny story actually…"

The promoter explains how their previous event had ended in a very messy druggy affair and that their designated driver hadn't really understood the one very simple rule of being a designated driver and crashed their car driving home whilst out of his mind. The passengers had come out of it relatively unscathed. Except one. Our sleepy friend. He'd taken the brunt of the crash and had required major surgery to recover. Surgery which included losing an entire kidney.

"So yeah, this party was paid for by his insurance compensation! Pretty sick, huh?"

I look across the back seat to him again, and for the first time during this surreal 24 hours, I genuinely feel compassion and sympathy for one of these guys. What a poor dude. What utterly *terrible* friends. This really is a fucked-up situation. I want to reach out and give him a bit of a pat on the shoulder or a respectful nod. I want him to know that I appreciate the money he's spent on my fee, my flights and (albeit shitty) accommodation. This guy is a verified saint among absolute weirdos. He's the hero I totally didn't expect.

Then I look down at his feet and take it all back. For he, too, is now wearing a pair of Kermit The Frog slippers. Gazing moronically up at me. Stupid and green. Mutely mocking. I take a deep breath, close my eyes and feign sleep until we arrive at the airport.

LOONY BALLOONY

This is a weird one. The main protagonist here is resolutely not the usual laidback DJ type. He oversaw this beach bar that was pretty famous and notoriously messy. A proper wronghole. 'DJ Stickler', the resident there, used to amuse me greatly 'cos he was so uptight. For a scene like ours? I dunno but if DJs are a 'type', he was about as far away from it as it gets. I mean, the booth was totally plastered in his neatly-typed passive/aggressive notes about what you could and couldn't do. Rules inside the booth for DJs. Notices outside for punters. He was like one of those people in a house share that is always making lists and getting in a tizzy about the bathroom and making rotas for the kitchen. Got his own shelf in the fridge and labels all the food.

At the mad beach he was like everyone's Victorian Dad. Everyone was day-glo and he was in black and white. It was most noticeable if you DJ'd there. Firstly no one got paid. The place made a fortune over the bar, but only he got a wage. But he made you feel like it was a BIG favour to play there. A favour being done for you, to be clear. It was a total madhouse and, most importantly, nearly constantly off the hook. So that vibe which, to be fair, was 99.9% down to the loony punters, was a very attractive gig to DJs. I mean, I'm not kidding when I say you could play anything there and they would go potty. Mainly as it was a daytime thing, and almost everyone there came from being awake the night before. It was fabulous chaos.

So you'd plot-up to DJ for this place for free around midday and it would be great and you got the odd free beer if you could some- how corner a member of the frenetically overworked bar staff. Then, early-evening, just as it was getting good, he'd roll up to fully take the credit. The first thing he'd do to let you know he was there was by being a massive prissy fussbudget. I mean, literally, he'd get a brush and start brushing sand and dust off the stuff while you were trying to use it. Cleaning around and sometimes on you. You know, like that thing the annoying housemate does? I used to have a flatmate who, whenever they were pissed-off or wanted the place to themselves, would start hoovering madly and cleaning and making out like you were a human stain on the face of the planet and needed to be eradicated. Stickler made that type of fusspot look like a hippy with a bong and a dressing gown. He'd tut and frown, and if you took a needle off, he'd barge into you and take the cartridge apart from the deck not currently playing. I mean, granted, a lot of DJs came and went there, and it was pretty manic, but all you have to do is talk. Just say what you want. Like, "this is my place, and now you are done," or at least tap your watch or something, but it was a really quite weird sort of soft bullying.

He was ultra straight-laced, too, you know. Like not just sober but really anti-fun. Really tutted and rolled his eyes at the punters. He sort of hated them, really. This was the time of peak nutters too. Everyone was off their chops, but not DJ Stickler. No, sir! Not on his watch. He was sort of sweet some days, like a Puritan Mum sucking a lemon. There was this sort of mock concern he had for people "not looking after themselves", which was frankly just straight-up superiority, but he could be nice with it, in the way a moody Mum can be. Then he'd swing to full-on furious Dad of the Old Testament if something went wrong with 'his' place. It wasn't his, of course, as we will see. He wasn't very popular, but I actually quite liked him. He was pretty deluded in the sense that he really saw himself and this tiny bar as the rivals and peers of the world's megaclubs. He really did. Possibly as a lot of big DJs would roll up there after work and play sometimes. He saw himself at the centre of that; ergo he was the Daddy. I guess I am telling you all this as a preamble as to why it was so funny to see him taken out of his natural environment.

Von Stickler managed to wangle having this beach bar as a stage overseas at a UK festival. He called us in one day, 'us' being the lads who played there for free the most often. He liked us as we never complained and did a good job. He showed us this elaborate blueprint, which looked pretty good, to be fair, and he was proud as punch that "tons of imported sand" was being used to create a mock beach. What could be more 'beach bar' than an actual beach? In a nutshell, this whole place was being transported abroad to England, AND we got paid for once. There were sponsors, which was an appropriate tropical beverage. It was a red-letter day and he was over the moon. Also, a very rare thing was happening, one of the owners was coming. Like all things in this semi-tropical place, it was owned lock-stock by the tiny locals who were all minted, related and thought the foreigners were either hilarious or awful, including us. They were pretty religious too. In fact, this guy was called Moses. Moses and his family owned not just the bar but that entire stretch of beach and everything on it, including a couple of hotels. I liked him. He was a man of few words and seemed perpetually amused by everything. I got a sense that the subtext here was Stickler selling world domination to Moses and Co. This was a planetary franchise. The start of BIG THINGS.

Thing is, the festival was in England. The Schticklegruber was actually English, but the sun may have gone to his head a wee bit and made him forget what his homeland was really like. We went there as a group, and he was Mother Hen. Scout Leader. He loved fussing about and bossing us around on the journey. As soon as we landed, the fun started. Literally, every one of us was in the standard DJ uniform of that time and place, which was flip flops, vests, cargo shorts and some sort of pointless keychain or bangle. It was about 35 degrees when we left, and we arrived to a bracing British summer of about 10 degrees. I mean, we had come from somewhere hot, granted, but this place was *not warm.* I can't say it was freezing, but for people who didn't even bring a t-shirt, never mind shoes or a jacket, it got *properly* Baltic, fast. Moses' teeth started chattering at one point, and he was the only one with grown-up clothes. Like all natives of where we had come from, he always wore shirts and long trousers, even in a 45 degree heatwave. England was like the Antarctic for him. It wasn't awfully warm for the rest of us either. It didn't help that we were all sort of wrapped-up in Stickler's mad sort of Captain Ahab vibe, chasing the White Whale of his perfect gig. An obsessive psychodrama of sorts, and we were his doomed crew. Reality was not cast in any role whatsoever. He said it was going to be awesome and sunny, so it damn well had better be. Never occurred to any of us to think otherwise. Never occurred to him that he couldn't control the weather.

The festival was hilarious. Shin-deep mud. None of us could even stand up straight, like a bunch of shit Bambis on brown ice. Couple of us lost our flip flops immediately and did the whole thing bare-foot. We arrived at his perfect stage production, and it was like that moment in Spinal Tap with the mini-Stonehenge and the dwarves. The whole thing was about half the size and plastered entirely, every inch of it, in the branding of the tropical drink sponsor. This was not the plan. Stickler had a towel with him from the bar, so he huffily started pulling down whatever branding he could reach and put the towel over the front of the DJ booth. It was a bit grubby and sad, and that was just the towel. Moses looked somewhat less than his usual slightly amused. The 'imported sand' was definitely there but had clearly been imported from the local quarry as it was a sort of shade I can only describe as 'cement grey'. Stickler was more Ahab than ever, chivvying us all along and saying everything was FINE, just FINE in a slightly quavering John Cleese-esque way that suggested completely the opposite.

The weather got worse and worse. It went from chilly Brit summer-time to actually torrential. So there we were. Six of us from the tropics in the middle of a good ye olde worlde Great British quagmire. Our 'tropical' stage actually had a wee bit of overhead cover, so we became quite popular with people trying to find shelter. We gamely played our happy sunshine vibes whilst shivering our livers clean out of our rib cages in our vests and tans, and then Stickler had his best idea yet. To "bring the sunshine" by inflating all these beach balls he'd had the tropical sponsor make up, which in keeping with the whole disaster turned out to be not the size of beach balls at all but slightly smaller than a football. We spent hours blowing them up and he happily threw them into the crowd. The crowd liked it and started a game of lobbing them back. Balls flew back and forth. This must be the jolly British Dunkirk spirit they keep telling everyone about.

Now, I'm no scientist, but as we took turns to DJ, I noticed that the decks and mixer seemed more and more fucked up every time I got up to play. The faders would grind, the knobs would stick and soon, DJ Stickler, who liked the cleanest, most ship-shape operation in the world, was going out of his mind. Then, as one of the blowup balls wanged into my face, taking a little bit of skin with it, it also left a strange residue. It dawned on me what the tech issue was. I worked it out. Stickler had basically personally invented the world's most efficient anti-DJ device. I mean, even I know that sand and water is basically cement. The balls were a beautifully designed crud delivery system. They constantly flew overhead, and we would throw them back and before you know it, it was a little like a food fight. DJs and crew versus punters. Stickler's 'operation bring the sunshine' was seriously backfiring by fucking-up everything electronic. Which was everything important. Seriously, if you got a drawing board and some big brains and tried to invent a thing to completely fuck DJs up, what could be better? A 'fun' device that essentially everyone wants to play around with that drops gritty glue on everything it touches. Besides the locally-sourced imported sand being manky to begin with, after about the millionth time a mud-encrusted raver shambled into our 'beach' and stood on it, it became even nastier. The rain made it into a sludge that eventually completely caked every ball.

I point this out to Stickler. Stickler looks horrified 'cos not only has nearly all the gear had to be replaced already, but the artillery barrage is also *constant*. Even as I explain it to him, there are hundreds of balls flying through the air and hitting us while we talk. Already the mixer and both decks have needed replacing. At this rate, the entire festival and possibly the whole of England will eventually run out of Technics, mixers, and even amps and speakers. Stickler starts to panic. He is playing too at this point; as always, he saves the top slot for himself. His boss, Moses, is right there watching this madness. You can see in his face he is formulating opinions.

Stickler starts, one-by-one, to personally confiscate every single mini-beach ball. The playfulness of 'operation bring the sunshine' is now officially *over*. It is now 'operation miserable pensioner neighbour'. The crowd boos every time a ball is confiscated. A lot of balls and a lot of boos. Stickler sort of loves it too. He's in his pure element now: telling off kids, tidying up and stopping fun. I turn around and Moses looks greatly amused at the total chaos. He just gestures and I come over to him and he points at me to look at Stickler from behind. I go backstage and there is our glorious leader literally waist-deep in balls. He has managed to catch every single one and huffily stuffed them all into the booth with him until he is literally DJing with his arms in the air, elbows out like a fun-killing chicken or giant mad Davros, King of the Daleks. Kids are coming up and asking if they can have their ball and he furiously shakes his head and waggles his finger at them. Lacking gravitas somewhat as he is up to his tits in cement-covered balls. From the rear, the booth looks like the world's worst kiddy play area. A ball pit from 'Threads'. Although he retains his jolly Buddha-like countenance and is seemingly genuinely amused by the nightmare, something in the eyes of Moses tells me the plan to take over the world ends here, today.

There he is right there, the most prissy, OCD and uptight man in the universe alone in the eye of the ravemuck hurricane. Lord of Chaos on the day of his triumph. Literally tits-deep in his own creation. The ultimate grumpy neighbour with every local kid's ball in his garden. And he ain't giving *anyone* their ball back, no matter how nicely they ask. No, sir.

SEPARATED AT BIRTH

Let's just say the festival was near a historic, beautiful city on the Baltic coast of a very big country famous for its furry hats, clear spirit and wooden dolls that fit inside other wooden dolls, that fit inside other wooden dolls (and so on). It was my first time in the country, at a time when its new class of billionaire kleptocrats were buying up English football clubs and Cypriot passports and starting to moor their megayachts in Ibiza. Accordingly, it was the best fee I'd ever earned in my at-that-time brief career as a touring DJ. A good enough fee to get me there a day early for the full experience.

Upon arriving, I found myself on a coach with a few other DJs I didn't know, a couple of tour manager types, some shy young people I took to be journalists or bloggers and a highly effusive English guide. He was suspiciously vague about why he was there or where he was from but incredibly excited about the event. Or, more precisely, the money the organisers were throwing at the event. "It's about prestige for these guys," he explained, leaning in to whisper conspiratorially, "they don't know anything about music or DJs! But money is no object."

I didn't really know whether to be insulted that I was clearly not there thanks to the passion generated by my middling brand of disco house, or regretful that I hadn't asked for even more money. The bill was impressive in a kind of grab-bag of random names kind of way: portly house DJs from the USA, a couple of humongous trance behemoths from the Low Countries, and even a former member of the Prodigy. The big names were supplemented with filler acts like me, most likely plucked from whoever (like me) had had a little bit of press recently.

I was delighted to learn that my grand concrete-but-elegant hotel was a famous one from the Cold War. This was where the former regime had placed visiting diplomats and attachés, explained our guide. I imagined the rooms wired for sound and surly men in raincoats in the lobby, peering through pinholes in newspapers. There was a bottle of vodka and a shot glass in the room instead of a bottle of water. It tasted slightly oily, the way I'd read in a magazine once that the good stuff should. A quick shower and change and another shot and I was feeling like disco James Bond.

The next day was the festival proper and I found out that it was split into two. The big trancey stadium acts would be playing on a massive aerodrome on the mainland. The more esoteric of us were playing a more select gig on a centuries-old island fort. It was pretty spectacular to get there by speedboat. Not even one of my fellow passengers falling through a big unmarked and un-roped-off hole in the jetty when we arrived could ruin the buzz. At least when we were sure that they hadn't died. After playing an early set to barely anyone in the exterior court-yard and watching the sunset, I decided to explore the fort a bit.

First, I walked around the ancient battlements as far as I could. The event had barely started, there was a distinct lack of liaison or supervision, and the DJ who was on was playing, of all things, breaks.

It was becoming increasingly clear that health and safety was not a big deal here. At several points, I nearly toppled from the sandstone walls into either the freezing water or the cobbles ten meters below like some sort of Medieval Knievel, a pleasing jolt of adrenaline that also anticipated the parkour-influenced opening scene of 'Casino Royale' by several years. Fortified by more vodka, and in the knowledge that danger was very much my middle name, I decided to try to penetrate the interior of the fort. As dancers dodged over-enthusiastic, unsupervised pyrotechnics bursting either side of the stage, I made my way behind it.

I discovered that the fort was laid out in a series of concentric and ever-smaller circles, like the famous dolls I literally hadn't seen anywhere. The first was a general backstage area. One DJ sitting on a flight case, a toilet cabin, and, on a shelf, my guide from the coach, fast asleep despite the decibels. I continued onwards and inwards, through a dusty arch hung with a velvet curtain and into a flurry of colour. This was the dancers' changing room, where impossibly athletic people, possibly imported from Ibiza, were sliding in and out of tiny outfits, professionally oblivious to my presence. I did feel like I was intruding, but I kept my eyes forward and aimed for the next archway.

The next 'ring' was empty, save for a brand new and incongruous purple sofa and glass table with a half-full bottle of champagne and two glasses, like the scene of a luxury kidnapping. One more empty ring, darker and more gloomy than the last and then I emerged into a room containing a handful of what was either soldiers or extremely paramilitary-looking police. Wearing balaclava things and machine guns... the lot. I set course for another curtained door, clutching my artist lanyard like a life raft. They turned around and watched me blankly. Afraid to turn back and expecting a little laser dot to appear on my forehead any minute, I blundered on and through.

And emerged into a raucous sweet sixteen birthday party. A table of ice buckets and imported spirits. More purple couches. Twenty or so teenagers dressed in skinny white designer jeans, boho style dresses, huge logo T-shirts. All of them visibly and loudly pissed. And all really, really, pleased to see me.

Why became clear when two lurched towards me, liquid swilling out the side of their crystal glasses.

"Tiesto! You are Tiesto."

I am, in fact, *not* Tiesto. The only thing I have in common with the Dutch megastar is that we both play records for a living, and we both have a lanky look and a (certainly in my case) undeservedly youthful appearance. All I know about him is the odd factoid that in Spain, his name means 'plant pot', which I imagine has led to many Ibiza locals mightily confused about why that garden centre on the billboards is so expensive. I mean, sure, this room is dark, but Tiesto and I simply don't have the same hair colour, haircut, eyes, fashion sense, aura of success and prestige or music taste.

A simple misunderstanding, and one I was keen to clear up. I had reached what looked like the final boss level of the pointless castle challenges I had set myself, and if I wanted to hang out with a bunch of pissed up teenagers, I would've been playing student union gigs (I'd played a student union gig the week before). Let the kids have their fun and I'll return to the action, maybe find someone I know, or wake up that guy from the coach.

"No, no, I'm not Tiesto," I explained, shaking my head paternally.

"You are Tiesto."

"No, no, not me, lovely to meet you, must be going." But the rest of the group had clocked me now.

"You are Tiesto." Not so patient now. I'm sensing a slight irritation with me at this point.

"We want picture. We want sign with Tiesto. Picture. Sign."

I'm starting to realise that I've stumbled across a colony of the children of the country's nouveau riche. The clothes should've been a clue, or just the fact that they were isolated here in the centre of the castle like so many little princes and princesses. Like royalty, they were clearly not people who were used to being told 'no'. But as a busy man with things to do, I kept shaking my head politely and turned back to the door.

Only to find my way blocked by a *very* large man in a suit with a face like a granite tombstone. The submachine gun he was carrying on a strap over his shoulder, very black, very space-age and heavy-looking, twitched as he cocked his head microscopically to one side. And back.

By now, the kids were getting a bit handsy: "Picture! Sign! Tiesto!"

Well, it was the biggest audience I'd had that night. I spent the next hour writing autographs, posing for photos – with individuals, with groups, with the whole bunch – and being pawed, mauled and man-handled. I think I might even have developed a shlight Dutch akshent at one shtage, to my everlasting shame. Eventually, they got bored of me, and the professional murderer on the door gently ushered me out. I'd like to say that we all became great friends, that the spirit of rave brought us together despite the language difficulties etc. etc. But we didn't. They were an awful bunch of spoiled, bullying little shits who should've been drowned in the Baltic. I still don't know if they really thought I was a very famous Dutch trance DJ. Maybe they were taking the piss out of me for invading their little sanctum. Maybe they were simply constructing their own reality in a way that only the very rich and entitled can do. But I spent the entire time worrying irrationally that the genuine article might walk in any minute, and I'd get shot.

I just hope Tiesto had a better evening impersonating me.

EL RAVAL

2010, summertime, and I'm outside a restaurant in Barcelona, having a post-tapas ciggie, minding my own business, thinking about how crazy life my fairly new DJ life has become. It's late evening, and the city is starting to come alive again as the locals head out to eat and drink. I can hear glasses being clinked, conversations and greetings in Spanish and taxis idling behind groups of friends navigating the narrow streets.

At this stage, I was new to touring internationally. Dubstep had recently blown up and I was riding that second big mainstream wave. One minute I was playing to 20 mates in a pub and occasionally putting some tunes online and it seemed like the next I was flying around the world. It was a dizzying experience and, at times, a bit of a culture shock. There's no way to control your environment when you're on the road. You're at the mercy of random people and you never quite know what random people are up to. Especially if they come up from behind.

Like this particular occasion, someone out of the blue on the street comes up and pinches my arse. Not a cheeky tweak. A full-on, iron-fingered clamp grip. They'd grabbed flesh and cranked it painfully, like the gain on the mixer when the sound technician's got his back turned. Now I was deep in my thoughts, taking in this pretty full-on Spanish city for the first time. I yelped like a chihuahua and jumped a few feet in the air. Then I turned around and did what I'd do in any other situation where someone's invaded my space; I lamped the culprit in the stomach. It was a completely knee-jerk reaction, and it wasn't until the punch had landed that I realised who I was hitting; a six-foot-plus drag queen in full regalia. Flowing wig, perfect make-up, electric blue dress.

She was rolling deep as two fellow queens flanked her… and right now, she was winded and coughing her guts up.

It was one of those frozen moments where everyone pauses to take in what's happened. I never expected to have my arse grabbed like that. She never expected me to punch her. And I never expected to be punching a drag queen. This has gone from a quiet moment of reflection to a possible public hate crime. I panicked and compounded it by pushing them out of the way, causing one of them to fall over the winded one. I ran back into the restaurant where the promoter, two other DJs, my friend and the MC were all sitting at the table with a great view of what had just happened, clapping and pissing themselves laughing at me.

"Did you put her up to that?" I ask them. Pretty pissed off, if I'm honest.

A chorus of head shakes. Apparently, it was clearly just one of those random things that random people do. The trio were proper drag queens. I soon learnt there was a bar around the corner famous for drag artists and various burlesque shows and cabaret acts. My pals had watched them talking and smoking, one pointing to my behind, another one twisting it and you already know the rest of the story. The problem was that they were now standing outside the restaurant, punching their palms in the universal sign language 'I am going to hurt you' gesture and shouting raucously. They wanted vengeance and I wanted to get the hell out of here. But the promoter merely shrugged and ordered another round.

"They'll be gone soon; they're performing round the corner. I just don't think they're used to being punched," he explains.

I'm not used to punching drag queens either if I'm honest. She was bigger than me by at least a head, but it just felt wrong. Anyway, we had another drink or two and, true to my man's prediction, they did disappear. I don't think we even saw them leave, we were busy chatting and they'd gone.

The next episode was a lot more pleasurable. My set was in Barcelona's most badass club. It was heaving, the crowd were pretty wild and I was very happy with my set. I can't stress how new all this was to me and how mind-blowing it was to be doing all of this. So, after my set, I decided to celebrate and search for something a bit stronger than booze.

"Cocaine?" The offer came from a slick-looking man of diminutive height, sporting a dapper moustache and had sidled up like he was on wheels. He looks like he's been selling coke since the 70s. So I think *yeah, why not?* The timing of it was too perfect. So I nod and follow him, thinking we're going to another room or the toilets, but no, we're walking outside the front of the venue.

"In. Car."

Okay, so he's very security conscious and he's not bringing it into the club. I'll roll with it. So we get into his car. An old battered VW Golf which is not very coke dealer at all. Well… it would be if it was Essex in 1992 instead of the home of Gaudi and Camp Nou. We sit and he proceeds to start the engine.

"Woah, woah. We're not driving anywhere. I need to be in *that* club!" I tell him, pointing forcefully. My jacket, my phone and my tunes are all in the club. I was not keen on a 2am sightseeing tour.

"Five minutes only!" he barks and off we go. I suck my teeth and decide to jump out the next time he stops. But he doesn't. It's like every traffic light in Barcelona has been magically switched green for the occasion. When we do indeed stop, it is smack in the courtyard of a square of old flats. The Barça projects. Even in the weak glow from the open doorway, it all looks pretty run down. Flaking paint on the walls in the few spots where there's no graffiti. Deserted balconies with moth-eaten canopies. The only sign of life is the rattle of battered air conditioning units intermittently hanging off the crumbling edifice.

"Five minutes, back with cocaine. You wait," he orders. Like I've got any choice in the matter. So I do wait. Five minutes. Ten minutes. Fifteen minutes. This geezer's taking the piss. I'm a stranger in a strange land. In the deep end. I think about beeping the horn but I'm in the middle of a pretty ghetto area in a city I don't know at all that speaks a language I can't speak a word of. I don't want to bring attention to myself in what is clearly an illegal scenario. Twenty minutes. Fuck this, I'm out of here. I get out and walk in the general direction we came. I'll ask for directions from the first people I see and I'll hail the first cab I see. Sorted.

Already I'm feeling better about the situation. I'm back in control. Then I hear some singing around the corner. It's English singing. Not bad harmonies, either. I pick up the pace and walk around the corner to see three men all singing away. My saviours.

"Excuse me, I... *Woah!*"

They turn around and all look at me in pantomime shock. I can't fucking believe it. It's the drag queens from earlier! Now wigless and dressed down a lot more, but still with their make-up on. Their cheerful singing stops mid bar as recognition dawns on them. They quickly assume the attitude of murderous rage I'd seen earlier and charge at me.

Without many options, I charge at them and, employing another knee-jerk reaction I didn't even know I had, I start doing this weird windmilling thing with both arms punching anything and everything in my path. I've had fights in the past and I've never tried such a move and I doubt I'd do it again but, fuck it, it kind of worked.

So then I get past them and *run*. I run as I've never run before.

They're on my tail. And the chase is well and truly *on*. In hindsight, it must have looked like something out of Benny Hill. Three off duty drag queens chasing a young wet-eared DJ in his first year of touring around the ends of Barcelona. But at the time, I am absolutely shitting myself. This part of the city is old, and the streets are narrow and confusing and silent, with street lights few and far between. Tall blocks of flats loom overhead and the sounds of shouting and footsteps echo off their scuffed, sand-coloured walls. Occasionally I see wider boulevards with trees and sparse traffic at the end of the corridor-like alleys, but I don't know whether the open ground is worth the risk of breaking cover. I jump behind bins, crouch in the narrow gaps between parked cars, behind scooters, in bushes, doorways. I bounce, rattling off metal shutters on shop windows and skid changing direction on the shiny cobbled pavements. My pursuers seem to have split up and every time I make a break for it and turn a corner, I see one of them coming the other way. I'd love to see my route on one of those jogging apps, with all the twists and turns I must have sketched out a maze over mad mileage. But I was running for my life.

Then came my lucky break. At a wide, otherwise deserted junction flanked by ragged-looking trees, finally I see a cab. I rush over, slam the door and keep looking around. I'm not out of the woods quite yet.

"[famous club] por favor!"

Twitching and looking around as we drive away, part of me wishes I could see them and give them the middle finger. But the overwhelming feeling is relief. Then the driver is laughing as we pull up two minutes later, right beside the club. In the heat of the chase, somehow, I'd not just ended up in the right direction, I'd nearly made it there. I tipped the man heavily for unwittingly saving my life and strolled back into the club, taking one last look over my shoulder. The coast was clear. I head upstairs and find my mate near the decks.

"Where the fuck have you been? Tried to ring you loads of times. I got your tunes, they are backstage. You been running or something? You look quite sweaty. You taken anything? What you got? I got a load of coke. Bought it earlier off a geezer in here, well sound. Want some? Why are you hugging me?"

FREQUENT FLYERS

I wanted to tell the story of travelling the world as a 'woman of colour'. I don't like that term, but I need to keep it vague to protect myself. The journeys were pure work, of course, my job. I have to say these days, it feels like a good time to talk about this sort of thing. It was in the past, so sometimes when I mention these stories to friends, *white* friends, of course, they always say something like, "oh, it was a different time". No, it really wasn't. It wasn't the 1960s. It was only a few years back!

This tour wasn't such a hard gig and it was to be one of many over some years. I've done far worse in terms of grind and schedule. It just left an impression on me as the first one. I think as well with the recent thing with Black Lives Matter and the change in attitudes, it seems timely. One of the things I find amazing is that the terrible things white observers see really gets to them, whilst I just totally shrug them off. The person I toured with in this story was a white boy, and he was constantly appalled and outraged at how I was treated and, honestly, it's totally the norm. Standard. This is the problem men have, denial. Denial can manifest itself as outrage too. You see that it happens but feel you have to be more outraged than those of us it happens to. By doing this, you deny us. That ain't right, honey.

First off, on this tour, White Boy is surprised when I tell him to always go for the man at the check-in desk because men are relatively laid back, but women are always meticulous, do their jobs properly and can be *far* more aggressive. He was shocked and saw it as the other way around, his privilege right there. I'd often just leave a queue that had a female attendant working and join a far longer queue for a male. And I have to say, wherever we had to engage with a female attendant, we tended to get difficulties and sometimes outright obstruction. I would just go through it all and then give my travel partner a knowing look after when I was proven correct. I totally recognise this is unpleasant to hear and shocking, but I'm just reporting what I deal with all the time. Yes, of course, this is not a universal issue. Not all men are lazy pushovers and not all women are obstructive nightmares. It's a huge generalisation but one I very much act upon and believe in due to experience.

I've been a travelling DJ for a long while now and speaking with White Boy who was also an old hand on the tour with me, he tells me the entire career for him he's literally never once been stopped, questioned, checked or even particularly inconvenienced other than the odd delay or lost bag. Almost every stage of every journey with me, something would happen. And he gets to see it first hand right next to me. I'm talking sinister plainclothes security types pulling me out of queues before we'd even checked in. "Can you come with me please?" and they would never say why. Sometimes grabbing and pulling. Then there'd be an hour, maybe two of stupid questions. "Where are you from? Where were you born?" You know, as if the passport they are holding right in front of their eyes is fake, and so am I. Sometimes missing the flight. White Boy would get to see the truth of the inequality of the world time after time after time. Sequentially. Trip by trip. Day by day. Passports would be heavily scrutinised. Officers and superiors would be called. Bags ripped apart, checked and rechecked. And listen, I'm a classy person. Well dressed and turned-out at all times. Just the wrong colour to be anywhere near an airport, apparently. And I can't stress this enough; at every stage of the journey, something would happen. Some trips had three separate flights and we would be taken aside six times, in and out. I say "we". He was, ironically, just a passenger in all this.

It wasn't just the travel. It depended a lot on the country, but all sorts would happen with drivers, promoters and hotels once we got there. Australia was the worst by some margin. Like I couldn't even get a cab to stop and got openly racist comments on the street. The USA was the worst for borders, but again, it depends. Like some USA gigs were very 'integrated' and felt relaxed, but others were really 'white' and would be problematic. In a sense, though you were sort of prepared for 'Western' racism as it is kind of familiar? But when you were in a 'non-white' country where I was somehow still the 'wrong' shade was really weird. I mean, Eastern Europe was *tough*. But it was places like India, Indonesia, Saudi Arabia and South America that I found really shocking as I was surrounded by people of all sorts of backgrounds and shades, but if anything, it could be even *more* overtly racist.

What I didn't understand was that in some situations my pale male touring partner was by far the *only* white person around and he never got any kind of stick at all. Not even so much as a mention. It's like a global get-out-of-jail card. You can sort of see why, in this weird culture war, how white people are so blind to racism. The whole world has been programmed to defer to them via colonialism. It's strange to talk about it, but it is important to me. It was this tour, though, that really opened my eyes in a big way. You could tell the story of the sexism and racism on its own, but it was really thrown into relief because White Boy was right there alongside. Like a control experiment. How I was treated compared to someone right next to me doing exactly the same job at the same time. I mean, there would be times where we'd be greeted or interviewed or met and the person would just immediately talk to him and never once look at me. Like a jacket of invisibility was on. I had to tell White Boy to stop trying to steer it, as out of embarrassment, he'd force the person to say hello or squeeze me into the small talk, but it was crushingly embarrassing sometimes. For all concerned.

I was inspired to talk because I liked your other books. Like what you are trying to do with it. But isn't it really interesting how the female stories in them are all about harassment and the lads are about having a big old laugh? There's the privilege again right there. The biggest problem white men seem to have is having too much fun, while the women and people from 'minority' backgrounds (sorry, I don't even know what is correct anymore!) don't have time or the ease of privilege to get fucked up and live the rock' n' roll life. We're too busy trying to be heard. Trying to overcome. Although telling all this reminds me of a great comeback from a black friend who is also a DJ...

Let's use the name 'X'. We were once in a very, shall we say fraught? I dunno, not violent but about-to-get-violent sort of situation. So I step up and I am quite small, but I get on my toes and get in this nasty guy's face who is giving us racist stick in the booth, and X is behind, smoking. Just when it looked to get a bit out of hand, X steps over and just asks nicely, "Is everything OK here? Can I help?" and while doing that, just gently touches the raging steroid guy on the face with the lit cigarette. It was amazing how it diffused the whole thing! Guy jumped about three feet in the air. Like you could see the gears working in this guy's tiny head. Thinking, "If X meant to do that, X is a maniac and very much to be avoided, but if they didn't mean it and it was an accident, then I am soft as shit", and he just sort of melted away. I turned to X and was like, "Whoa! Did you mean to do that?" and X just looked at me and took a big theatrical drag on the cig and replied, "Mean to do what?" and just turned, smiled, and walked off.

GAY FOR PAY

"Here you go, dude, home sweet home. Drop your bags and let's hit the town. What a night we have planned!"

Touring at home in the UK, the best an underground DJ can expect is a drive from the hotel to the club. If they're lucky. But when you arrive in almost any other country around the planet, you're given the luxury treatment. It's something I've never failed to appreciate, even after touring internationally for over 15 years, and it's something I definitely appreciated after my epic ten-hour flight from London. I followed my chaperone's orders, dumped my bags in my room and we quickly hit the road. It was my first set in San Francisco for several years. I was there a night early, the city had never let me down on the party stakes before and I was keen to blow the long-haul cobwebs off and have a blast.

"You hungry, bro?"

Of course I was. So my two new companions and I take in our first stop; Hamburger Mary's, an LGBTQ+ friendly burger chain. It's 8pm, I'm in that floaty, sleepy jetlagged state, the vibe is fabulous and the menu is mouth-wateringly fattening. Heaven. I order much more than my belly could possibly fill and drink as much as I can. My new friends seem really cool and I'm settling into the groove very nicely.

"You ready to hit a bar?"

Damn right I was. So I'm taken to a venue around the corner. Like the burger bar, it's bedecked in rainbows and they're pumping out some serious disco belters. I figure my two friends are clearly gay and they're showing me their favourite spots in San Fran, so I continue to drink, dance and laugh my way through the evening. At some point, we hit the shots. We get high. Soon my jet lag is well and truly behind me. I enter that dangerous phase any touring DJ will recognise; the classic up-for-36-hours-now-high-as-fuck-anything-can-happen type of state where you feel you could crack on for days and days. It's the phase you usually hold on to for *after* the set you're booked for but these guys sure know how to party. My show wasn't for another 24 hours, so bring it on!

"You ready to hit the club?"

We bundle into another cab and before long, we were being ushered into a very lively club, cutting the queue completely. Of course, it was an LGBTQ+ venue; I'd have been disappointed by now if it wasn't. And once again, I was welcomed with open arms and treated to more shots, more jokes and more random encounters with San Francisco's most fabulous party people. This was great and one of the best arrival parties I think I'd ever had. My flight seemed like it had happened weeks or even months ago and I was already a rainbow veteran of the San Fran scene. I'd well and truly landed!

"Okay, let's take things to the next level! You ready?"

I was born ready! These guys had just scored a session hat trick with the perfect burger joint, bar and club. I knew I was in safe hands. I just wanted to keep the party going. More shots, more bumps, more giggles and another taxi to our next destination, which appeared to be at the end of a lane. One of my new friends turns and gives me a wink as we stroll towards a very private looking establishment. Unlike the spotlit and spangly bars we'd been to, this was extremely low-key. They knock on the door and we're ushered into a lurid pink and scarlet boudoir. It looked like a wild west style brothel. But strictly full of chaps.

"Surprise! It's a massage parlour! Let us know what you want to do and we'll take care of it. There's even a glory hole...."

I pause for a second. This was an odd twist and one I'm not massively comfortable with. Bars, drinking, partying, dancing, flirting... sure, bring it on! But massages and glory holes? This was too much for me. I needed to come back to earth a bit and work out how I'd ended up here.

"I'm not sure I'm up for this bit guys, you knock yourselves out. Maybe I can meet you in a bar later?"

"Oh, we're not gay. We were instructed that you were?"

The conspiracy unfolds. The thick plottens. A friend back home had DJ'd for the same promoters just a few weeks before and heard I was due in town later. He thought it would be hilarious to tell them I'd just come out of the closet, that I'd ended my marriage of ten years and I was very keen to make up for lost time. He told them that I was still quite raw and emotional and quite confused about the situation, so didn't like to talk about it publicly, but he advised that a night out in San Fran's famous gay scene would really do me a power of good. All of this was nonsense except one thing, the night out *had* done me good. I hadn't had this much fun arriving at a booking in years.

I guess, ultimately, I'm just not a glory hole kinda guy.

There was one final postscript. When I'd first arrived at my hotel to check-in, I'd just opened the door and dumped my bags; I hadn't looked around or taken anything in at all. But that following morning, when I got back, I turned on the lights, pulled back the covers, and discovered that my bed was covered with a veritable rainbow of gay porno mags, DVDs and a bunch of sex toys. All neatly arranged on display.

That's the kind of attention to detail you've just got to admire.

ENGAGE AUTOPILOT

It was summertime and I had a weekend where I had two gigs. One on the Friday and one on the Saturday. I played the closing set on Friday at an East London club and that went really fine. The last two hours, I started to have a drink.

I wound up getting invited to this after-party. So I thought, "You know what, I'll pop down for a couple hours" but I wanted to be fresh for my set the next day. I went along and by this time, it was around 7 o'clock in the morning. I promise myself, "I'm leaving by 9am. Latest"

It gets to 9am... Push it back again. 11am... push it back again... 1pm... push it back again....

By this point, I'd come so far out the other end that I had to carry on, like a transatlantic flight that's halfway across the ocean without enough fuel to turn back. I'd reached the point of no return.

I had my set put together for that night already, and I had my stuff with me, so it seemed like the best option even though I was in this real druggy headspace. Especially as I remembered it was one of my best friend's birthdays and he was having a barbecue in the afternoon. So I took my mate from the after-party and headed there. It was really sunny and people were dancing. The vibe was really nice but we were fading fast. So we decided to resort to various options from her bag to stay awake.

A few more drinks on top of that and it's now about 8:30pm. I was playing the opening set at another East London hot spot at 9pm.

We're on the way, and I'm just gonna make it on time, when my mate says, "Look, I have half a pill on me, why don't we do it and that will make your set even more fun!" I'm not really in the best headspace to say whether or not having this pill is a good idea, but it sounds like a species of plan in a totally plan-free environment. So I take it.

Everything is *great,* we're having a laugh, I'm suddenly feeling pretty good. Like, "shit, this pill has brought me back to life!" The club is already pretty busy with a lot of people waiting for my set. So it's like, "Bam! set up quick and start playing". Ride the momentum. Fresh start. Played my first track, second track and people are vibing. The downstairs is filling up.

And I'm starting to feel the effects of this pill more and more. I'm seeing everyone kind of wavey and I'm feeling happy, it's really nice. I put my headphones on to listen to the next track to check where I was going to mix it in from.

My eyes are closed. I'm dancing away. I am deep in the zone. In fact, I get completely lost in the zone listening to it... 'this is good, this is gonna go down *great'.* Suddenly I get a tap on my shoulder from someone, and when I open my eyes, he's pointing to the crowd.

I had completely omitted to mix the second track in. The main track that had been playing had stopped about two minutes ago. I've been dancing away, eyes closed with my headphones on while the club has been completely silently watching me.

Everybody in the basement is staring at me with these massive grins on their faces and then the whole room starts cheering. I have never been so embarrassed.

It was like having a typical DJ anxiety dream where you get to a show and you forget your CDs, or suddenly you can't mix or some shit like that. But it was actually happening to me in real life.

After that, I played like a man possessed and somehow managed to save the set. But the guy who was running the night wasn't impressed one bit. Apparently, he regularly tells this story now and, of course, everyone thinks it's just *hilarious.* Just not hilarious enough to get me booked at that party ever again.

WRESTLEMANIA

It was the fanciest hotel in the entire Midlands and many parts of Leicestershire. The restaurant had a dedicated sushi chef and a far eastern fusion menu. The bar was designed by a famous architect and the lampshades were each worth as much as a small car. It served elaborate drinks, including a vast selection of obscure bespoke rums. Famous people would regularly stay at the hotel after their massive show nearby: Oasis, Stereophonics, Snoop Dogg. One time it was these older guys who just said they were in a band. "Oh, what's your band called?"

"Oh, we're called The Doors." I mean, *fucking hell...*

The hotel bar also had me as a resident, every weekend, drinking quality rum for free, getting rather high and generally lowering the tone.

Occasionally, though, I had help with that. Like when a huge American wrestling show hit town and essentially took the whole place over. Everyone was in the bar. The DJ booth faces the bar, then to the left is the swanky restaurant. And this pack of wrestlers, all built like giant condoms full of walnuts, were telling me, "You've gotta get out of here; this is the VIP Area." They'd just re-lacquered the bar and spent loads of money doing so and the manager, this very laid back Italian dude, was calmly watching all the women wrestlers dancing on the bar topless, smashing the fresh bar top up with their heels. Everyone else who worked there had their heads in their hands.

The wrestlers kept coming up to me and saying, "Yo man! Play some hip-hop! What the fuck is this shit?" So I put on 'Witness The Fitness' by Roots Manuva, and they were like, "This isn't hip-hop, this is fucking *techno* man!" I mean, they really, *really* hated my music in a demonstrably steroidy way. They wanted 'In Da Club' or something like that. So there are all these 9ft tall women wrestlers with their tits out on the bar and the guys had a hold of this 'young buck' wrestler as they called him, a prospect being 'initiated'. So they were pouring beer on their hands and, in their own words, 'bitch slapping' him on his bare chest as he screamed, "Oh daddy, daddy no!"

I was just really pissed off that they were questioning my musical taste, so in turn, I started questioning their masculinity. Frankly, because I was very coked up and also very drunk. "Fucking look at you guys, you're all slapping each other and oiling each other up. Think you're all tough and macho and look at the fucking state of you!" I mean, I was basically offering them out. There was a guy who was the width of three people who focussed on me and tried to talk it all down. Triple Torso and some of his older wrestler mates were giving me the "listen, son…" kind of speech, trying to keep me out of trouble with the younger, more aggy ones. At one point, I had a *literal* tag team leaning over the decks promising to beat the shit out of me.

But it was one of those gigs where my lowly status actually gave me a weird freedom. If I'd been booked as a celebrity DJ, I'd have had to kowtow to them, but I was the resident who was there every week while they were just passing through. Also, I simply didn't give a toss.

Some time later, some bloke with the Stereophonics wanted to fight me because he didn't like the music. "Play some fuckin' rock!" he squealed. What could I tell him? Mate, I once picked a fight with an entire Royal Rumble over my music. I'm hardly gonna change my style for a skinny Welsh rocker, am I?

THE PHANTOM DJ

I was closing an open-air stage at a festival when it absolutely, manically pissed it down. I played Purple Rain, about 12 mad punters stayed for a soggy group hug, then even the plucky damp dozen vanished.

Thirty of us made a decision and bundled the decks and monitors into a small backstage tent, keeping them plugged in for audio and power thanks to the massive stage cables. We zipped it up and had our own mini festival party. After a few hours, we started hearing whoops and cheers outside our hermetically sealed sesh. The rain had stopped, the sound from our mixer's output was still booming out of the main stage's massive speakers and people were having a tasty dry rave outside. It was beautiful.

The crew and dancers all rushed onstage and made it a jam, but we kept the decks where they were inside the smaller offstage tent, so I was playing completely hidden. The actual onstage DJ booth looked weirdly empty, so like genius magpies on ketamine, our mates started assembling a pretend DJ booth out of the kind of stuff you find lying around on a Sunday night at a festival.

A dog biscuit was the crossfader. Bottle caps for the EQs. iPhone leads as tonearms. Various citrus fruits as effects knobs. Then they started picking really up-for-it punters to give them their shot at stardom and have a go in the 'booth'. I could see it all from the side, through a gap in the tent. It was sublime! People living their DJ fantasies, punching the air and occasionally waving a dog biscuit.

The stage curfew was 3am. As the time approached, a beefy phalanx of security appeared, ready for an orderly end to the fun and to usher everyone off. But none of the security noticed that the decks were made from trash or that the DJ in the booth was just a miming random. They definitely couldn't see me controlling it all from the side. So… well. I just carried on, didn't I? 'Last songs' kept fading out then, bang! In with another.

Security was *very* pissed off. They rushed the booth after my third cheeky encore only to encounter a sweet, young and totally terrified rave lad who, bless his soul, uttered the immortal phrase "B-b-but I can't make it stop… I'm playing a lime…."

TOXIC

In South Africa, in the club scene, there's so much toxic masculinity. If I have to go to the bouncer and say that a guy's harassing me, I know there's a high chance nothing will happen, or he'll get kicked out for five minutes and be straight back in again. Sometimes it reaches a point that makes you question whether the whole industry itself is rotten.

I was playing as support for this very famous female South African musician. A Big Star. It was still during the beginning of my DJ career, so I was quite happy about the gig and pretty hyped. I thought *yes! This is my perfect break.* As a DJ, you always think you've made it when you work with specific famous people you've idolised or that have a lot of status within the industry… at least until you actually work with them.

Many leading female Joburg DJs play balls-to-the-wall techno to distract from the fact that they're girls. But I don't hide my femme energy from my sets. The way that I am, the way that I dance, the way I DJ, the way that I dress is all very free. But sadly, anything that's 'free' for many men makes them think, O*kay, I can do whatever I want.*

We were playing at a festival in Swaziland, but the night before, we had a gig at this nightclub in Johannesburg. I walk into the club to set up for my set and it's packed with men. I mean packed, like chock-full. There are a few hunnies, obviously, but it's mainly a super masculine space.

I go to the bar and these two guys straight away come over and offer to buy me a drink. When I say "no, I'm fine, thanks", they start getting aggressive. Now I know exactly what kind of space I'm in.

Anyways, I try to make the best of it. I'd seen a group of guys hanging out behind the DJ booth while a male DJ was playing. I'm up next, so I go over to the tour manager of this big lady artist I'm supporting, and I say to him, "When I'm playing, can we please make sure that there are no guys standing behind me in the DJ booth?"

"Okay, cool"

I start playing my set and the men are still there. I'm looking for this tour manager as I'm playing but I can't see him anywhere. For my entire set, all these guys are shouting at me, making remarks and saying stupid things. The proximity between them and the decks is so close it's like we're basically on top of each other. You can imagine the intensity of that kind of energy.

I'm super upset. I feel fragile, vulnerable, not safe at all, and there's no one around to assist me. These men weren't just sitting there; they were invasive. One of the guys kept coming up and trying to grab me and make comments. But I just kept thinking, 'I need to get through this set'.

When I finished, I went to the bathroom to have a bit of a cry. It was so overwhelming.

I pull myself together and go back and try to find this tour manager. When I see him, I'm like, "Where were you? I asked you specifically to get these guys away from me when I played." His response was, "I'm not working for you. I'm working for the Big Star."

About 30 minutes after this chat, the same tour manager is clearly starting to get drunk.

Meanwhile, I'm still trying to brush the experience off because this is literally the first night of my tour with these guys, so I'm dancing in the roped-off area for the headline artist when I feel someone touch my ass. I turn around and I'm like, "What the hell?!" It's not some random guy, it's the tour manager himself. He does it again, and again, and *again* even though I tell him, "the next time you do that, I'm going to break your hand. You have to stop."

Of course, I'm now thinking to myself: *fuck, this is the person I'm supposed to liaise with. This is the tour manager. This is the person that, if I have a problem, is the one I need to speak to and is meant to help me.*

Luckily, one of the ladies who worked with another DJ on the team came over to me and said she noticed what was happening and asked if I was okay, and if what was going on was consensual. Again I burst into tears and explained that no, it isn't, but that I didn't know what to do or how to say anything. This man, this tour manager who is harassing me, is not only supposed to be responsible for my welfare; he's basically who I'm working for.

She was like, "Cool, leave it with me. I'm going to speak to the talent". She goes to the Big Star, chats to her and of course, she says, "Oh my god, I'll sort this out".

But they don't sort it out.

Eventually, we all leave in the early hours of the morning and Big Star, at this point, has her phone out and is taking videos. When we get out of the tour van, they're still taking videos (so because I'm also a trained dancer and love to dance), I start twerking for her video to a track they're playing. While that's happening, the tour manager gets out of the car, comes up behind me, and slaps my ass again, then walks away.

The next day when we get to Swaziland, Big Star watches the video back. She finally stands up to the tour manager, tells him, "Yo, this is terrible. I didn't believe it before, but now that I see it, I know she was telling the truth. I had better not see this again."

So I think shit is fixed. I get back on stage to play again, and I was free, dancing. I had a great set and did what needed to be done. After the show, I get off and the tour manager comes over to me shouting, saying I messed up part of my set. I don't mess up my shit. I'm a perfectionist at my own thing, and it's very rare that I will mess up any element of my set – and if I do, there's a good reason why. I prep everything and for this gig, the one that was supposed to be my big break, I did more than ever before.

Eventually, he works out that it was a live musician playing on stage during my set who had fucked up. But for the rest of the festival, the tour manager keeps saying snide remarks to me and making stupid comments about everything I do.

Fast forward to the end of the night and we're back at the hotel. We were eating in the artist area, four doors away from mine. The tour manager is downstairs somewhere. I get tired and say goodnight.

I walk out of the room but I've got all these things in my hands; you know, as hunnies, we can have four coffee cups, a bag, a laptop open and still be doing life and running our business. Anyway, this tour manager pops out of nowhere and sees me and offers to open my door. He says, "Can I help you?" I insist I'm fine. He then grabs the key off my finger and walks inside my room.

I'm standing outside and my heart is pounding. I was like, "What are you doing?"

He says, "I'm just putting the key down."

But as I'm walking in and he's walking out, I see the door is closing. He's still inside. I turn around and he was like, "Don't you wanna kiss me?"

No dude, get the fuck out," I shout. You know how that goes. He perseveres.

"Come on! Come On! You know you want to."

Eventually, I force him out of the door and it slams and I'm just against it there thinking, *what the fuck?!* Why, as females in the industry, as DJs, as musicians, as dancers and women who are confident and free in how they dress and express themselves confidently do we then have to experience this shit?! Why do we have to experience men harassing us, and why does it just slide on by? Why must the show always go on?

BIBLICAL SCENES

It was the second time we'd been invited to play the Movement festival in Detroit. It was a tremendous honour because it's probably still to this day our favourite North American festival, if not our favourite festival, period. It's just so epic to be in Hart Plaza with all the history and the energy and the types of people that show up. It feels like being part of the threads of underground electronic music culture.

We'd been playing the city for about five years and building a cult following, playing these druggy underground gigs in old theatres and skating rinks and basements. We're not from Detroit, but we felt like we'd solidified our relationship with the city, building relationships with the people there, and we'd been going into Movement for a couple of years. It's always a big deal for us to go to Detroit.

At the festival, we were playing the pyramid stage right by the river. Before we go on stage, the sound guy takes us aside. He says, "I've got some really bad news for you. There's a tornado warning. We may have to pull you off the stage; we may have to shut it all down because of the weather."

But we start playing, thinking *this is gonna be fine. The weather is always in our favour, we're going to be okay.*

But the wind just starts kicking up more and more. From our vantage point, we could see this dark mass of cloud and rain coming up the river towards us. We could hear this otherworldly 'hisssssssssss', getting louder and louder. We were very, *very* meticulous about these bigger DJ sets, especially in Detroit. Maybe we could be more improvisational at something smaller, but at a gig like this, we had a set to follow, all worked out in advance, mostly vinyl. But by this time, the wind was blowing the table back and you can't really play records; it's blowing the records right off the platter, it's blowing the arm on the turntable off the grooves. We end up playing almost all digital stuff and the wind is getting fiercer and the sound guy comes up and is like, "we're gonna have to take you off" and we're like, "No, no, no one more minute, one more minute." Because I remember thinking that whatever happens, we must, we MUST play this one record. We must play this new track I had: Claude VonStroke, 'Who's Afraid Of Detroit.'

So we keep playing and we play 'Who's Afraid Of Detroit' and the people in the crowd go into this frenzy, this crazy moment of perfect energy. It's not just the weather that's causing it, or the excitement of our fans or new people getting turned on, or even the music! It feels like all the threads are connecting, all at once. We were at the nexus of something that happens once in a lifetime at a certain, special place. Then it goes very dark and the rain and the wind and the outer wall of the tornado come crashing in, things flying everywhere, but not a single person leaves the dancefloor.

There's this breakdown in the middle of the track, and as it draws to a close the biggest gust of wind comes in suddenly and actually blows the whole console, which is on wheels, across the stage. I'm running alongside it like a madman, somehow reaching to twist the knob on the mixer to throw the bass back in the track. It was just the most epic moment I've ever experienced. And after that peak, the tornado veered away back into the river, the wind and rain started to recede, and the sun returned. We felt like somehow, as DJs, but also as part of that moment, with that crowd, in that city, we'd saved the whole festival. Together.

THE COLDEST DISH

So about 15 years ago, I was asked if I wanted to go and play in Seoul in South Korea. Now I'd never been to Korea, but as someone who'd pretty much obsessed with Japan, Seoul was also one of those Bathing Ape-obsessed kind of cities that I love. So I said, "Yes, please!" and I went over to play at this club in South Korea. Very happy to be asked, actually.

But then I got to the club and no one spoke English at all. Apart from one girl who came up to me in the bar, who said she was a promoter. So I ended up hanging out with her and we were having a drink. And I was a bit nervous, I'll admit. I was saying to her, "Very young isn't it, in here?" And she was saying, "Oh don't worry, the older club crowd will come later."

But looking around everyone was about 14 or 15 and they were all girls, dressed in that kind of Harajuku style which the Japanese kids had been dressed in a few years before. We were in this kind of closed-off bar area, kind of a VIP type spot. Packed full of older people who were a bit more dressed up – mainly men, not many women in here, though.

So I started watching what was going on and there was a kid onstage playing really, really terrible EDM. I was saying to the local promoter, "Oh, they're gonna hate me now." But she was telling me that when the kids have gone, the proper house people will turn up. I wasn't convinced... but I was slowly getting drunk. So I eventually got to the point where I didn't care. I was in Korea, for fuck's sake. Sometimes you've gotta do what you've gotta do. Be professional. Play the music you think might suit them, rather than the records you really want to play. You're there to entertain, so do it.

But then suddenly, the bouncers came over and manhandled my new promoter friend clean out of the club. I was like, "What the fuck is going on?" and someone from the club came over and, in very broken English, told me that she worked from a rival club and thus wasn't welcome here at all. So that was a fucking shock for a start. Very strange behaviour.

By now, however, the club is absolutely packed and there are at least a thousand of these young girls looking up at the DJ. So I thought, *Oh no…* One thing I hate is crowds who just look at the DJ. I'm not one for dancing as I work, I'm not the best looking guy, and I feel a bit conscious of being an older DJ; are they gonna be "Oh, who's this guy? He's too old to be the DJ, surely?"

So I was getting really, really nervous and there was no one to speak to about it. So a guy came over and was letting me have some updates on time. They took my record boxes, two of the old metal ones as I had in those days; they carried them for me. Then, suddenly, the DJ stopped and these, well, very young boys came out on stage. Like a boy band, all in suits. It was like a scene from Korean Pop Idol or something. And the place erupted. Like absolutely erupted. These boys of 16 or maybe 17, all suited up and doing dance moves, had the place going berserk. And I thought *I'm not on after them, am I? Please God, no.*

After about 15 minutes of that someone came and grabbed me by the hand and walked me through the club… and right out the front door. Then round the back, through a goods exit and then we went up from the basement. By now, my anxiety level is huge and it's mixed up with my alcohol consumption in the worst way possible. So we went up one or two levels in this goods lift, then I was ushered into another one and stood there for ten minutes, then it shut and I started to go down. And I could hear the club below me and the screaming of the girls. Then suddenly I realised I was going down onto the stage. Slowly.

I mean so slowly that I could see the first row of the crowd of fourteen-year-old girls. And then the second row, then the third. By the time I got to 30 rows, they could see me and it went from screaming to utter silence. And I mean utter silence.

I then had to walk on, open my record boxes, assess the decks and then actually get going. But they didn't have vinyl decks, so I had to get busy with a small package of CDs that I had on me. And it took me a good five minutes. I remember I had bought a couple of cheesy tunes that I thought, 'If it really comes to it, I'll play these'. A version of [Orbital's] 'Chime' by one of those early Dutch producers. It was alright, but it's one of those records that you keep as a 'Get out of jail' kind of tune. First one on and we're already trying to mount a jail-break. All these girls in the crowd and there was absolute silence still. 30 seconds into the track going on and half the crowd had, literally, left the building.

And by the end of the record, the crowd of a thousand was down to twenty people. Within about half an hour, the people from the bar came down and started dancing and it turned around up to a point. I believe it was about what they expected. But it was probably the worst DJ booking I've ever had, especially for something I was so excited about doing. I was half jetlagged, half drunk and I had a massive issue with how that poor woman was treated – I mean, that was really nasty. I didn't know whether I should have jumped in or not. I didn't know what the etiquette was. In the UK, I'd definitely have had a go at someone who worked there. But back in the bar, a lot of the guys did have that kind of Yakuza look and I wasn't sure what the deal was, being so far from home. Maybe killing their dancefloor stone dead was the best revenge I could give her.

LES SYBARITIQUES

One of the things you get to do in this business sometimes, at least if you're lucky, is create an environment where people can be free. Free to be themselves. Especially people who might not be free in the outside, daytime world. The space I helped run, book and that I DJed at in New York (until it finally imploded a few years ago, owing hundreds of thousands of dollars in rent) was one of those places.

It was grandest in its second incarnation, a huge dilapidated building that had previously been a banquet hall where a theatrical set designer would 'create your fantasy event'. He'd left loads of his props inside when he left, so we just continued the fantasy. But the spirit was born in our first venue, which looked like a regular house on a quiet street in Brooklyn. Inside was a disused strip club which we turned into an illegal club space slash queer community centre.

After four years there, the parties were total carnage. I don't even know how to describe it. It was like Noah's Ark, two of every beautiful animal on the planet. We were constantly experimenting with the layout, trying to get it right, and at one point, I moved the DJ booth into one of the private strip rooms, which had wall-to-wall mirrors. We'd knocked a hole in the wall, so you could look onto the dancefloor, but it was the *worst* idea. You couldn't hear the sound in the main room and people just kept coming in and out.

One night I was playing with a female DJ who runs a local label. It wasn't a particularly special party. Then we both looked around and she just said, "What the *fuck*?" There were these two trans girls in the mirrored room and one of them was fisting the other. All I remember thinking is, *I can't believe they're not using any lube right now*, which may have been triggered by the blood I could see. The entire space was gross at this point. It was pre-Covid, but I was already walking around with anti-bacterial wipes, so the thought of all those germs going into this person's body was too much. We just carried on DJing and didn't look back again. Next track!

That's just what kind of space it was. Trans people, women, anyone… they felt safe enough there to have sex in public. It's a real achievement if you can make that demographic comfortable enough to get fisted. It was its own little world with its own set of rules and regulations. There were restrictions and limitations, but in a way, also none at all.

Once while DJing, I really needed to piss. It was packed, the busiest the club had ever been, and there were no bottles around. In a normal club, you'd put on a track and go to the toilet, but you just couldn't at this place. It was the complete chaos and dysfunction of the place that actually created the magic. A person I was seeing was doing drugs and whatever else under the DJ booth, so he just said, "go in my mouth". I had the longest piss and he took it all like a bad flask. Nobody had any idea what was happening whatsoever.

Freedom comes in many different forms, I guess. Even if sometimes it's something of an acquired taste.

THE LESSER ROCK 'N' ROLL SWINDLE

I never intended for this whole making tunes thing to be more than just pure fun and for posting on my music social media platforms. I was anonymous for a long time. I had no plans to make this into a career. My ambitions at the beginning were completely non-existent, really. Then there was a late night a while back I spent on the computer and drinking a couple of beers. I uploaded a track and passed out. I woke up hungover, barely remembering what had happened and the comments and views started flooding in and it looked like they would never stop. That was the first time I thought I could make something out of this. Then I started getting gig bookings.

The thing is, I'd never DJ'd before. Never! Enough time has passed now for me that I can actually admit that. It was terrifying, but I didn't want to miss out on the chance. I would be booked without any experience at all. Fake it 'til you make it. I'd never touched a CDJ or a mixer or anything in a booth. I would sit at the airports and watch tutorials on how to beatmatch and stuff like that. It wasn't like a grand arty hoax or anything; when I started accepting bookings, I took it very seriously. I worked hard and knew the basics after a very short period. I took every opportunity possible to practice. I already had a big enough imposter syndrome and I didn't want to be contributing any more to it than was already there.

My first big headline gig was in Dublin at this old club called The Hangar. I was so nervous I ran back and forth from the departure gate at the airport seven times because I thought I'd lost my passport. Turns out it was in my back pocket the whole time. They had sold out the event in two days and I still felt like I had no idea what I was doing. I thought I was going to go up there and be a massive failure. I was completely shattered from the nervousness and the pressure. In the end, it somehow went well, and that was the one that made me think, "Wow, maybe I can actually do this for a while."

And then I started to enjoy myself, finally. Things took off from there and I was blessed enough to have more and more amazing shows offered. After a time, I became confident about performing. I hadn't been 'found out' while I'd literally learned on the job.

But, having been so nervous about being an imposter, now I realised I couldn't bring myself to say no. For me, it felt like *I don't know when my expiry date might be. I don't know when I'll ever be asked to play again.* You never know what could happen tomorrow. I was driven by this fear of saying no and turning down things. At my busiest, there were weeks when I'd play three or four festivals in one or two days in the UK. Then I would fly to Colorado for ten hours to do one show. Then a few hours later, fly back to the UK. And on it went.

There was one weekend where I was supposed to play at a big festival. I remember being more tired than I ever was and I'd been on the worst red-eye flight you could ever imagine, turbulence, crying babies, crazy passengers, everything. When I landed at Gatwick airport in London, I just sat down outside a Costa coffee and started crying. I'd completely broken down. I was so burnt out. I texted my manager and was like, "I can't do this".

When you're that tired, you no longer enjoy what you're being offered, no matter how great that is. There had been a few moments like that where I felt like I was sacrificing far more than I was receiving. There was a point when I even stopped getting nervous for shows. And I thought: *this is not how it should be.* I would look around and I saw more excitement in others than I felt myself. Mental health in this industry is something that's getting more attention, but it's still at a point where it's difficult to draw the line. It's difficult to know what is too much and what is enough. Then the pandemic came along and suddenly enforced this big break in things on everyone. It should have been a nightmare, and I know it was for many people, but honestly, I think it saved my sanity.

After a year-long hiatus and having a breather of sorts. I had my first gig back recently in Berlin. It was incredible. When I got into the venue, the nerves came back for sure. I realised, *Fuck, I'm actually really nervous! What if I don't know what I'm doing? I haven't touched a DJ set up in over a year! What are all these buttons?!* But even at half capacity, the vibe and energy were unreal. After 20 minutes or so, I felt like I got into the groove of it and it was extremely cathartic. There was one thing in my mind, a feeling I hadn't felt for so long. Not an imposter. Not a burn-out. *Alright*, I thought. *Now I remember why I love doing this.*

SOUND ADVICE

Somehow 'The Soundman' and The DJ seem so often to be natural antagonists. There's a thing about the techs and the acts being slightly at-odds. They see us as dimwitted children pretty much, and I don't blame them, really. DJs are constantly breaking carefully set-up tech, are arrogant and off-hand and turn up to work for a couple of hours while the techs are there all day and night and get paid almost nothing in comparison.

It has changed recently, but it was always sound 'men' back for a long time and always a difficult encounter for me. A ponytail and a large torch was the uniform when this incident happened. The Sound Guy at this famous club was always easy to spot because he rushed about shoving people aside and had a face like a disappointed space hopper. He was literally the only person not having a good time. Overall he looked like a furious deflated goth, which helped to pick him out of the crowd when he was needed. His thing was always madly over-complicating anything if it was at all possible. "Can it go a little louder?" would result in a 30 minute lecture on why you can't re-paper cones, married to a list of how much each speaker cost and were you willing to pay for them etc.? He also left loads of little passive/aggressive notes around about chopping fingers off and how only morons go into the red. You get the picture; he's not unique.

Sometimes the DJ becomes the focus when something dramatic happens, usually to be fair because we kinda are the focus of the event. On the very rare occasions there is a fight we sometimes end up as referees or some sort of shit sheriff. On this night, some folks came piling into the booth with a medical crisis. Contrary to what my Mum and, frankly, an alarming amount of punters think, there is no mic. Certainly not in this deeply 'underground' venue. A microphone is rare. Something you have to book in advance in many places as they will need to hire one. They were clearly agitated, so I cut the monitors completely, took off the headphones and asked what the matter was.

There wasn't much detail other than someone was having some kind of fit or collapse. They were being helped by staff, but the ambulance was stuck. As usual, cars from ravers were parked at mad angles for miles down the road and the emergency services couldn't get past. We needed to find the owner of the offending car. This was serious. I knew enough about clubs, and particularly this one, to understand such things can damage your license permanently. Over and above being a human crisis.

It needed dealing with quickly and efficiently. For all I knew, a life was at stake. I saw the Sound Dude over in his corner, doing the lights (which he always made clear was beneath him but secretly enjoyed, and did not laugh at all when someone gave him a T-shirt that cheerfully said 'Only Fit For Light Duties' on the front) and looking as ever like he was in a special Hell designed especially for him and him alone. I waved madly at him to come over, something that would usually get a contemptuous sneer at best, but something in my alarmed state was authentic and actually drew him over to me. Albeit like a reluctant teen being asked to do the washing-up. I shouted at him: "SOMEONE'S COLLAPSED ON THE DANCEFLOOR AND THERE IS A CAR BLOCKING THE AMBULANCE, WE NEED A MIC!"

"Yeah?"

"YES!! LIKE NOW!"

"Yes, I heard you the first time"

"WHERE IS IT?"

"What kind?"

"WHAT??"

"Mic."

"DO YOU HAVE A MIC? THIS IS AN EMERGENCY!" "What kind though?"

"NO, YOU MISUNDERSTAND; SOMEONE MIGHT DIE!"

"Yes. I heard you the first time you asked. I am asking you what type of microphone? Omnidirectional? Ribbon? Diaphragm? Unidirectional...?"

"ARRRRRGGGGGH!"

DO THE HUSTLE

Over my time throwing parties in Kampala in Uganda, I've seen some weird sights. Sometimes you just have to admire the hustle. This one dude was a known figure in the sort of alternative music scene. One of the guys that was there first played EDM before anyone else. He never got to play at our parties officially or get his name on the bill… but somehow, he always managed to get on the decks, mostly because he had a bad habit of hawking the decks and eventually getting guests off of them by pretending he was on the line-up.

It got to the point where he would just rock up to the party and crash behind the DJ booth, which had a little bench behind it, or if not somewhere else in the club. He'd hibernate like a tick. At the very tail end of the night, when most people had left and every DJ was tired, he'd wake up from under the booth, plug in his controller or USB and sneak on. Most times he'd be playing to a totally empty club, but he was always so happy to play his tunes. I guess he was pretty well-rested as well, ironically. The weird thing is that it totally worked. He got better, he got his name out there, and now he gets booked. Sheer hustle.

We've also had some legendary after-parties with legendary people. One that always comes to mind was at 'Hollywood', the infamous hostel/dive bar in Kampala where we used to rig up fat sounds and dance like mad. We did this party that went on for two days straight from Friday-Sunday morning.

The last DJ on the decks was a guy from this crazy Dutch crew. Twenty minutes before he got on, he popped acid and MDMA. But when he stepped into the booth to play, nothing worked anymore.

There was no sound. The place was already rigged up on matchsticks and loose wires everywhere... It's now ten in the morning, lots of people leave because it's already been an hour with no music by now.

By this point, the DJ is *mad* high. He said he thought the whole booth was upside down. He's taking the whole system apart, unplugging and replugging every wire in the fucking club until he finally realises the problem is a fucking filter knob on the controller! The beauty is that he played for about seven hours after that in the end. The guy is such a mad selector that he blissed everyone out. People were coming back in; he finally finished playing at 5pm, I think until he finally felt like gravity was the right way around. All out of pure love for the after hours.

THE OMEGA MAN

I know that unless I'm very careful I have a tendency to peak way too early. I don't know if it's some kind of self-sabotage, not knowing my limits or just that I get a bit excited, but I'm the one who tends to go off like a firework on the first night of a festival and then sleep through the acts I was desperate to see the next day. Or instead of saving myself for the cool afterparty just gets too crazy at the main event. Or stays up all night the day before a big gig. But I think the very first time I got booked to DJ in Ibiza, I can be forgiven for getting excited. It was a villa party, you see, on a Sunday afternoon, and the flight from my hometown of Paris was in the morning. Me and my DJ partner were playing our residency the night before, so of course, we thought we'd go straight to the airport from the club, get some 'sleep' there and get straight on the plane.

There was no sleep to be had in the airport. It was bright and bustling and we were massively overstimulated. Ibiza! We snatched a few minutes each on the plane, but by the time we set foot on the White Isle, our enthusiasm was flagging. We couldn't face the big queue for a taxi. So I hired a scooter and we both jumped on it.

What I didn't know, what no one had told me, was trying to find a villa party by yourself in Ibiza at any time is hard enough, even with a local taxi driver doing the navigating. We didn't know that GPS and Google Maps might as well be guesswork there (something to do with the magic of Atlantis?). When it's your first trip to the Island, it's about 40 degrees celsius in the blazing sun, you're hungover and you've had no sleep for 24 hours, it's even harder. We drove up and down dirt tracks and driveways, meandered through pine trees and gradually got more and more dehydrated until, as if by a miracle, we found the party. Hundreds of supercool people and a great sound system in the grounds of a slick and modern whitewashed villa, miles from anywhere.

By now, it was nearing noon and there wasn't much time for hellos. We jumped on the decks and, dead tired but still quite enthusiastic, we played our b2b set. It was good. I mean, we were kind of on autopilot, but it went down well. But after a couple of hours, I was flagging.

I asked if there was somewhere I could sleep and was shown to a basic but clean room inside. Despite the thud of the bass and the hiss of the crowd, I was out like a light.

I think maybe it was the silence that woke me. It took me a few minutes to realise where I was. Ibiza! Of course! At an amazing villa party. But then why is it so quiet? I stretched, arranged my clothes, and headed back to the party.

But there was no party. There were stacks of empty bottles and plastic cups in every corner and on every table. There were cigarette ends by the thousand, dotted about the grounds as if dusted from a giant salt shaker. There were the obligatory little plastic baggies trampled into the dry dirt. But there were no people. No DJs (including my partner), no promoters, no sound. The system was still there, but the decks were gone, their dusty outline remaining like the chalk that marked where a body fell at a murder scene.

It was dusk now, and the shadows were getting long. Wandering about, dazed and confused, I felt like the last man on earth. I remember my eye being caught by a plastic phone cover, bobbing in the pool, the only thing even moving for miles around. My phone! Of course! Battery dead. I plugged it in, waited a bit, and called my DJ partner.

As you'll probably have guessed, it wasn't the biblical Rapture. The police had arrived in numbers and shut down the party shortly after I'd gone to bed. Apparently, there had been arguments, tears, a near riot and then a mass exodus, and I had slept through it all, and for another few hours too. My fellow DJ had blearily decamped with the promoters to another party and assumed I'd just been swept up in the chaos like everyone else. He actually sounded a little jealous that I had gotten some sleep. I jumped back on my scooter and headed out to join them, refreshed and ready for a new adventure. *Ibiza!*

SCATMAN AND ROBIN

"We were in Costa Rica for a festival, and our whole crew of DJs and managers and friends were staying at this little hotel, along with the artist liaison for the festival. This guy has worked at several festivals, especially in Central America and had actually become a really close friend of ours. He's fucking funny – he's hilarious with quite a large personality, the personality of a fucking superstar DJ and the ego to go with it – but it's all in good fun. While we're playing the festival, at some point, he disappears.

Everything at the festival goes down without a problem, everybody plays well, everybody has a good time and we go back to our hotel to kind of kick it and wind down, and homeboy – the liaison – is tripping his balls off on acid.

He's somehow moved some of his shit in my room and is just taking over the room I'm paying for and I'm like, "What the fuck is up with this, homeboy? I paid for this room; this is where I need to sleep, I'm an old man, I like to go to bed when I want to and not be bothered."

But he's like, "No, no, I slept here last night because I was here a day earlier than you and I'll just crash on the couch or whatever" and I'm like, "Okay, whatever" and head down to the verandah. We fast forward and it's lights out. I'm kind of tripping on mushrooms by now. I go to change my clothes in the room and there he is. Holding onto the dresser, squirting a fucking massive diarrhoea shit all over the floor.

He's squatted down like an animal really close to my bag and my bag is open. My clothes are there and all my stuff is there. I'm like, "What the fuck, dude, what the fuck" and he just looks at me. He's like, "It's okay, I'm just..." and I'm like "What? What!?" and he continues to shit while I'm fucking berating him, tripping on mushrooms which means I'm staring at him for a while just trying to process this, which somehow makes it even worse. I'm like – is this really happening? Is it the mushrooms? Then: is this guy trying to, like, make some sort of statement? Does this guy not like me? Have we gone back to some kind of territorial instinct? Is it because I wanted the bed?

I couldn't handle it. I was fuming mad. In my younger years, I probably would have literally rubbed his nose in it because I was that kind of person, but I was like, 'fuck it'. I shut the door, I walked out and I said to the other DJs: "Yo, homeboy went feral. I'm fucking outta here; call me when that shits cleaned up cause I'm not coming back here when there's that in the room." I just fucked off to a bar on the beach. So one of the other guys, one of the headliners at the festival, apparently tells the other guys, "I'm not scared of any poo." He got the bucket and the mop from the maids' place and cleaned it all up. They called me later and were like, "Hey man, everything's okay" but I didn't care, I'm not going back in there, so I slept on the fucking couch and threw away the clothes in that bag because they had poo particles on it. I'm not like a super germaphobe, but that is way over my line.

The liaison woke up the next day and was so apologetic but I was still fuming. Seeing that guy squatting like a wild animal. The noise of it. The smell. It was just incomprehensible. I'm like, "You owe me for the room", and then after that for a whole month I texted him every day, text after text after text of puns: 'I don't mean to raise a big stink but you kind of fouled up this weekend' or 'I don't like leaving a bad odour but that was kind of a shitty thing to do' etc. Probably a bit cruel. But imagine seeing a grown adult shitting in your room. I think he got off easy.

FACING YOUR DEMON

I'm a DJ, label boss and radio host now, but this story is from a while back and from the other side of the booth. I was a promoter in Paris at what was honestly the coolest club in town, and we had a residency on a Tuesday.

The club paid me, and I was responsible for paying the guests and any other staff we'd brought in, and I paid them at the end of the night. Those are the rules in this game. Even if the night fails, the fees have to be paid as agreed, even if it means taking a big hit. Our night was always pretty busy. But one evening after I had done my party, the club didn't pay me. I took an advance and paid everyone and then invoiced the club to reimburse me. One month passed, two months passed, three months passed, and I still had no money from them.

It was not a huge amount of money, but it still felt really shit not to be paid. Not only had I sorted the DJ's fees out from my account, but it didn't feel right because, as I said, this club was really, constantly busy. I'd followed the rules; why shouldn't they?

I'd written messages, left voicemails to them, and of course, no reply. Eventually, they finally called me on a Friday to say, "We have your cheque, come and pick it up from the office at the club." I went down there at about 4pm or 5pm in the afternoon, but when I arrived, they said, "Oh shit, the guy from the accounting department is already gone for the weekend" I became a bit annoyed. I was like, "Man, it's been three months. I've been waiting for this money, and you're telling me now at 5 o'clock the accounting guy is gone?!" I was yelling and getting really furious. So eventually, the security assistant found my cheque, and I went back home.

But I'm not finished. I was back at home chilling, and the club owner called me directly, super aggressive. I mean, this guy was known all over Paris as being really, really tough. He had a bad reputation. All of a sudden, he's shouting down the phone, "Who the fuck do you think you are?! Do you think you come to my club and shout at my staff?!! You think you're the boss?!! I'm going to break your legs! I'm going to kill you! If you go out in Paris at night, you'll be dead in the streets!"

I was really nervous because I knew what he was capable of, or at least I'd heard about it. I was really stressed. So after he hung up, I said to myself, "OK, I need to go down there and have a proper chat with him face-to-face and sort this out and explain the background story to him." We are both adults, after all.

I jumped on my scooter and drove straight there. Right as I arrived at the club, the guy was leaving the club. He sees me, and he goes, "That's it, I'm going to fucking kill you!" I said, "OK, that's cool, let's have a fight, and then we talk", and I removed my glasses.

The staff saw this and came running out of the office and were holding him back, saying to me, "What the fuck are you thinking? He's going to kill you!" We started swapping punches right there in the street. I'm explaining to him how long I waited and the misunderstanding with the cheque in between him swinging wildly at me and me dodging him. Me calm (on the outside) though very much trying not to get hurt, and him redder and angrier by the minute. Eventually, he stopped and left. He had to pick up his daughter from school. Obviously, he didn't kill me.

For a few weeks after that, I was nervous that my time in Paris would be over, that I wouldn't get booked by other club owners because he would spread the word about me, but he never did. In fact, it was the opposite, and I became known as the guy who stood up to this infamous tough guy. I'm just thankful it was a school day.

THE HOUSE OF PAIN

It started innocently enough, as these things often do, with a Sound-Cloud follow. I regularly check out my new followers and noticed this particular person had some pretty nice uploads on his page. So I sent him a message that I was pretty impressed with their tracks and DJ sets (something I had never done). We quickly hit it off and eventually, he tells me, "I can get you booked to play in my city." I was actually pretty excited for this as I don't get too many international gigs.

Fast forward a few weeks and I get a phone call. The gig is booked if I want it. I obviously accept the invitation and I start planning everything out. The promoter (let's call him David) tells me that I can stay at his house and the flight will be taken care of, as well as a little bit of money for the gig itself. I tell him that I don't stay at people's houses and I'll just get a hotel for the night. He strongly, overwhelmingly, insists that I stay at his house. After some thought, I figure: *Why not? It's just one night, right?*

So after a couple days, he tells me that I now needed to book my own flight and would be reimbursed after the gig. Normally I would never agree to such a thing, but I really wanted this gig, so I agreed and paid for the ticket. The night before the flight, he assures me that he will be at the airport to pick me up and we'll go get food and head back to his house.

The day has arrived. I fly into David's city and give him a call once I land. "Sorry, bro, I can't pick you up at the airport; I don't have a car," he tells me. "I only live about five minutes from the airport. Can you take a taxi here?" he asks. At this point, I am starting to get a little frustrated, but no big deal. I roll with it.

I arrive at David's apartment and call him to let him know I am there. He comes to the lobby to greet me, noticeably dishevelled and sleep-deprived. His gut peeks out over dirty gym shorts; a cigarette hangs from his bottom lip, a condition I soon learn is permanent. The building is a tall, condo-style building with his apartment on the ground floor. It is small but modern and quite clean. One problem I notice right away, though: there is only one bedroom. David shows me to this single bedroom and tells me this is where I will be staying. I ask, "If I'm sleeping here, where are you gonna sleep?" He tells me he will sleep on the couch. This seems super weird to me and I am already cursing myself for not booking a hotel – 30 seconds after arriving.

Over the next few hours, so many people start to come and go that the sitting room resembles a McDonald's drive-thru. It has become evidently clear to me what is going on here and I am starting to sense a very sketchy loser vibe. Among those seemingly nonstop visiting the house, one particular individual insists on having a private conversation with David; he's visibly irritated by my presence. After he leaves, David tells me, "These guys think they can just come and take my money, I'll make one phone call and they'll never bother me again." I really should have just left and gotten a hotel, but I again reminded myself, it's just for one night. How bad could it be?

It's now about 9pm and someone else comes by who wants to show me his studio, and although I am exhausted from flying all day, I oblige. We all get in his car and David asks if we can make a stop along the way. This stop turns into a two-hour ordeal of David hopping from place to place, collecting money from people. I didn't sign up for this, but I am a very patient person and yet again, I remind myself, it's just for one night.

Now we're at the studio and we hang out for about an hour. Everything's pretty cool here, but we're all so tired we decide to call it a night (not having anticipated two hours of driving around beforehand).

Now we're back at David's house and it's 2am. I decide it's time for bed but as I lay down, I am overcome with a strange sense of fear and uncertainty. A weird, tingling, Spidey Sense. After about 45 minutes of trying to clear my mind, I finally fall into a light sleep. Then, not 15 minutes later, I'm awakened by the door of the bedroom bursting open. I sit up, alarmed, and someone is staring at me. I glance out into the living room and I can see two more guys in the apartment having a very heated exchange with David. I quickly get up and start getting dressed as I am fully aware something is very wrong here.

"Please, I just need more time. I will pay you everything I owe you!" David shrieks in the other room. I hear the sound of him being hit, knuckles on flesh, over and over.

My heart is racing and I know I need to get out of this situation fucking immediately. My first instinct is to call a taxi so I can get going. Luckily the app says it's only minutes away. I jam my stuff in my suitcase with the three heavies periodically checking to see what I was doing. Knowing damn well Plan A isn't going to work, I try it anyway: walking into the living room with all of my bags and saying, "Guys, I have nothing to do with this and I barely know this guy. You can handle your business and I didn't see anything. I am going to go now."

One of the heavies looks at me and shoves me back into the bedroom. "You're not fucking going anywhere," he says. "Stay in the room and shut up. I don't want to see you messing with your phone either."

They slam the door shut and I am now in a full-blown panic. Shortly after, David comes into the room and tells me he needs all of my money. He swears he will pay me back. With little choice (I didn't really want to be present at a murder scene), I give him all the money I had, which was luckily (for me) very little. He closes the door behind him and I check down at my phone and I see that my car is just a minute away. Luckily, there is a sliding glass door and the apartment is on the ground floor. I roll the door as quietly as I possibly can, heart-pounding, see the car arriving and take off sprinting to the car. I get in and tell the driver, "Get me away from here as fast as you can."

Like a bad caper movie, the driver steps on it, his Hyundai Sonata tires squealing weakly and inching away at seemingly glacial speeds. But finally, David's apartment is in the rearview, and we head to a hotel that I look up along the way back into the city. For the first time since arriving, I feel at ease. After some thought, I decide it's not a good idea for me to proceed with the gig as my wellbeing is not worth sacrificing the chance of being around this guy again. I book the next flight home and head to the airport two hours later.

All in all, this was a hard lesson learned for me. I lost a ton of money on the flight, hotel, and additional fee for changing my flight back — but I was certainly happy to be back home. It was tough to learn but worth every last penny. So I hope this is a learning experience for others to always trust your gut instinct — and whatever you do, don't stay at the promoter's house. Ever. Even if it's only one night.

THE BEERHUNTER

It was New Year's Eve 1995. I was part of a DJ duo at the time; we had been playing some of the best clubs in the North of the UK for a few years already. This particular club was legendary and one of my favourites still to this day, 26 years on. Normally in the past, we'd played in the upstairs bar, which had crazy energy and magic all of its own, but we'd been given a coveted slot on the main floor this time, and boy did we enjoy it. The actual night itself is something of a blur, which is hardly surprising. What happened after is somewhat clearer in my mind.

We were all invited back to one of the promoters' houses for some afterparty shenanigans. We're in there for five minutes, still reeling from the gig, when the host makes a suggestion we weren't expecting.

He pulls out a gun. And he asks us if we want to play Russian roulette. Buzzing from the club, in our collective, ecstatic states, we actually went along with it. It seemed natural. It couldn't really be happening. It was a collective hallucination, another jape on a long night of japery.

Out in the back garden, on a chilly but sunny morning, blue skies and frost crispy underfoot, he pressed the gun against his temple. The trigger is pulled. Click. Another volunteer holds it against their temple. Click. Another volunteer, another temple. Click. Then the host takes the gun. He puts it to his temple, then all at once, he grins and points it up in the air and fires. It was the loudest BANG! I'd ever heard. We all looked at him in shock. It hadn't been loaded with a real bullet, of course. He'd fired a blank up into the sky. I know now that blank cartridges aren't empty. There's still something in there, and at close range, it can do a lot of damage. It can kill. I'm not sure a blank exploding in the ear would have been great for a DJ's hearing, either.

Now I look back on it and truly wince. What the fuck were we thinking? I assume the two volunteers thought either there was no danger or absolute death was imminent, neither of which are sane responses when you think about it. That is just it though, no one thought about much at all back then. At the time, we all just laughed and moved on. Honestly, we'd forgotten it after about three minutes and proceeded to party our way through the rest of New Year's Day. And pretty much the rest of the decade.

SCENE AND NOT HEARD

OK 'straight' away, pun intended, I want to say I am not 'The Gay DJ'. Maybe write that in bold type. My career and possibly my whole life is a constant battle straddling a line between what I am being told to do by outside pressure and what I know deep in my soul is the right thing, and god, it is so very exhausting expecting the two to ever meet. My partner and I have a running joke that 'scene' things are hideous and we avoid them like the plague, then collapse laughing when we have a great time on the scene.

"Just because it is 'scene', why does it have to be awful?" is what he always says. I get this. It's like a mantra. This may as well be a tattoo for me. I play *music*; I don't play 'Gay Music' although granted, most great music is made by LGBTQ+ people and didn't we start it all? That is a fact. Deal. I've tried so hard over decades to shake off the shackles of being forced into a corner. I have to say it is a very cosy corner! It is so easy to live in. Guaranteed gigs and 'pink pounds' by the plenty.

Forgive my sarcasm; it's good to unload. Yes, the scene can be a safe place, a sanctuary and also quite definitely a prison. A life sentence if you are not careful. And why should I stay in there!? Stay in your cupboard, boy! I don't like that message one bit and you know what? The worst ones for that are my own people. Really.

There's a lot of 'damned if you do, damned if you don't' in the game for me. I get shade if I don't do 'scene work' and step outside like I'm some sort of traitor, and I also get shade if that is all I do. It is almost like you are not a proper DJ if you don't work outside the scene. I suppose I just wish that borderline didn't exist. And then again, you should have the right to choose to exist in the scene if you want.

Complex, isn't it? I also see that 'a scene' doesn't just apply to gender or sexuality. Scenes are everywhere. Some of the 'straight' scenes I see are so funny, way way more bitchy and hardcore than ours! Scenes are terrible. I hate them and love them. I mean, I would be nowhere without it; it is where I started. And by the same token, you get a sort of 'we made you, so we can break you' thing too. Moving sideways or upwards is treated as a defeat instead of a victory. It's so very English too. 'Stay in your place', that sort of thing. For everyone, big or small. Rules, rules, rules! So boring.

How can I describe it if you are on the outside looking in? Well, inside the box, you just can't do anything but play a certain kind of vibe. I mean, for sure, things have got a little better lately, especially with a certain fantastic disco-on-a-Sunday, but still, I can end up playing dreadfully over-fast material at super 'butch' places with chicken wire around the booth that are really quite dangerous. I don't mean, how can I say it, peril? I mean dangerously bad for our development.

Of course, also 'boys will be boys', but there is this push and pull. It stunts our growth a little. On the other side of the tennis court, I have to be butch at straight gigs. Tone it down. Which I have actually been told to do. And I honestly don't think it had anything to do with what I was playing and everything to do with prejudice. I don't think those words or 'pieces of advice' would be used on a straight DJ. Not ever. I even get told before I play what I should be doing. As if I'm going to play the Village People all night or something and haven't been a pro DJ all my life, thank you very much. If you take offence, they look at you like you are exactly what they were expecting. An arsey queen.

So yes, Miss Secret DJ asked me to talk about something that personally means a lot to me. And I think you will live to regret it! Perhaps this is all about society rather than me complaining. I don't have much to complain about really as long as I stay in my little box. Prejudice is about denying individuality. All about labelling. Generalising.

Limiting. Shackling. And not in a fun way. I want to talk about sexuality too, but maybe not in the way you think. Being 'homosexual' is a spectrum, and I use that word advisedly. We have people who are what I might call 'oversexed' in the way that many of you are, and I mean the mainstream by 'you'.

There's plenty of people who need spaying and putting in stocks across the board. I'm joking, obviously, but there are people at the extreme edge of that spectrum and clearly, that spectrum goes the other way too. I didn't have a boyfriend for a very long time. I'm quite prudish, really, or so I've been told. Often! To me, I am 'normal', whatever that is, and perhaps I give a bit of side-eye to the more excessive bits of my world. And there are also friends of mine who are completely celibate. What I am trying to say is we get judged by extremes.

Like every member of a society has to be accountable for the actions of a crazy minority. That might be a bit dramatic, but it sort of makes sense that we are also judged by cartoon ideas of who we are, imposed by the mainstream. You know what? This may be disappointing not only to you but also to some of 'my people', but we can be pretty boring and ordinary. In fact, part of suffering under the yoke of conformity, part of equal rights, is the inherent right not to be exceptional. Like we have to be funny, especially entertaining, 'colourful' or can only be interacted with as a joke and covered in glitter and sequins. There is the basic human right not to be discriminated against, but also this contains the right to be boring as hell or be very serious. Like everyone else. Equality also means being free to be equally dull.

When I was just starting out, I had a sort of breakdown. Back then, there wasn't quite as much care or even names for mental health issues but what really happened, I think, is that I felt so strongly that I wasn't wanted in the world and did not belong at all that my brain decided to take me out of it. I think also it was connected to a sustained physical attack I survived near Soho about six months before. Like a sort of delayed reaction. This was leaving a bar when I wasn't even working. It gave me a real fear of the night. I don't think people realise how dangerous it can be to work in the disco business. You get looked after a little bit by bigger venues, but I tend to work in smaller places and the level of blasé attitude to safety is just staggering.

Like you have to fight tooth and nail to get looked after. They treat a request for a taxi like you are the Queen of Sheba herself asking for a limo when all you want is not to be beaten to death. Security doesn't care about the staff in some places; they are just there to stop insurance claims and look out for the licence. I've been attacked too often inside a venue and there has been no reaction at all from the management. This is another thing that keeps you in your little box. Fear. I'd love to play more 'serious' venues and to a crowd that is only there for the music; it's my dream and so rarely happens. But honestly? I'm petrified sometimes.

The anxiety is off the charts and taking drugs stupidly for years didn't help. I won't lie and say it was self-medication; it was hedonism. I really wish I hadn't as now I am older, I can see that some of my fears were me not looking after myself properly. There is anger as well as fear. I'm angry that the music we invented has been stolen and we've been edged out of it. I'm angry that I am marginalised. It's mostly fear, if I am honest. There are real reasons to be fearful, and then there is paranoia. Took me a long time to separate them. Trying to break free. The fight for equality is not easy. We don't want more than you or to take anything you have; we just don't want to live in fear.

I feel a real kinship with illegal raves and it's so, so far away from my comfy world but I'm getting more and more fed up with all the factions and really wish people would pull together. I'm scared we are pulling in the opposite direction of where we need to be. It's all so, so selfish now.

Oh, I don't know what I'm saying here. That I'd love to just be known as a DJ. Someone who knows about music and can rock the discotheque. To be just that. But to be 'heard', to get ahead of the pack, you get labelled and gimmicked and forced to wear a hat that doesn't really fit but kind of serves its purpose at the time. And you know what, it's no different for me being pigeonholed than it is for a straight trance DJ to be forever stuck in that genre and driving that bandwagon. Being stuck in our little boxes doesn't just apply to me. There's such great pressure from new people coming up too. You don't get a second chance or to go home and change into a new outfit; you get stuck wearing what you've been given until it gets tatty and out of vogue. You've got something fab lined up but no one will let you change into it. For people like me, we really had to fight to get where we are. I mean sometimes, literally. Spilt blood for it. It wasn't a career choice, more like a vocation. To arrive in the big city, come out and be proud... being a DJ and the music that came with it was part of that for me. Identity and something that was mine. I owned it. I made myself. In defiance of what convention told me I should be.

Hey, I can only speak for myself. Don't cancel me for not representing properly! I was asked for my story. I know there are lots of others and I like what you are trying to do. Let voices be heard. Listen to the stories of all the people. Oh, I don't know. I really don't have any answers but it is good to talk about things. Be open and proud. You wanted to hear my little story. I actually feel like it's not my place to talk like this and that can't be right, can it? Thanks for listening to my voice, though. I really liked your message in one of your books about 'togetherness' and what 'dance music' used to represent. Would be nice to remember that original feeling. Hear everyone's voice. Come together. Wouldn't that be lovely?

PREPARE TO FAIL

I played a DJ set in Japan as part of my co-owned label, which I'm an artist on. Our main artist had been booked by this really cool venue in Tokyo to perform, so she and the other label head and myself decided to go and play the show together.

I splashed out on all the flights and getting everyone there. I booked Airbnbs and arranged everything to arrive a week prior. It was a really nice time. It was a good trip, leisure wise. Eventually, it came to the night where we had to perform, but we'd never really rehearsed anything for it. We'd planned to be quite spontaneous.

The three of us showed up early in the day to introduce ourselves. We did a soundcheck, and that was alright. We were confident and really hyped for the gig. When we went back into the venue at night, it was packed. Local Japanese trap artists were playing on the ground floor. It was really electronic and just a super good atmosphere and vibe.

It came to our main artist doing her set, and in the booth, there was this light and sound engineer who was also the promoter, running the night. We soon came to realise he was doing absolutely everything from this huge MacBook Pro. He had all the electronics, the audiovisuals, the projections and the mixers running through there.

We'd given him my video, the other label head and the main artist's videos to put on there. But when it came to actually playing the set, we went to the guy to cue the video, and he'd done so much LSD that he couldn't remember the password to his laptop.

We were all laughing about it in the green room behind the DJ booth and this laptop mainframe. The soundtrack in the club was on loop. My main artist was naked, wearing this costume of only diamonds that she had planned for months ahead of this gig. I was basically battling between wanting to kill the guy, giving up on everything, and being in hysterics.

In the end, we chose option four, and all got really drunk. I didn't actually get to perform, and neither did the other label head, my business partner. Somehow, luckily our main artist performed in front of a stock photo we could pause, and we somehow rigged her sound to work. But it was a pretty long way to go for a drink.

T.W.O.C

I don't believe in stereotypes at all. Like, not all Scottish people are misers or violent drunks. The Welsh don't all have powerful singing voices and prefer to live underground in big caves (or was that dwarves?). Mancunians don't all strut about like Liam Gallagher. Lots of nonsense.

But the very first festival I played was in Liverpool and it was stereotypical enough for a 1970s sitcom. Myself and a couple of other DJs I did a night with had driven up from London in an absolutely knackered old van we'd borrowed. This thing had no radio, the seats were ripped and flaking away with old foam, and there was basically nothing between the steering wheel and the engine except a stalk for the gearstick. It was so LOUD, we couldn't hear each other speak on the way and I had mild tinnitus for days afterwards. Max speed uphill was about 40mph and I'm pretty sure that climbing the M62 we were getting overtaken by skateboards, lawnmowers and mobility scooters.

The van didn't have a working lock on the back door either, so given that we had arrived too early for our set and didn't have a hotel room, we parked in the production area and lugged our overnight bags with us to the festival. Making contact with whoever was in charge of our stage was proving difficult, so puffed up with self-importance after checking out our names on the lanyards, we headed to the massive VIP tent to hang out. I realised this was a mistake when I pulled back the flap to the tent and a chair came flying out and hit a girl who was walking out at the same time a glancing blow. She just shrugged it off and headed back inside to find who had thrown it and get some Scouse justice.

Inside was absolute bedlam. A full Wild West-style saloon fight was kicking off. Apparently, in order not to upset any of the local gangsters, the festival organisers had been extremely conscientious in inviting them all for the full red carpet treatment. The problem was that some of these guys had been feuding for decades and this was the first time they'd been in one place together in all that intervening time. The security had either been caught unaware or had more wisely decided not to get involved.

The only person who was attempting to calm things down was the DJ, who'd reacted to the carnage by turning up his Hed Kandi-style lounge-ready funky house as loud as possible, maybe in the hope that the power of Barbara Tucker ft. Blaze would pour oil on troubled waters. To this day, I can't hear "preciouuuuus, precious love" without a mental picture of two women bent double with their hands deep in each other's hair, spinning round and round while swearing and screeching at each other in accents so high-pitched only bats could hear them.

By this time our contact had turned up and she took us away to a nearby empty tent with a couple of sofas and sorted out some drinks while they called in an air-strike or mounted police or whatever to get the VIP under control. We stayed there for a while, it's only occupants, getting our pre-set buzz on and congratulating ourselves on what we thought was our own personal green room.

Unfortunately, we relaxed to the extent that we left our bags under one of the sofas while we went to play, and when we returned, well… you can guess the rest. There wasn't really much of value among our underpants, towels, chargers and deodorants. However, one of our party had recently invested in home contents insurance, which made him absolutely determined to get a police report. Being slightly smug about not having broken a single law at the festival (those were the days), I tagged along for the hell of it as he made his way to the police area. The senior superintendent or whoever we talked to was another stereotype: barrel chest, bushy moustache and pristine uniform. But his professional air soon left him when we explained how we'd left our bags unattended for about four hours. "You did what?!" he said about five times, with the "you stupid London dickheads" not said out loud but clearly implicit. "You've got to understand," he explained, like a patient-but-exasperated father to a toddler who'd just stuck their hand in the toaster for the tenth time: "People… people… people COME. HERE. TO. STEAL."

Oh well, you live and learn. And it seemed to turn a switch on in my mate's head, as he decided that he would have his revenge on the city or festival or whatever and embrace his own dark side. Over the next few hours, he somehow convinced several bar staff that his artist badge gave him carte blanche to nip behind the bar and retrieve large quantities of whatever he liked: first beers, then bottles of foul brightly-coloured spirits. At one point, he even swiped a bottle of champagne. Finding an abandoned inflatable sofa in the main stage field, we stayed there and just got steadily more drunk on purloined booze, gradually collecting a small crowd of local hangers-on who ended up inviting us to an after-party, which totally beat sleeping in the draughty van, and did end up proving that Liverpool people were properly sound.

There was one more unfortunate incident, though. The festival was surrounded by an outer fence built of those 8ft high wire panels, each one like the side of a giant shopping trolley slotted into little brick-like weights at intervals. A little the worse for wear, when I finally made it to the end of the maze to get out, I leaned back on the one at the end and it toppled over, in turn toppling the other 300 or so connected to it like dominoes in what seemed like slow motion as I stumbled away in panic, once and for all proving that London people are twats.

THE OLD SWITCHEROO

I've been going to the same festival in East London for four years or so. And the strangest things seem to happen there, every year. I remember I was doing artist liaison in the Ambient Tent one Sunday morning. I'd already done the Saturday night to Sunday morning graveyard shift. Not been to bed since Thursday night. And the Ambient Tent is where everyone goes when they're on acid, which tells you everything you need to know.

So anyway, this one DJ had squatted down behind the booth to light a cigarette and unbeknownst to him, his trousers had fallen down. Me and my friend were just saying to each other, "Do you think he's gonna do a shit on the rug? Why's he got his trousers down?" We couldn't see the cigarette or anything from where we were. I said this and someone said, "Mate, you're the artist liaison; why don't you go over and stop him?" But I just sat there and waited it out. It just did not occur to me to get up. I was just so invested in waiting and seeing what would happen. As I said, things just happen there. Or fortunately not, in that case.

The following year I was actually performing in the Ambient Tent. So that meant playing ambient and leftfield techno, all while doing 'sexy' vocals over the top. In lingerie and platform heels. It was pretty extra, not gonna lie.

It was about one o'clock in the morning by the time I went on, and I was feeling a bit worse for the wear. So I asked a friend if they had a little pick-me-up, which they gave me. But then they turned around and told me, "Oh no, I've given you the wrong bag". Shit. I'd actually had quite a lot of said pick-me-up, which turned out not to be a pick-me-up at all.

It was a bag of ketamine, and it was also a portal to an interdimensional hell-hole.

Twenty or so minutes later and I was being particularly 'unwell' under the DJ booth. A friend came in to help me. Several friends, actually. One to stroke my back, one to put my records on for me, etc. So as I sat under the DJ booth with my record bag in front of me, puking to the side, someone stroking my back, me looking through my records, handing it up, it going on, then puking again, doing the vocals, putting the mic down, being sick, going back into the record bag, being sick, going to do vocals, putting the mic down... over and over for my whole set. I never want to repeat anything like this ever again; I can't stress that enough. It was just awful. When I stood up, very wobbly, I actually got a round of applause. That's the kind of state I was in.

I somehow managed to finish most of my set, though I think the DJs on afterwards had to come on early. A friend was like, "Do you want some Valium?" because I was visibly shaking. So I took some and tried to calm down. I mean, it was genuinely a horrific experience. I can laugh about it now, but at the time, it felt like an endless tour of hell.

And the weird thing was that because I was doing live vocals, my friends were walking in and hearing my voice, but they weren't seeing me – because I was under the booth, unable to stand up. They were just seeing my friend DJing while hearing the voice of the person they'd come to see, possibly interrupted by puking noises. This was Friday night. There were still two days and nights of the festival to go.

TEXTURE LIKE SUN

Heroin was my thing for a long time. Maybe seven years, but it sure felt like longer. I suppose in medical terms, I was what they call 'high functioning'. I could operate just fine, but I'm probably a producer because I could stay at home, function and take drugs too. It was always a solo thing, not at all social. I didn't even take drugs at the party or DJ gigs. I couldn't wait to get out of there and go home to do them.

I didn't shoot up, to begin with, oh no, that would have been terrible and dirty and would make me an addict. It was smoking. The works came later. The problems really started when I started to get more travelling gigs. First off, I just flat-out made excuses why I didn't want to work in a particular place. It wasn't cool enough. Didn't like the government's politics. I'd never heard of the venue. Whatever. But there's only so much bullshit you can come up with before you have to cave in. The stuff coming out of my mouth started to sound ridiculous to me, so I can't imagine what it sounded like to someone else. I always wonder how much my agent suspected. She sure never asked. But they never do, do they? Not as long as you are makin' bacon. By then I was on speedballs.

The thing is, when you are as covert as I was, you had to take it with you everywhere. If you roped the locals in, your secret was out. I was in prison for a while when I was a kid, so I was pretty savvy when it came to smuggling and good at keeping secrets. It was pretty small amounts. I'd pretty much take just enough to function, not to have a good time. My idea of good time did not involve standing up. I think people see discos as a happy, clappy sort of place generally, but there is a very dark side. The venues I play take themselves very seriously. They are quite joyless places. Dark tunnels full of plastic people.

Don't get me wrong, I am very committed to the job and especially to making music. I take my studio work very seriously. I'm cleaner now but for a while, the whole thing was very dark. You could argue the scene itself was dark. Maybe that was my perception of it but when the focus shifted to Berlin and I moved there, it all made sense. Like it was made for me.

Maybe there is another reality. You can disappear in this world of discos. You really can. Go into it and never emerge again. Live and die there. Like an undersea kingdom. Drexciya knew it. You can inhabit another place, a fairy world. Like Alice down the rabbit hole.

To emerge from it, you have to examine why you do it. It's totally obvious what you are doing, but until you ask 'why', you will just go around in circles. It is amazing how little you analyse it. It is entirely about what you are doing, or maybe you vary it by blaming it on 'where'. "Oh my God, I'm doing heroin again, in Berlin!" sort of thing. I guess that is the point, isn't it? You take it so you don't have to think about things. What opiates do is roll up every single issue you have, old and new, and make them all into one big problem. One that is an easy fix. Why do you think we call a dose 'a fix'?

Thing is, I was good at it. I did well. I was happy. Really. I look back and I was never happier. Mainly as I was completely oblivious to everything. That is the point of it, though, isn't it? I think I only stopped eventually because my youth ran out. I mean, I am not that old but there is a window where you can absolutely destroy yourself and your body just pings back like a rubber band. I'd probably still be doing it now if I could. Eventually, you substitute any kind of exercise or good eating or wellbeing for an artificial high and you quickly start to decay. You just stop bouncing back.

I could get pretty pure stuff, so I got away with it for a while without major incidents. Most of my issues came along later from not moving or eating much. I have a friend who is also into it but exercises on it for kicks, which is weird. She is super healthy and takes heroin every day. Weird, right? Maybe it is less weird than you think and there is a lot of it about. Maybe one of us is in the room with you right now?

Why am I telling you this? Maybe it is a postcard from the dark. A warning flag. Also, you know, maybe the person you think is having a great time and nodding along to your boring monologue is just tripping balls and has no idea you are even there. I'm a terrible example. I don't even agree there is anything wrong with it. I'm a textbook nihilist. Real freedom is the freedom to be awful. I loathe ambition and go-getters. For me, the whole thing, the industry I am in, it's a murky place. Also, it is totally a refuge for no-hopers like me. I am a spider and this is my hole. The planks under which I exist.

TIME OUT

Despite what you might imagine from its heritage, when I was coming up in Chicago there were no opportunities and everyone seemed like a hater. By the late-2000s, after six years of DJing, I was burned out, disillusioned with music and tired of getting shit from my family. I decided to give up DJing and get a real job. That was it for three years; I didn't go to clubs, couldn't even listen to dance music in the car because I felt so traumatised.

Everything had started promisingly. Barely into my 20s, I was the opening DJ at the city's best club. My first release had come out on one of the city's big labels of the time, although the owner had put out the wrong track. When he played the record for the first time, looking over at me proudly, I realised with horror it was an unfinished demo I'd included on the CD I gave him.

I also loved touring England, which had started when someone had flown me over to play a birthday party and I'd used the trip to get some other gigs and build contacts. It ended up so that each year I'd stay in Manchester for a month or longer on someone's couch and travel around the UK, playing places like London and Leeds.

On my fifth tour, the last before I quit, I came to Liverpool to see another Chicago DJ play. The music was changing at that point and back home, we didn't really know why. Dirtybird was coming along and what I suppose you'd call minimal and tech-house. My UK friends had to explain that whatever music was popular was down to whatever drugs were popular. The UK is always ahead of the curve when it comes to fun and drugs. For a long time, ecstasy was huge, so everyone was into house and happy stuff.

But now it had shifted to ketamine, so this minimal/tech-house sound was taking over. It sounded really boring to me because I was used to listening to classic house. Where was the soul? Minimal was cool for a track or two; I was into some of the producers, but not two hours of it.

So with a bump-tism of K, my friend led me into the main room where one of the scene's figureheads was in the booth. For thirty minutes it was the best music ever. I wanted to listen to it for the rest of my life; every detail just seemed so clear. When a hi-hat came in, it felt so exciting.

Going back to the house room, it sounded like everything was 'in' at once. I physically couldn't listen to a saxophone, a vocal, or too much of anything melodic. So we went back to the Minimal room. At one point, I had a camera tripod and was firing it like a machine gun out the green room, battling anyone who came in. It made sense of what was happening. Once it wore off, though, so did my enjoyment. I don't want to blame minimal or ketamine, but when I got back to Chicago, I was completely uninspired by the music that was around. Around 2006, it just got shitty. House needs a little more flavour for me, so a couple of years later, I quit DJing.

It was really sad because I'd left school to DJ and hadn't reached my goals. I didn't know how to turn that first taste of success into a career and it had fizzled out. The question that kept going through my mind was, had I just fucked up my life for the last ten years? When you're young, it's easy to talk yourself out of success because of the constant battle with your inner critic.

It turned out to be a figure-your-life-out period. I started a live project and met the vocalist I now run my label with. Then around 2012, the music started to get groovier again. When I came back, I knew exactly what I wanted and how to do it properly. If you want DJing and making music to be your career, you need to treat it as a job and take the proper steps. I now know more about publishing and running a label, how to deal with agents and managers. It's very different from when I was in my twenties.

BULLY FOR YOU,
CHILLY FOR ME

Not sure if this qualifies as interesting to anyone but me, but one long weekend I may have experienced the most diverse weather conditions of any human. Think about it. What other job on the planet has as much travel? There really aren't many. Pilot? Crew, defo. Who else will do three or four flights in one day? All the time, too, not just in a one-off extreme situation.

This particular weekend was a monster. It was a UK bank holiday, so as well as the usual miles on a Friday or Saturday, there were big gigs on Thursday, Monday and even Tuesday. It sometimes happens that, for various reasons, a weekend really creeps up and mugs you. It can be a particularly harsh weekend just gone that makes you groggy. It can be that in your mind, you see the busy week on the calendar, but your brain is telling you it is not the one approaching but the weekend after. It is very, *very* easy to get disoriented in this game. At the peak of it definitely. So it was a case of: *whoa, what do you mean I'm playing in an hour on the other side of London?? It's a THURSDAY.* And then it dawns on you that you got the week wrong.

The hectic run across town means any thoughts about anything else just pour out of my ear. By the time I've huffed and puffed into the makeshift booth at what is technically still daytime and pretty sun-shiny, I'm just pleased to have made it. Then I do a double-take on the piece of paper; there's *another* gig this evening. Dammit. About an hour to spare, so again, just about get there in time and get the job done.

Then feeling like I pulled off a coup, go to an after-hours. Then a Random's house. I'm still there Friday lunchtime, just about getting double vision when the panicked text arrives about a change of plans in flights. WHAT FLIGHTS!? Oh shit. It's THAT weekend. The one on the calendar that had so much overlapping text and notes you could barely read it. The weekend of doom I'd been mentally avoiding. I had to be in Scotland in about six hours time, play, then get a connecting flight to Amsterdam for Moscow.

By the time the car raced past Newcastle and I got out for a piss break in my shorts, sandals and standard-issue ket vest, I realised it was a bit bracing. I'm fairly solid, so I shrugged it off, but when I got out at the gig, it was clear I wasn't down south anymore, Toto. As expected, most of the girls were wearing as little as I was, but they were way tougher than I. They lived there. Anyway! Press onwards. Do the gig! Get to the airport.

Airports are a doddle. Toasty. When I arrive in Moscow, I realise that my mistake is a very large one. It was properly sub-zero. And I thought Scotland was chilly. I had nothing suitable and it was way too late/early to buy anything. The locals thought it was hilarious, and naturally, a large coat was found and in the car, I had magazines and newspapers wrapped around my arms and legs. In the club, it was not an issue but the extreme change from steamy near-naked bodies to sandals on ice on the pavement outside was getting silly. But it was only Friday. Or was it Saturday? Tomorrow I vowed that no matter how tired I was, I would sort some clothes out. I'd been caning it, so naturally, I went out like a light and woke up to someone hammering on the hotel door. I had a very short window to leave.

Luckily now I was in an airport at a reasonable hour this time and you can buy clothes. I got kitted-up like a Cossack and felt relieved. I called the agency and they said change of plan. It's not Italy now; it's Malaysia.

I got off the plane in Kuala Lumpur literally looking like an arctic explorer straight into 90% humidity and 35 degree heat. I tried looking in my bag, I didn't have a lot of luggage other than records, and luckily

I'd kept the t-shirt but not the shorts and sandals. I often ditch things on the road to save baggage weight. The t-shirt properly stank and it didn't help the whiffy combo that my lower half was woolly socks, boots and thick trousers. In hot countries, the locals get annoyed if you open windows as it is all about controlling the climate with air-con. Within minutes my hosts had opened both their windows. They'd rather be cooked to death by a torrent of boiling steam than smell me.

Next, we started climbing and climbing on the steepest motorway I'd ever been on. The country was in a heatwave and this resulted in a vast, grey overcast that was oppressive and greenhouse-like in temperature and humidity. We were heading for a resort in the clouds that would apparently be above the smog and haze. Judging by the volume of traffic, half the nation was trying to climb above the smog. When we got there, the entire thing was cloaked in dense fog and called off. I mean, you literally could not see your hand in front of your face. I was laughing to myself and just as it started to snow, my laughter got just a tad hysterical in tone. I retreated to the oddball circular hotel at the summit of the mountain. At least tomorrow was Sunday. Or was it a Monday?

SUNDAY MEANS IBIZA! Hurrah! I arrived an absolute wreck to a highly catholic place that had almost nothing but clubs open. No shops of any kind were going to sell me anything. Luckily I spied one of those sort of tourist gaffs that has a load of inflatables and buckets and spades that was open and sweated my way to the counter and the lady took one look at me and pointed at some flip flops and bikinis and no more needed to be said. I did that gig and it was almost pleasant. Once again, as the sun went down it got a wee bit chilly, but that didn't matter because I was off my chops again and due back to Manchester soon.

It was fucking freezing and pissing with rain when I got there, of course. The 'bank holiday' vibes were daft. It was an 'Ibiza party' in a derelict part of Greater Mancunia and was outdoors at Easter. Even I knew it was silly thinking it wouldn't rain. At least I had a stupid Russian hat. The rest I'd left in Ibiza because it was too bulky. Once again,

I was not suitably attired for the seasons. Naturally, when I got back to London for the Tuesday gig, it was oppressively sweaty and grey in town, having been a very pleasant weekend for a change in the capital. If only I'd got to see any of it.

Unsurprisingly, I got the flu and did the next mental weekend of work, both hungover and feeling horrendously awful. Since that epic weekend of bizarre temperature extremes, I made sure I always travelled with some thin thermals rolled up in the bottom of the bag and had the local weather on the itinerary.

MAKE 'EM SHAKE

So this happened towards the beginning of my career – and actually, it was almost exactly the time when DJing started to go from being my hobby to becoming a career. I was still pretty starry-eyed about the whole thing. And when I say 'starry-eyed', I mean that I just wanted to play out. I wanted to play anywhere. I was like 23, 24. I had maybe a couple of small releases out. I had no real credibility I could use as currency to question how things worked at gigs, which will become relevant later. I just wanted to play music to people.

So anyway I was offered a set of two gigs playing in hotels for what was to me, at that time, a LOT of money. Now I was warned that these would not be life-changing gigs [credibility-wise]. But one was in Asia and one – and this is where the story takes place – was in Russia, St Petersburg to be exact. So I was happy with that – I mean, I was being offered a decent amount of money to go there, plus I had just been hit with a pretty debilitating tax bill, which this gig was able to get me out of. So everything added up, at least on paper.

So I got to St Petersburg, which looks exactly how I thought it might. It was incredibly, incredibly cold, it was snowing and as I walked out of the airport, I couldn't help but notice a really ridiculous black Porsche, which really stuck out amidst this snowy Russian scene. And then my heart both leapt AND sank at the same time when I saw that the driver of this ludicrous vehicle was holding an iPad with my name on it. So he was here for me. Brilliant.

The hotel staff were so, *so* keen to impress me that I was immediately very uncomfortable. The concierge laid out a program as I was checking in: "Your dinner is booked in for 7pm," so I thanked him, but then he went on, "...and you'll be having it with the head chef". So I say "Well, there's no need for that," but they insisted. The head chef in question was an exhausted Frenchman who was, he told me, trying to make a new life in St Petersburg with his family. So there we were, doing our best to get through this rather awkward dining experience, me thinking: *well, this is different... it's something to talk about, at least.*

Now I give all this context because the gig did not match up to the level of effort that had been expended so far. I mean, when they showed me where I was playing, it turned out to be the hotel's reception. About four people were sitting there, but that did rise to about 12 people at one point in the evening. And it was just... surreal. I mean, I wanted to just stop and say to someone, "You know how much you're paying me and this is all you want me to do?"

So I played background music to a few disinterested people as they sat around in this hotel reception. I just got my head down and played until I was told to stop. Then I went upstairs to my room, thinking I'd had a strange experience but might at least get a funny story out of it. I was just about to crash out when my hotel telephone rang. So I picked it up, out of curiosity more than anything, to hear a voice asking, "Is that X? I'm a good friend of the booker of the hotel and I run the coolest club in town. We often work with the hotel and we've got a party on tonight. I can pay some extra money and you could play some records if you like?"

And I'm like, "Yeah, I mean alright, sure."

He continues, "it's the coolest club, we play the best EDM, we love Black Eyed Peas...."

And you know I think I just stopped him there. "I'm sorry, no offence, but that's not the kind of thing that I do and I don't really have any music like that."

But he was all: "Come on, come down, you can make it work! I know you like cool music, come and play some of your cool music here." So I just convinced myself: *come on then, this is a new experience at least – I'm in St Petersburg for one night, let's go!*

So he said there would be a car there in 20 minutes and right on time there was. Now, the first alarm bell was the music policy, obviously, but then the second alarm bell was arriving at the club and ALL of the bouncers were wearing balaclavas. As I walked in, this guy met me – and I swear there were actually guns on display in a kind of decorative way – and dragged me into the back room of this actually quite glitzy club (guns notwithstanding). Immediately a camera crew swung around the corner. "Hey, we're making a video of tonight; you want to be in it?"

"Oh, no, not really."

But they were all, "Come on, it's cool!" And it was a professional crew and this guy was right in my face, saying, "So how do you like St Petersburg? How do you like the women here? They're pretty sexy right?! Pretty sexy...." And this is all being filmed. He just kept on and on... He kept telling me that he didn't drink, but he seemed like he'd maybe been to Alcoholics Anonymous and replaced booze with high-grade imported coke.

And then I actually have to DJ at this very mainstream Russian club. I just had no idea what I was supposed to do. In the end, I just mustered the best mainstream music I could find in my records, which was New Order, Human League, I think I probably had a Prince record tucked away somewhere. So the guy before me is slamming out EDM and then I come on sounding pretty fucking weak in comparison. After about ten minutes, the promoter guy comes back and says, "Man, you gotta play faster, you gotta play faster!" I said to him, "I don't really play any faster man, this is what I do." But he was insisting, "Come on, man, you gotta play faster! You see those hot women there with the big fake titties! You gotta make them shake, man. I want to see them shake their titties along the bar!"

To which I could only reply, "Well, ok, I'll do my best."

So then, ten minutes after this, he comes back and basically repeats the same thing. So I'm just gritting my teeth and thinking *I have to get through this now*. Which is what I proceeded to do, until out of the corner of my eyes I saw a guy with a saxophone come up beside me. And he goes, "Hey man, I'm gonna play sax over you now!" So on top of everything else, I've now got a sax player going for it over my limp 80s pop rhythms...

Anyway, when I finally came off, the promoter's previous enthusiasm had visibly drained away. He handed me a bunch of money, which was actually far less than he had promised me, but at this point, I just wanted out of there. So he told me he'd get me a taxi back to my hotel and he took me outside to this car park, which looked like one of the scariest places I've ever been: it was just a barren grey wasteland with the occasional burly man just drifting around to add to the lingering air of menace.

Then this tiny little car pulled up – the complete opposite of the Porsche from earlier – and I don't even think it was a taxi. How the mighty had fallen. But I got into this tiny thing and then as we got on our way, two things became clear: one, that the driver didn't know the hotel as it was so new. And two, that he didn't speak any English – and I, of course, didn't speak any Russian. So discussing point one was pretty tricky.

So we drove around in circles as he got more and more irate, rumbling away in Russian. All I could tell was that the price was going up and up. And I told him how much I had on me, showing him so he'd understand. And I really thought *I might die tonight. I might actually not make it home.* I mean, it was really scary and this guy was getting seriously angry. I really felt like this could be it. And it would be a sad way to go, especially with that as my last set! But after about half an hour, he eventually found this hotel, took all the money out of my hands and slapped me on the back as he started laughing. I started laughing too, out of sheer relief at still being alive, I think. Then I ran back into my hotel, desperately hoping that not all my touring days were going to be like this.

GABBER GABBER NO

I was DJing gabber when I would consider it really good, at the beginning around 1993, which is how I got chased out of town after being accused of being a Nazi. Mostly I played in London, but there were other parties up and down the country, so once I got booked in Stafford. It's quite a small town, but I grew up there, so still had some connections. This was the era when you'd drive around the country every week, sometimes playing three gigs on a Friday or Saturday.

The party was in a large wine bar in the centre of town, which in retrospect seems quite amusing. But it was a big open space and the people promoting it ran the only dedicated hardcore record shop in the town, so they were a hub for the rave scene. This was a mid-weeker, a Wednesday or Thursday night, so it probably finished around midnight.

My friend, a hardcore-turned-jungle producer, offered to drive me up there – about a three or four-hour journey. It wasn't a dedicated gabber night, there was more breakbeat-oriented stuff earlier on, but I played the last set to about 50 people. 'Alles Naar De Kl--te' by Euromaster was one of the anthems of the time that I remember – very aggressive with big vocals in Dutch.

The party finished, and after the lights came up, there was the usual traipsing outside, saying our goodbyes. We made it to the car park, then were confronted by four Asian lads who'd followed us out the bar. For a moment, I didn't know what was happening, although it was obvious something wasn't right. Then they asked, "Why were you just playing that racist Nazi music?"

They had it in their heads it was white supremacist music. A few things going around in the press at that time linked gabber to that way of thinking. If that was any link, it wasn't coming from the producers, and it definitely didn't have those connotations to me – quite the opposite. In London, it had emerged out of breakbeat hardcore, a very mixed crowd that brought together all different kinds of people. Gabber was one of the offshoots it had taken in parallel to jungle.

Who knows how it would have unfolded if my friend hadn't jumped in his car, a Ford Sierra Cosworth, and zoomed off as soon as we joined him. That wasn't the end, though, as the lads jumped in their own car, some kind of souped-up GTI, and started tailgating us. They chased us out of town at about 70mph till we hit the motorway.

I'm not sure if that incident left a mark or if it was just gabber getting cheesy very quickly, but after a year or so, I'd moved on.

PAS DE DEUX

Sometimes you arrive and it's totally obvious the whole thing is just *wrong*. Like nothing about it feels legit. I don't just mean the sadly frequent gangster type of set-ups, but the ones where they are clearly doing it for the first time. I mean, yeah, everyone has got to start somewhere, but there's a limit. This one always sticks in my mind because I really felt awful about it all. I arrived and the pick-up was basically a kid and his Dad. We got in their family car, full of baby seats, toys and rubbish like any family car, and set off to the venue. Dad did all the talking and I naturally engaged with him in the standard car small talk. We got to the venue and it was magnificent! Like a sort of Oxbridge building or ancient meeting hall. Beautiful baroque palace, not just an architectural wonder but loads of character, like totally perfect for a big disco.

The kit is top-notch, with a crew of pros hired in. The newest sound and lights. Place looks great! I'm second on the bill to a big name, but there doesn't seem to be any resident or warm-up there, so I turn to them and ask if they want me to start right away? This is about 10 pm, opening time. I've never minded starting the night off; I quite like it. It feels good to get the thing going. Catch the vibe and mould the party into shape. So I start playing.

One hour later and there's still not a soul in there. The sound is bouncing around this huge space. Could easily pack 1,500 in there. In the distance, at the door, I can see Dad and lad. Hopping from one foot to the other, doing the nervous dance. It happens, late starters. Two hours later and it was coming up to midnight. I've promoted a fair bit as well as DJ'd. There's a rough rule of thumb, in the UK certainly, that if it's not happening between 12 and 1, it ain't happening, period. Maybe lately, a little later in some big towns that go until 6 but not a lot more. Listen, I'm a pro; I'll do the job regardless. But it's torture playing to no one, especially with a place like this, all dressed up and nowhere to go. Besides, the kid looked about 15, must be way past his bedtime.

I don't know about you but I'm the sort who'd rather put something out of its misery than watch it suffer. I put a long one on and went out to the entrance. Asked when DJ Big Name was coming and "you know, maybe think about a Plan B?" When your name is attached to something, you kind of get emotionally attached too. It's on you too. Part of me was thinking, *get out of here before anyone sees!* And the other voice is thinking of ways to fix it. I suggested maybe placate Big Name by telling him to enjoy a night off at the hotel and I'd carry on. Dad had already cancelled him. Dad was slowly going purple. Kid just looked blank. Hell of a double act. Laurel and Hardy.

The thing was, it was perfect. Everything about it was spot-on; there just weren't any people. The crew knew the score, rolling their eyes at me but doing their best as well. By 1am, Dad comes barrelling over and cuts it all off. Calls it a night, to my tremendous relief. It only takes a handful of folks to turn up and see a disaster for it to get around town. And if a meme picks up, around the world. What is it they say? 'Someone will tell two people they had a good night, but will tell 20 if they had a bad one'. Something like that.

Promoting is a funny thing. When the socials became big, I'd see things like this one-off happen more often. People thinking that someone pressing 'interested' on Facebook and a virtual online 'guestlist' equated to a real-life amount of bodies on the dancefloor. I mean, another rough rule of thumb is that if you absolutely have to guess with confidence, you get about 10% back of what you put out. This goes for the guest list too. A list of 100 means you can only really bank on ten of them definitely coming. It might be more, but it's a number you can bank on, sort of. If you need 300 people in your place, you need to be absolutely certain at least 3000 people have been seriously approached about coming, with no maybes about any one of them.

The socials may tell you that this has happened, but more and more studies are showing that this is not true. And their numbers are not reliable. Hey, you might be at the peak of youth and highly sociable and have 300 mates and acquaintances you can bank on; that's great. I'm talking about cold promoting to an indifferent public here. Say, for example, you go to a different city other than your own and can pull off a gig to total strangers, then you can call yourself a promoter. Yeah, there's not a lot of certainty, and as such, I have a lot of sympathy for anyone with the guts to try. It's not a job for optimists. You have to be quite calm about expectations.

So back to this – and Dad is volcanic with rage by now. I venture that you know, hey, it happens! Maybe there is another big thing going on in town? Promoting is always spinning the wheel a bit, never 100%. You did a great job with the place etc. He looks at me like I am stupid.

"Me?? This isn't my fucking calamity! It's *this* idiot!"

He gestures to the kid, who, as per looks mute and blank. Turns out he's not a teenager, he just looks really young. He's a senior student in town and this was supposed to be his career. He was 'Ents' (events) Manager at the University. The following car journey to the hotel was grim. Dad shouted everything. Turns out he paid for it all too.

"I TOLD HIM! THE UNIVERSITY IS IN ANOTHER BLOODY TOWN NEARLY! THEY HAVE FREE STUFF ON! THEY AREN'T GETTING ON A TRAIN!"

I felt awful. I said I didn't want paying (it was a full-fee job, in keeping with the size of it). My name was on the bill, too, so if some locals didn't come, it was partially on me.

"WHY WOULD ANYONE FROM HERE COME!? GENIUS HERE DIDN'T TELL ANY OF THEM! JUST HIS DAFT MATES A THOUSAND BLOODY MILES AWAY!"

The kid was obviously used to this. The entire time I was there, he never said a word. I insisted I was OK; accidents happen and let's waive the fee.

"NO! I WILL PAY YOU EVERY PENNY. EVERY. SINGLE. POUND AND PENCE. AND EINSTEIN HERE WILL PAY ME BACK IF IT TAKES THE REST OF HIS LIFE! AND IT PROBABLY WILL!"

I was in full cringe by now, almost doubled-up with embarrassment. I knew DJ Big Name alone would be costing him at least 10K. I suggested I should take half my fee?

"NO! NO, SIR! THIS ONE HAS TO LEARN THERE ARE CONSE-QUENCES! YOU WILL GET EVERY. SINGLE. BEAN. YES!"

Then with one hand on the wheel and the other in an envelope, he starts measuring out my wage one note at a time. Glaring at the kid as every note slapped down. I wasn't kidding; if it meant relieving this horrific atmosphere and crushing guilt, I'd have given them every penny back. I even tried to leave the envelope in the car and Boiling Mad Dad just followed me out and crammed it into my jacket. I think it was the worst car journey of my life.

MANAGER MELTDOWN

I should have known my first South American tour would be cursed the moment we arrived at Heathrow to fly to Bogota and realised my manager had booked the flights for the following day. Even for his levels of what you Brits call 'scattiness', this was pretty out-there. He was a classic party boy clown who, like far too many people I met in the industry during the mid-90s, seemed to care a lot more about the lifestyle than the music itself.

But he got results, so I didn't complain. How could I? I was in my early 20s, I'd moved over to London from Europe and had found myself in a very sweet spot of that first wave of progressive house artists. All the right DJs were playing and releasing my music and I had a busy international schedule. Waiting another day to start my three-week tour of South America was hardly a problem. I'd played out there before, but always for one-off shows, then fly back the same weekend. This time it was for a tour and my manager decided it was best he came along with me. He swore it was for 'business reasons', of course, but when Colombia is the first stop on the route, it was obvious why he came.

Personally, I was sick of the sight and smell of cocaine. I'm no Mother Theresa, I enjoy a drink once I've finished performing, but the white stuff has never been for me. Even in the slim chance it might have been, the behaviour I saw when I came to the UK and saw how the DJ' gentry' behaved on the stuff was enough of an advertisement to not partake. At best, it turned people into sweaty, swollen-ego chatterboxes. At worst, it turned (usually) switched-on, (sometimes) thoughtful people into furiously greedy, sex-hungry monsters.

Every weekend was the same whether we were in London or touring around the world: the show closes, the punters leave, we retire to a bar or the promoter's place to unwind. I would never decline the invite, I like to be sociable – but one or two drinks to say thanks, meet some cool people then back to the hotel for some sleep is enough for me before I move on. Hey, if I'm really lucky, I'd get to have a nice experience and be able to get the hell out of there before the escorts were called in.

It happened at almost every big show I played at. More than a lot of the big DJs from that era will admit. A manager, promoter or some other seedy 'industry professional' would leave the room and return a while later, parading the girls around the room, offering them like sweets from a jar – to a room largely comprised of married men with young families at home. Some of the DJs even had wives who worked in the industry, but everyone in the room seemed to be comfortable with it, so I would say my goodbyes and make an exit.

As I say, I'm no party pooper, but it just wasn't what I'd come into music for. I was very lucky in terms of my age and where dance music was at when I got into it.

I'm old enough to be considered old school but young enough to come in during that second wave. Unlike those paving the way into the unknown, my generation could see that careers could be forged in this industry if you did your hard work and didn't party too much. I was very serious about this and was incredibly focused. I'd spent more than my 10,000 hours in the studio and I was reaping the rewards; I didn't need meaningless sex or drugs that turn you into a dickhead. But each to their own and the clubs themselves were incredible. So I'd keep things polite and leave whenever I encountered the dark behaviour at the end of the night.

When you're on tour, however, that's not so easy to do. And by the time we reached Bogota (three days later due to a bomb threat in the Colombian capital delaying all connecting flights – leaving us rattling around New York for two days), my manager was chomping at the bit to get his 'beak'. So imagine his delight when we finally arrived in the Colombian capital and were picked up by what was clearly a cartel goon in a bulletproof BMW with completely darkened, inch-thick windows – and offered cocaine within seconds of getting into the car.

As usual, I politely declined and enjoyed the scenery as we drove. And drove. And drove. A few hours into the journey, I asked where exactly we were heading. "Private booking, in the mountains," my manager explained between sniffs. He was panting like a dog and covered in a thin film of sweat.

I took his word for it and continued to enjoy the journey as we drove deeper into the mountains, going further and further off any type of main highway. Then suddenly, the dense trees gave way to a view of a stunning villa. Still to this day, I've never seen anything like it. A sprawling, brilliant white complex of luxury buildings, perfect gardens, multiple pools and mean-looking men with machine guns at regular intervals. I looked to my manager for reassurance but he was just as gobsmacked as me. He just gave me a look that I understood to mean, "this is uncharted territory for me too mate, let's see how this unfolds."

In fairness, it unfolded incredibly well. I avoided eye contact with anyone carrying large firearms but the main host was very general, jovial and well mannered. He told me it was his birthday, he thanked me for coming and gave me $5000 in $100 dollar bills as a tip then showed me to a green room, told me his casa was my casa and pointed to a huge salad bowl loaded to the rim with cocaine. My manager was instantly as happy as what you Brits describe as a 'pig in shit' and buried his head in the trough. The cartel man laughed heartily and left us to make ourselves at home.

The next few hours were a blur. They always are after long flights and car journeys. I took a stroll around the villa, spoke to a few other DJs who were booked for the event, had some incredible barbeque food and enjoyed a disco nap in the shade before heading to a ballroom inside the villa where around 2000 people were all having the time of their lives. Had you teleported me into that room I'd have had no idea we were in some cartel boss's castle all, I'm assuming, paid for by high-level cocaine manufacturing and smuggling. It was a lively, peak-time club atmosphere I'd seen many times in Latin America. Who are these people? I wondered. Are they cartel people? Are they criminals? How did they get here? Have they been here the whole time? And while I think about it, where the fuck is my manager?

All these questions run through my mind as I start getting into the groove and study the dancefloor. I never felt scared at any point, but there was niggling worry in my mind that if I messed up the set or killed the vibe, then things might go awry. I mean, I'm thousands of miles away from home playing at an unlisted, private event. The only person who knew I was there was also there with me... and I had no idea where he was. He's old enough to look after himself, I decided, and I focused on playing a great set. Then, around 20 minutes into things, I looked up to see him about three metres directly ahead of me. I wonder how I could have missed him – on a raised bit of stage gyrating around every woman in his vicinity with his shirt undone to the very bottom button and his eyes bulging out of his head on their stalks. I could tell he was on another planet – I'd seen him in some pretty awful states in the two years I'd known him, but this was next level. Every vein I could see in his neck and his face was bulging. He looked like he was about to burst. Well, at least he's still alive. I carry on about my business.

Thankfully my business went well and everyone appreciated my set. Relieved, I spent time talking to my new cartel amigos and enjoyed a few drinks to be social. They made sure I was fed and watered and around 3am they offered to drive me to the hotel. I have to say, cartels might have a nasty reputation and be responsible for all manner of gruesome things, but when it comes to hospitality and booking you for DJ sets, they're faultlessly professional. Far more than most promoters I've played for. I took them up on the offer and ask if anyone had seen my manager.

"He's fine. Still partying. We'll make sure he gets back."

That was more than enough reassurance for me, so we drove into the town, I checked into my hotel and fell into a deep, satisfying sleep. Suddenly I'm awoken by the room phone ringing.

"Sir, we have a problem."

"Oh, okay, how can I help?" I ask slowly in that dazed way you do when you've been rudely awoken by a stranger in a strange room. I look at the clock; it's 10am.

"Your guest is causing a commotion. If you don't remove him, we'll have to remove both of you from the premises."

"My guest?"

"Yes, sir, please come down to the reception."

I quickly get dressed and head down to the lobby and before my elevator even reaches the ground floor, I know what's happening. I can hear him long before I see him.

"I NEED COCAINE! I NEED WHORES!!"

It's echoing from the hotel's cavernous ceilings, along with various crashes and bangs and screams, and I'm turning inside out with embarrassment. I turn the corner and see him, this topless sweaty mess covered in random cuts and bruises, his eyes like a wild dog and his flies undone. He's stooping over a glass table, trying to lift it up and flip it up while screaming demands about hookers and cocaine.

"YOU!" he's looking at me, but his eyes are glazed.

"YOU! Let's get more cocaine. Let's find the prostitutes!"

I'm not even sure if he recognises me or places me accurately. But it's clear enough to the hotel receptionist that we have enough of a connection for him to be my responsibility.

"Get this man out of here now, or there will be a lot of trouble," he says gravely to me. "This is not how we expect your host's guests to behave and they will not tolerate this."

"GET US SOME FUCKING HOOKERS THEN!" screams my manager.

By now, I've gone the colour of scarlet with embarrassment and rage and fear. I clamp my hand around my manager's mouth and literally drag him across the foyer and into the elevator. I can feel his drool and sweat under my hand; he's literally slobbering like a rabid dog. I force this sweaty, grubby mess across the hall while all around normal, regular people and families eating breakfast are staring at us and silently judging us. I finally get him to his room and start the process of bringing him back down to the earth as he continues to froth at the mouth and rave about hookers.

First, I pour him a vodka. Surely this will calm him down a little? Nothing. It doesn't touch the sides. If anything, it puts more lead in his pencil. So I pour him another, and another and another. Eventually, after about a litre of vodka and a litre of rum, he turns the volume down and agrees to other conversational topics beyond coke and whores. Things like the next destinations on our route and whether we should continue our business relationship or not. He seems to calm down a little, so I make him shower and decide to take us out for some fresh air. He has the shakes, he's twitching, he still looks like he could explode any minute and now (thanks to me), he stinks like a distillery. But he's not ranting and raving about coke or whores, so it's as much as I can ask for. I take the risk and nervously lead him downstairs, hoping we don't cross paths with anyone we'd seen in the morning.

"Sir!"

I pretend not to hear it, keep my head down and hope it's not for me.

"Sir!"

Shit. It's definitely aimed at me. What's happening now?

"Sir, the driver for your other guest has been in touch. His flight landed in Bogota and he should be with you in time for your evening meal."

At first, I felt relief. This new information is not more fallout from this morning, therefore great news! Then I feel confused. *Other* guest? I check my watch. I check the date on the clock behind the reception. I proceed to absolutely shit myself; in amongst all the delays and bomb scares and cartel villas and lunatic drug-addicted managers, I'd totally forgotten that my girlfriend's father was joining us for two days of sightseeing in Colombia before joining us for two more dates in Brazil and Argentina. And he was a matter of two hours away. I look at my manager and assess the damage. He looks like a cross between Spud from Trainspotting and Phil Mitchell from Eastenders and he's muttering to himself like a man possessed, so I do my best to make him presentable.

First, we go for a stroll but the heat of the day makes him even sweatier and reduces him to a grunting animal. Then I take him for a swim in the pool and, after a few sketchy lengths, my work starts to pay off. He begins to yawn and agrees to have a lie down. I leave him on a sun lounger in the shade, finish my swim and get ready to meet the man who could potentially become my father in law. I was momentarily free of my caring responsibility and was actually looking forward to the company.

My girlfriend's dad was in IT, was well-travelled and had an interest in the arts. He'd joined me on several trips before when our schedules allowed and had seen me perform in Australia and quite a few locations in Europe. He was in his early 50s and painfully straight. But, in comparison to my manager, I was pretty damn straight, too. I even began to wonder if things would eventually be alright – I just needed my manager to stop looking and behaving like a depraved crack fiend, and maybe dad-in-law-to-be might not pick up on any awkwardness.

At first, this seemed to go well. I meet the dad in the lobby and arrange to meet him in the bar in half an hour. I then head to the pool to find my manager stirring in his lounger. He's a bit sketchy on the details, so I fill him in, send him up to his room and encourage him to sleep for the night and that he'd be fine in the morning. He agrees and heads off and I start to relax a little. Could this be okay? Maybe they won't even see each other for the next few days and by then, my manager would have come down and appeared 'normal'. Perhaps I'm overreacting after all.

The next two hours were very pleasurable. I enjoyed an adult conversation that didn't involve sex workers, enjoyed some delectable Colombian cuisine and planned our next few days sightseeing. My entire day of mothering a drug-addled moron began to seem like a dim and distant dream. Then I see that my company is peering over my shoulder and frowning.

"Bit obvious," he murmurs.

"Sorry?" I ask, completely oblivious to the fact that this could possibly be something to do with me.

"Some type of suspicious transaction in the lobby."

I shrug with a 'welcome to Colombia' type of grimace and continue my meal. My well of suspicious transaction tolerance had run completely dry. I had no intention of even turning around or being witness to any type of situation. Druggy idiots everywhere, I surmise and continue talking, thinking nothing of it. Twenty minutes later, the conversation still flourishing, I see the dad is distracted again and looking behind me into the lobby. This time, sensing something is up, I turn around and my heart stops. It's my manager, steaming at the ears once again, and he's with one of the goons from the previous night. They're laughing far too loudly and embracing each other in a hearty 'we've just had a monster line of cocaine' type of way. The goon leaves the lobby and my manager is shouting something about being with him in five minutes.

"SHIT!" I think to myself. I need to hide; I need to turn away now. I can't let these two men meet. But as these thoughts race through my mind, my manager clocks me and strides over as if the entire day of me looking after him hadn't happened.

"BOYS!" he shouts over to us. "We got half an ounce of coke and whores on tap for the night, come on, driver's waiting. Chop chop!"

The brazen tone of it all made it seem like I knew he'd be there and that this was all part of the evening's entertainment. I was painfully guilty by association and the look on my girlfriend's father's face was one of total horror. I could see him moving me from the 'acceptable, upstanding, potential son-in-law' category to the 'complete waster' category in a flash, and there was nothing I could do to change this. I wanted to explain myself. I wanted to tell him that I'd been caring for this man and trying to stop him from killing himself or getting us killed all day, but it didn't matter. Nothing mattered any more. I wasn't in Colombia; I was a resident of Awkward City. Hell, I was the Mayor.

"You crack on, you know that's not my thing," I say to my manager, laughing it off, but I knew it was too late. In my girlfriend's dad's eyes, I was now officially a grubby cokehead who slept with prostitutes and that was final. He looked at me like I looked at so many of the DJs I'd met when I came over to the UK and, even though I was entirely innocent, I felt complete and utter shame. A shame of being part of this culture where this is accepted, a shame that would fester in me for five more days in his and my manager's company on this cursed tour.

Mercifully Colombia was the most hedonistic stop on the tour and the rest remained relatively cartel and sex-worker free. The presence of my girlfriend's dad did calm my manager down a little, but the conversations were ice cold, stilted and wrought with tension and the dad didn't attend any of the shows in fear of what he might see. Needless to say, when I returned to the UK, my girlfriend called off our relationship – and I called a halt to my partnership with my manager.

ANGER DJING

We were introduced to the organiser of a new festival in our native Portugal two years before it happened. He had grand ideas, a vision of something between BPM and Burning Man – not our vibe, but as we run a radio station, he was keen to have us involved. Originally there was talk of us hosting a stage. Then we were going to do a boat party. Neither of those panned out, but he insisted on booking me and my partner, another female DJ I co-run the station with, to play individual sets.

As far as we knew, everything was fine as we set out by car from Lisbon to Porto, a journey of about 300 kilometres. And the festival was in a beautiful spot, a turn-of-the-century warehouse near the waterfront, really charming, with a beautiful, ornate wrought iron gate at the entrance. Since time was tight, we pushed through the big crowd outside to tell security we were DJing soon. When we asked for a stage manager, though, we realised that there was trouble in paradise.

There wasn't a stage manager to be found. There wasn't any type of manager. The entire management had gone AWOL. Already in uncharted territory, we decided to head to our stage. But there was no stage. Our stage no longer existed. Looking as bemused as we were, the security guard pointed us towards the main bar as the only possible source to try to get more information.

Inside there was a lot of glitter, people with feathers in their hats and steampunk goggles, all very cheesy. Everyone looked really high, so there was a party vibe of sorts, but it was obviously less busy than it should be – maybe a third of the 600 or so capacity.

The guy in charge of the bar had the same expression as the security guard, complaining the promoters hadn't been around for two days. In their absence, he and his team were holding it together, some staff having cut their losses and quit. The rest were obviously frustrated. We stood around nervously while he made some calls that didn't get answered, then he moved us on again, this time to wait by the sole remaining DJ booth on site where one of the directors was meant to meet us. By this point, it was obvious the whole thing had gone rogue, so we were freaking out.

After we watched the unfolding chaos for a while, a friend of the promoters turned up to give us some kind of explanation and offer drinks. He was the highest person we'd met so far, so when I asked for a Coke, he replied, "The drink?" We found this very funny.

Eventually, a woman involved turned up and some semblance of order was imposed. She told us they hadn't sold enough tickets, so they were putting every single DJ they had booked on one stage. This meant most people were playing for just thirty minutes. Our two sets, however, were being reduced to a 45 minute back-to-back.

We've also been pushed back to 3am and now had a couple of hours to kill, so we went to our hotel to get some respite. When we returned to the DJ booth just before our new time, though, there was another guy waiting expectantly, headphones around his neck. I explained what had happened and that we were on next. He disagreed. We scrambled into the booth together and as I plugged in my headphones, he put his USB in and loaded a track, victorious.

We found someone to complain to and were met with more apologies before being given a second, definite time. The same thing happened again, two DJs from Berlin insisting it was their turn. This was the penultimate slot of the whole show, so this time I stood my ground. I put my USB in, then one of them put their USB in. A stand-off.

It got tense. They were arguing priority as they'd just got off a plane and we were just 'local DJs'. One of them tried to elbow me out the way, so my ego kicked in and I started shouting about how I'd played better Berlin clubs than they had. My partner was trying to say she needed to play because she was on her period.

In the middle of this, someone else 'from the festival' turned up. But there was no help from that direction. He was the most fucked person we'd seen so far, completely and utterly lost. I asked if he was OK, out of genuine concern, and he gave a distressed "No" then faded back into the night.

Humbled by this human tragedy, the Berlin DJs relented and we finally started playing. This is when the guy who'd originally booked us arrived! Only to shorten our set again, this time cutting it down to thirty minutes so the Berlin DJs could come on afterwards. He was so destroyed he was actually hanging onto us like a drowning man while we were playing, talking non-stop into our ears about how much money he'd lost. Only at that point do I realise: shit, I'm probably not going to get paid.

Our set actually went down really well. Maybe it was because we were 'anger DJing', letting out all the night's frustration into our performance, somehow capturing the mood of the weekend. Even the Berlin DJs who we'd been fighting with came up afterwards to say, "Good set, guys."

I think I got half my money in the end after my agent chased it. It seems obvious, but if you're a promoter and want to put on a festival, don't underestimate how much organisation it takes. Don't disappear when things don't turn out the way you wanted. And... make sure to manage your drug intake at work.

SCHOOLBOY ERRORS

It's generally like 90% great when you DJ. Good times. So you tend to remember the ones that go wrong. I mean, it all goes a bit 'DJ complaining', but I think that sort of thing only really applies to the rich ones. Most of us are not wealthy at all. Just getting by, really. I mean, the various global economies have a lot to do with what you get paid.

For example, Argentina got properly shafted and their currency tanked big time a while back. They couldn't afford much at all, never mind silly bollocks DJs. It's a big trip too. The planet isn't flat no matter what idiots tell you, and if you look at a globe, Buenos Aires is really far away. So the flight is not cheap. For the promoter, not me. What I am trying to say is, for some countries, you kind of have an agreement where you really aren't going to make any money out of it. You have to flex with reality; it feels dead wrong as well to try to rinse people who're struggling. Then again, you have to pay the rent. I guess what I am saying is; you don't play these places as often. So I was made up with my first booking in Buenos Aires. I met a lot of folks from there in Ibiza. Amazing people. Always in the thick of it. Party people.

I'd not been there before, so it was a big honour to be asked and when they sort of half apologised about it not really being worth it financially, I was like, "pfft! I'm in. Don't care!" So I got on the plane, and it was a monster journey. Had a transfer like most cheap flights, so something like a 20 hour journey. I'm not great at sleeping on planes; I get a crick in my neck. So not only is it silly o'clock in the morning when I arrive, it's the southern hemisphere, so I've gone from freezing winter where I am from to their summer. Humid and steaming even at this hour. It's like about 5am, and I get out of arrivals and not long passes before I am the only passenger left standing there. It's depressingly obvious no one is meeting me.

This is more alarming than you might think if you've never experienced it. Other side of the planet. Middle of the night. Loads of hustlers there too. "You need a ride, señor?" sort of grift. Looking around, as well as everything being shut, it's pretty run-down. Schoolboy error number one: didn't arrive with local currency. Not a cash machine or bureau de change to be seen. I have a telephone number for the promoter but no relevant coins for the payphone, as it was early days for mobile phones and mine did not work outside the UK. Eventually, I negotiated with a hustler (I'm surrounded by now) who I picked because he was the biggest. I got him to chase the others off and I luckily had some American dollars stuck in a crevice of my bag. He was happy to give me some coins and take me into the city for what was easily three times what it would usually be.

I rang the promoter's number a few times. I didn't care if he was asleep, he should be here. Eventually, he picks up and he's not pleased. Nowhere near as displeased as me though.

I cut him off: "Mate, I don't even know where I'm supposed to be taking this taxi to!" I was a day early and was here for two nights and three days as "a holiday", according to the promoter. I had no instructions whatsoever. I'd got on the plane with a boatload of promises but nothing at all on paper. Promoter told me to hand the 'taxi' driver over and gave him some instructions on the phone.

"Man no have hotel for you, but I have friend" says Drive.

Oh fuck. I'm not small or easily intimidated and by now I had a proper death stare coming out of me. I just turned it on him full beam and said "no tricks", and he did a big theatrical "who me?" sort of pose and off we went.

Thankfully due to the hour we missed BA's famously chokka traffic and even though I was new to the place, I could tell he was driving pretty straight and purposefully. No sightseeing detours. Fairly soon, we were passing through the centre. Can't miss it, got the biggest obelisk you've ever seen. BA has a wicked mix of grand municipal architecture in the dead centre and then these beautiful big, wide old tree-lined streets radiating off it. Eventually, we pulled up outside a pretty grim looking gaff on what felt like the outskirts of town, but by now, I was so exhausted and apathetic I was just happy to get out of the car and lie down in the gutter. Drive hammered on a door and an old lady came out sleepy-eyed and annoyed. I was hustled up to a sort of guesthouse/apartment that was low-key but functional. I hate not knowing where I am, geographically speaking, but I was grateful and conked-out immediately.

I didn't sleep long, as like I say, a sort of background radiation of discomfort is there when you are disoriented and unsure of your location. Very aware you are in a strange bed on the other side of the world. Hot too. It's around midday and I have a few coins left over and try the promoter again. No answer. I venture off to try and get some bearings. I find a bank and get some pesos. No clue where the centre is now or even vaguely where north or south is.

No one speaks English, and why the hell should they? I get paranoid that I will lose my bearings regarding the 'hotel' if I wander too far, so I resolve to harass the promoter until he pulls his finger out. I call and call and the day starts to fade and eventually, he answers in the early evening. Loads of mock surprise and half-arsed apologies. Hints of I'm a big bothersome diva for expecting him to do anything. It's not like I was asking for the moon on a stick or anything! Just to be met and a place to sleep. Then he says he is busy tonight, I'll see him tomorrow. Oh great.

So I think *fuck this!* and by force of hand gestures and desperate willpower, I move into a proper hotel in the centre. Now I'm high up, and I can see for miles. Totally get my bearings. Much improved scenario. I'm not fancy, I've stayed in all sorts of places, including on people's floors and sofas, but as I say, I don't like not knowing where I am. Most city centres are easy to navigate and very easy to find once you've left it and need to return, and it's smart to have a central hotel that every taxi driver knows.

So next day comes and it's the night of the gig and the promoter comes and gets me, immediately says "no way I'm paying for this place" (which was fully expected so I didn't even consider asking), and took me on a sort of publicity tour. I go to radio stations and something that was like a day party and he's sort of basically showing me off to people. This happens, but after such a poor show from him, I was pretty uncomfortable with it all but did my best. Everywhere we go, people are drinking and so is he, so by the time the sun starts to set, I am a bit tipsy too, so I make the second colossal schoolboy error and ask for some cocaine.

Promoter looks really surprised. I'm like, *don't look so shocked, mate: this is South America*, and he sort of laughs and says something like, "Yeah, you want cocaine? We got cocaine! It's just that it's the sort of thing kids do; we tend to grow out of taking it quite quickly here." Which I interpret as a bit poncey and haughty, but then discover what he means when he gives me this huge bag of it later. It's 100% pure.

Now you will have been told by your pub gak dealer that the nonsense he is giving you is "flake" and "almost pure", etc. No. It's really not. This close to the source, it's a different story entirely. In fact, it's almost a different drug. Everything about it is unfamiliar. It doesn't make you wired and jittery; it makes you feel really, *really* good. But it's STRONG! Like several degrees more potent than anything you've ever been near before. But because it doesn't make you feel shit in large amounts like bad gak does, you aren't careful at all with the dosage. I got to the gig and I was out of my mind just on a couple of fat lines that the promoter was gobsmacked to see me put out. They do tiny little pinches in each nostril. Our daft Viking method of giant slugs was insane with stuff this powerful. Before we started, I was almost tripping. I just about managed to play, but when they all sat down on the dancefloor I properly freaked out. Thought it was some sort of protest! About 700 people just sat down on the floor. Maybe it was some sort of attack? The promoter had to talk me down like I was a hysteric.

"Wait, WAIT! You will see. Wait!" but I was so high the few moments they were on the floor seemed like hours. Then they all leapt in the air when the track came back in and I nearly jumped out of my skin. This was some years before the Italians in Ibiza stole the sit-down move. Never seen it before in my life or even heard of it. Then later, a plastic cup hit me in the face. If they love a track, they really love it. When they don't, they also let you know. It was a very odd gig, such a responsive and up-for-it crowd compared to what I was used to. They really know how to party in Buenos Aires, but I was too fucked up to appreciate it. This was a pretty legendary venue too called 'New York City', which was ironic considering what America did to their economy. But I digress. Due to my second schoolboy error, the gig was quite tense. But it went OK.

Got back to the hotel and once again left to my own devices by the amazing disappearing promoter. Left alone in a hotel with a giant bag of pure. For a change, the flight wasn't at daft o'clock in the morning, but the following night. Nearly 24 hours stretched in front of me and my new 'luggage'. I started to unpack with gusto. It was ill-advised, naturally. Schoolboy error number three. Sleep was impossible and before I knew it, it was the afternoon. I was OK but very, very awake and starting to get bored. I couldn't just sit in a darkened room and shovel pure into myself! It was obscene.

Now I don't know if you ever get this, but acoustics can act up a little if you are high up in a building. Sound drifts on the wind and bounces and reflects off buildings. I was sure I could hear a party. I have a radar for these things. Maybe it was a parade, maybe I was having auditory hallucinations. I was certainly off my chops enough to be hearing things. I craned my neck out of the window into the blazing light and thought I could see a carnival below. Certainly a large group was out on the streets. It would be in keeping with my low-level British racism that South Americans constantly salsa-d around everywhere, no one worked for a living and every day was a fiesta.

I thought *fuck it* and I dressed and made my way downstairs. I was on a third or fourth wind now, not so much intoxicated as just on a wave of energy from being awake for so long. You get them, weirdly enough. Like your body knows it is being asked to do extreme things, so it obliges now and then by sobering you up and giving you an hour or so of juice. I steamed past reception and out the door into the baking heat and there was indeed a carnival of sorts going down this huge main road. I was really pleased with myself. I wasn't a drug-addled loser anymore, totally wasting yet another opportunity to see a great city; I was in the thick of it. Proper. A pro traveller. Mixing with the real. Plus it was a party. No one who has been up for days on gear says no to more party if it means putting off the comedown. Bear in mind I'd not slept on the journey either so it was coming up to three nights awake and somewhere, lurking underneath all the bullshit was Satan's very own personal jet lag with a forked tail and horns.

I joined in with gusto. This was quite a long time ago and very few Argentinians spoke English. Indeed it wasn't nearly as widely spoken as it is now anywhere back then. I spoke no Spanish at all. So I was cheerfully hand-gesture talking to my new friends. Smiling at anyone in a circle around me like a deranged lighthouse. It was noisy, so no speaking happened at all, really. I was possibly a little over-energised. Maybe dancing a little too madly. Whooping a little louder than anyone else. Then the fiesta seemed to slow down. People had stopped moving. The energy waned a little and everyone seemed to be facing in a particular direction.

There was plenty of space between people as by now we'd arrived at some sort of park. I figured maybe a band was on, so I started moving through the people to the 'front' of whatever was afoot. Then I heard an amplified voice and thought *great!* and everyone cheered. I cheered loudest of all. Then I saw a small ersatz stage with someone on it with a megaphone. Behind them was a huge plinth. Ah. Some sort of protest? Then I looked at the brass plaque on the plinth and while I didn't have a word of Spanish in me, I did see a long list of names and two words writ very large.

"Las Malvinas"

Now I come from a military family and I myself had a short dalliance with it. I missed the Falklands War by a few years. I would never call myself a soldier but it was a big BIG part of my life growing up. I looked around with immediately very sober eyes and suddenly noticed what were clearly a few veterans at the head of the crowd. I mean, not a lot of ravers have arms or legs missing, and there were quite a few here. Everyone was silent now and listening to the announcer. I'd read it not just completely wrong, I realised in that moment of total clarity that the last half hour or so of the 'fiesta' wasn't really quite as fun as I'd perceived, and that along the way, I was the only one dancing and whooping at some points. I was literally the only English person there, right at the front of what was essentially becoming an angry, anti-English rally and memorial for the brave dead. I started to back up, very, *very* carefully.

I got back to the hotel, took one look at the still half-full bag of gak and immediately engaged in what I can only describe as 'drug bulimia'. I knew I couldn't take it with me, and lordy did I want to! But it was too good to leave behind. So I literally started shovelling it in and then almost immediately washing it out with water. Sniff, spray. Sniff. Spray. It's only through the lens of time I see how insane it was, but at the time, it made perfect sense. I may have just come very close to being killed by a righteously furious mob perhaps and this was my reaction. Like wanting sex after a funeral. I wanted LIFE!

I was still at-it seconds before the taxi came. I got on the return flight like a recently embalmed corpse. Including the hotel, the entire fiasco had cost me substantially to go there. I think I slept for about a week when I got home. I subsequently went back a few times and had some of the best gigs of my life. Also, Punta del Este over the water in Uruguay was rather special. I had learned my lesson by then, however. It's a different world is South America. They are party professionals. It's not a place for the weak or foolish. And there isn't a day that goes by that I wouldn't go back there in a drug-fuelled accelerated heartbeat.

THEY DON'T REALLY
CARE ABOUT US

Comparing it to Fyre Festival probably paints an overly-grand picture, but my debut festival booking was the closest Scunthorpe will get. It was the festival's first (and last) year, and on paper, its promises ticked all the 'boutique' boxes: gorgeous country estate with camping in bell tents, unspoiled woodland, an antiquated folly tower and a 24 hour bar and gourmet food trucks. However, what sealed it was being booked by a promoter I knew who was helping them out. His past adventures had included taking over a four-story housing co-op in North London, the night before Islington Council evicted all the residents, where you received a 'helpful' hand-drawn map on entry and there was karaoke amongst the multiple themed rooms.

Club promo usually makes me cringe, but the festival's video was something else. Subverting the usual 'time of your life' after movies other festivals put out, it used stock footage of the most perfect, basic-looking people texting one another, details of the event edited over it, and ended with a crowd dancing at a glossy Coachella-type event. It was perfect for filtering out the kind of people I don't usually vibe with. The soundtrack was Michael Jackson's 'They Don't Care About Us' slowed down to a sinister drawl, really weird, possibly inappropriate, but kind of amazing.

'Supermarket DJ' was the next bit of 'promo': me going around Lidl doing a festival shop while being interviewed by a drag queen in an orange fur coat and wig. It probably didn't sell any tickets, but it did ensure onsite fame at the festival itself.

The line-up was mostly newer DJs, but there were some bigger head-liners too. Things started to feel strange, however, when my guestlist of four was extended and word came down my guests could bring guests of their own. Doing a rough calculation, we worked out that if each DJ brought seven free guests, like I was, it would still be a good number of people, even if nobody else came.

The festival made a point of telling everyone you couldn't bring alcohol and there was food available on site, but luckily, given the slight air of trepidation, we did a pre-festival shop. Then, on what felt like the hottest day of the year, we piled onto an ancient coach with no air-conditioning or toilet and set off on the four-hour-plus journey.

The stage I played, built by the people who booked me, is still the coolest design I've ever seen, up there with anything at Glastonbury or Boomtown. I mean, the entrance was a giant, upholstered, pink and purple vagina whose cushioned lips you squeezed yourself through. Entering the womb inside, you made your way to the stage in a clearing surrounded by trees through a corridor filled with tree trunks that poked through the ceiling. It was magical.

Later in the weekend, part of the stage opened to reveal a chaotic, interactive maze, which we'd heard rumours of the day before. It started in a waiting room, where a drag nurse and a BDSM nurse inspected you. Inside weird soundscapes and disembodied voices floated through the air as you explored different zones. There was a dressing up area filled with vintage clothing and a karaoke room with an ancient CD player. At one point, we were sitting on a bed chatting when the wardrobe next to it opened and a group of people came out from a hidden space we had no idea was there.

The rest of the festival, arranged by the main organisers, who were mostly absent, was shambolic in comparison. The artist liaison let me in, then disappeared to get drinks tickets and never came back. Despite the strict encouragement to buy food on-site, there was one food van and it only sold dumplings and rice – leaving just rice for my coeliac best friend. By Sunday, rice was the only option for everyone, the dumplings having run out, so we rationed the food we'd brought. The 24-hour bar closed for seven hours a day. But worse than this was that one of the stages didn't exist. Nobody had told the irate DJs arriving to play it.

My set still haunts me, which is my own fault. I was really excited; I hadn't played many big things at this point but wasn't on until 5am. Thinking I wouldn't be able to stay up and vibe with my friends without taking a pill, I had a cautious half at midnight. By 4am, despite having had a lie down in my tent, I was inexplicably higher than I've ever been. The stage was really busy, dawn was starting to break, and the girl playing before me was super confident, voguing behind the decks as she played off four CDJs – which made me even more nervous. The last thing a friend saw before I went on was me swaying in the smoke with my eyes closed and a grin on my face.

All I remember are flashes of looking at the record playing, realising it was about to end and freaking out. In between putting on each record, I was just standing there, not even mixing. As an act of mercy, one friend stopped another who was filming it.

I'd just got Carl's Cox mix of Slam's 'Positive Education', so it's one of two tunes I remember playing. Seven minutes into it, the sound guy came over and pointed to the filter, which had been on the entire time. Another man kept coming in to offer me shots of Jaeger, which I mostly refused. I'd thought he was another sound engineer, then halfway through my set, he started asking to play b2b.

As the comedowns piled up over the weekend, so did the bad feeling and uncertainty. A vacuum of official announcements meant rumours started to circulate. We heard that the owners of the festival were actually titled aristocrats who'd turned their annual jolly into a festival. An online news story was shown on a man's phone, allegedly one of the organisers, who'd been caught drunk driving, high on cocaine and in blackface. Real minor royal behaviour.

The only person we really knew in any position of authority was a friend who'd blagged his way in as an official volunteer, his job seemingly to get on with his normal activities, just in a hi-vis vest. Like a fun pub St Bernard, he was constantly on-hand to perk up your tent rave with a pocket full of sachets of flavoured vodka. These, he eventually revealed, swearing us to secrecy, were from a disused bar behind the maze where there was an enormous tartan laundry bag filled with hundreds of them. Were they meant to be frozen vodka pops? We'll never know. By the end of the weekend, everybody was doing shots of sickly-warm raspberry-flavoured vodka.

The final night was cut short, but the last set by a Scottish DJ had brought everyone together on a high, closing, somewhat ironically, with the League Unlimited Orchestra's 'Things That Dreams Are Made Of'. This could have been the abiding memory, a drug-assisted triumph of sorts snatched from the jaws of disorganisation and disaster.

In the boiling morning sun the next day though, with the site's drinking water turned off and nowhere to buy any, we learned none of the coaches home were coming – except for one tiny artist mini bus, which I'd given my place away on to stay with my friends. Mouths were dry and tempers flaring. One DJ threatened action of the stabby kind. Another, who'd arrived last night to find the festival already over, had an altercation with the organisers over a loud afterparty they'd held in the same pub they'd put him up in. Our artist liaison briefly appeared in an open-topped sports car, swigging a bottle of prosecco, then drove off, never to be seen again.

Five hours later, a lone coach finally pulled up. By luck, rather than judgement, everyone fitted in – though only because those who could afford it had already gone to get trains home. There was a crash on the motorway, of course, leading to standstill traffic and a detour through a tiny village, whose only shop got cleared out of booze and ice lollies.

Recriminations continued for weeks. DJ payments were chased. Cheery official online announcements crumbled as those who were there told their stories. 'See you next year' posts faded to silence.

It lives on in my memory, though as the best and worst festival I've ever been to, rolled into one. While I barely remember it, it was actually the gig that led to a few more gigs, which led to a lot more gigs. As one promoter said to me after: "All my friends were asking who you were. They said the tunes were great, but the mixing was weird."

ROCKY XII

Violence so rarely happens in our scene. It's one of the beautiful things about it. I'm not that old, but I remember when you could almost bank on there being a tear-up on a night out. I mean proper scenes. Murders. That was booze. Booze on its own is deadly. I come from the football terraces. I've seen all sorts. Peace and love for me all day and night though! It's why I got into DJing, in a way. That scene saved me. And a lot of my mates. We embraced it. It was a way out of it. So thankfully, after some years, I can't say I ever saw any aggro. I mean now and then (and mostly outside venues rather than indoors) but really, if you forced me to guess a number, I'd say physical violence is down about 75% thanks to ecstasy and house music. Maybe more. I'm trying to be as objective as possible. For me, it's more like 100%. Then again…

I was playing on the South Coast and some of those towns can be a bit rough. I mean those abandoned seaside towns that are like massive damp crack houses, but like have a lot of navy. Tough lads. It was a cool club, loved it. Town was a bit aggy-like, though. I dunno. I just felt it, like I get a vibe from any town with a rough edge. I used to go to matches all over the UK, so I've been around. I know which towns are soft and which are hard. I'd put this town somewhere in the middle of the scale. I wasn't on my toes but wasn't relaxed either.

So I'm playing and it's fairly early and about three-quarters full. People still queuing and coming in. Maybe midnight? Just started. So I'm minding my own business and turn to check my tunes and this smiling kid is grinning at me through the glass. It was one of them booths with a low window or glass fence around it about chest height. People group around the booth a lot. So he's friendly and sort of makes gestures like he wants to talk, so I go over and he reaches over the glass for a handshake and you know straight away something is off 'cos he grasps way too hard, he pulls himself up onto the top of the glass holding my hand and screams over the music "YOU ARE FUCKING SHIT!!"

Now, this can happen. I call it 'negging'. People sometimes come like they are making a request, but it is to criticise. Sometimes they are wannabe DJs and want to big up themselves. Sometimes it's genuine; they just aren't happy. Or it is a 'Karen', you know the type, male or female. Usually they are just off their heads. Normally it's water off a duck's back to me and also very rare, but this was different. Maybe it was because it was so early and I was 100% sober and not in that groove yet where you get super focused and don't notice much. Maybe it was because he grabbed me. Might have been that some spittle hit me in the face. Dunno.

Once in a while when you get negged it can totally ruin your vibe. And then ruin the night for the whole place when the person doing the music can't shake it. I mean, this is a once in a blue moon sort of turnout. Happens once every two years or something. Anyway. I was fucking furious. Tired too. That doesn't help. It was one of those weekends where the travel was epic and you arrived at every gig knackered. I have to admit, I totally lost it. Red mist.

Now a lot of punters see us like newsreaders. Like we only exist from the waist up. We are like ventriloquist dummies. Just an upper half, for entertainment purposes only. This kid just dropped down to the floor and strolled off. His great escape was walking about ten yards onto the dancefloor right in front of me. I just cued up the long one I usually reserve for when I need a piss just in case, but left the current track playing as it had some time left. I took off the headphones and walked out of the booth. It wasn't rammed yet, so I easily got through the dancers. His back was to me in his little group; I just spun him around and knocked him out. Like old school one-punch laid him out. To be fair, he was not expecting it at all. Must have thought I was chained to the booth or something, like a pen in a bank.

So let us be very clear. It is *not* something I do. Something I had not done since I was a kid and do not want to ever again. I wasn't myself at all. I turned on my heel and went back to the booth. Whole thing took seconds. No security came. The night seemed unaffected and I didn't even need to play my piss record; it was done and dusted before the previous one ran out. The night continued. The boss of the venue was by the booth and saw the whole thing and never said a word. I think there was a look in my eye that forbade discussion. It felt like justice at that moment. I was OK with it at the time. The fact nothing happened seemed to verify it.

At this time, I was still a smoker. More of a nerves thing than a proper habit, though. I only smoked when I worked or drank a lot. Never bought a packet of fags in my life, but I was a terrible cadger. I told myself I wasn't a smoker, but at every single gig, I'd manage to blag some. Most of the venues on my 'circuit' already knew this and would sometimes bring some for me. Then the smoking ban came and this, for me, meant putting on a piss record and rushing outside for half a cigarette. It was purely a nervous thing. Never smoked in any other situation.

Eventually, I just stopped because it was so hard to press through all the people just for a few puffs. So anyway, on this night after the dancefloor knockout scenes, I was a bit stressed, so I put the piss record on and legged-it outside for a smoke. For this venue, that meant out the front door and into a little twat paddock. A horseshoe of velvet rope that you could squeeze about six people in but currently had about 20 in there. I turned to ask for a light as part of my denial was never owning a lighter and the person smoking next to me turned around with a swollen face and the start of a juicy black eye, and it was him. The kid.

Only now that we were outside and not in the dark with flashing lights I could see he was taller, broader and way younger than I thought.

Fighting someone that much younger than you could see you lose just through lack of stamina. I'd collapse in a heap from exhaustion while he'd still be warming up. I looked him dead in the eye and asked for a light as you have to brass these things out. I held his gaze and he suddenly just burst into tears. Like a proper bawl.

Then it was apparent most of the people around me were his mates. Arms came out to comfort him and lots of scowls in my direction. I couldn't think of anything to say other than "all I did was ask for a light!". Then it all comes out. Between sobs, the kid says he is devastated. He'd travelled miles to the show, is a huge fan and only did it 'cos his mates were taking the piss out of him being excited to see me. They clubbed together and bet him 50 quid (a lot of money then!) and a pill that he wouldn't go up to me and call me a cunt.

Some of his mates around us backed the story up and started apologising too. Kid was still crying and everyone else was apologising from every direction and I have to say I don't think I've ever felt so low. I was like a tiny little man. Reduced to being the villain. Absolutely gutted. Rug pulled from under me. The worst person in the world. I honestly don't think I've ever hated myself as much as I did in that little area of roped-off nonsense.

I assured the kid it was all a dreadful misunderstanding and he kept apologising, which made it even worse and I did what little I could in the few minutes I had left of the piss record. Told him to come to the booth and I'd sign some records for him and generally make it up to him and all that. Which I did, also got him into some gigs in the future.

So the end of the night came and the kid has a full-on shiner by now and is in the booth with me and a couple of his crew and he is happy as Larry as well as 50 quid richer and on a pinger. Then the boss turns to me when the music finally stops and, in his very dry manner, says the first words I've heard from him all night. "Great to have you here again as always. Great set. Next time try not to kill any of my customers; I need them alive to spend their money. It's better when you make them dance, if at all possible. Thanks."

ONE STEP TOO FAR

This is going back a few years, to when myself and another DJ were asked to do a B2B set at Secret Garden Party on the Saturday night. We got the train down and started having a couple of beers, and by the time we got to the festival, we were quite merry. This was the same year that Faithless were performing, and they were on that night, so there were quite a lot of people there. We unpacked our stuff, watched a few sets and thought, *oh, let's go say hi to the Secretsundaze crew before we play.*

We had a few more drinks… got, even more, merry. By the time we got to the Sundaze stage, there was this massive queue of a hundred or so deep snaking going down this hill. We had to play ourselves in a couple of hours, so we decided we'd walk up to the front, show them our artist passes, and see if we could swerve the queue. There was a lady at the entrance checking everyone's wristband and the other DJ I was playing with was doing all the talking while I stood behind. He's asking her, "Look, can we come in? We're artists here," but she's looking at our passes and is like, "no, those passes don't get you access to this stage." Then my mate gestures to me: "What about for Maxi Jazz?"

Now, I've been compared facially to Maxi Jazz on numerous occasions. I find it hilarious because he's about 30 years older than me (though, to be fair, he does wear it well). But anyway, the woman sort of stopped in her tracks and looked at me. It was dark, it was late, I had a baseball cap on with sunglasses and a pair of dungarees, so I guess that made it harder to be sure.

She looks at me for a long time and then decides she can't risk upsetting a headliner. "Shit, okay, hang on a minute" and goes off to get a few 'higher-ups' to come out. They say hi and introduce themselves to 'Maxi' (it takes me a moment to remember that's me). Once there's a bit of momentum, it's like people in a group just see what they want to see. They escorted us in. They took us to a little artist area. They started bringing us drinks.

As we were moving through the crowd, people were staring at me. Someone came by and was like, "Hey, Maxi!" and gave me a hi-five. We're both dying to laugh but obviously can't. I'm just keeping face and pretending I'm Maxi Jazz. Mustn't break character. What would Maxi do? Stay chill, stay cool, act like you've sold a million records and you're still not sick of performing 'Insomnia' three times a week all summer. Fast forward a few beers and the music is starting to get kind of cool. I start dancing and get lost in the music and completely forget at this point how or why we got in there… and just wander on to the stage and start vogueing.

As soon as I did that, a security guard quietly materialised next to me: "Put your drinks down and leave the stage, now" So we put our drinks down and were gently escorted off stage, out of the backstage, and told not to go back again.

In the end, we didn't even see The Secretsundaze crew we'd gone to say hi to in the first place. But we did drink a lot of free beer. And most of all, I really hope the security guys still think they chucked the lead vocalist of Faithless off their stage. "I bounced that Maxi Jazz once. For illegal vogueing."

INTERNATIONAL FRANCHISE

This is a short one, sorry, but I'm a fairly mid-range DJ. Always have been. Still am. But on the millennium, NYE 1999, I don't think there was a DJ in the world that didn't get paid silly money. In fact, I think Secret DJ in one of their books calls this night the fulcrum point on which everything changed for the industry. They might be right. I got paid ten times more than I'd ever been paid before and, to be honest, ever was again. It was a bit weird. I asked if they could put the crazy wage behind the bar for a free party in the room I was resident in. My agent told me they'd sack me off if I did. I didn't know what to do with it (boo hoo!), so I decided to take my mates on holiday.

I'd not been on 'holiday' since I was a kid. Bucket and spade sort of turnout. My life was a holiday! But we ended up hooking up with some other mates, and we all went to Barbados, which was actually pretty boring for reasons I won't go into, so we ended up chartering a plane to go to a tiny remote island. Bit of adventure. Eight of us chipped in; I wasn't paying for everything. It wasn't THAT much money! But this island could only be reached that way. It was a dream for me, as someone who travelled for a living, to go somewhere with zero tourism. You'd be surprised how hard it is to get away from that. I always reckon that it's about commerce. A tourist has to pay for everything, a traveller mixes with local culture gratis. I always find that until I am invited into someone's home or do something that is free, I'm just a tourist. A wallet on legs. Anyway, the fact that you couldn't get there until you paid for a pilot and seaplane yourself, and apparently it had no hotels... this was a very good sign for me. Exciting.

We got there and immediately knew we were in paradise. The 'airport' was a jetty with a shed. The taxi was a bloke with a flatbed truck and there was only one road anyway as we slid around in the back of it, riding our luggage. Almost no vehicles. I won't name it, so it stays off the beaten track. We stayed with a family right on a pristine beach next to a turtle sanctuary. The London mates that came were funny. Kept asking why everyone was being so nice. Dead paranoid and couldn't relax.

The thing I loved more than anything was there was so little noise. All you could hear was the sea. I don't know if other DJs are like this, but in my downtime, I can't bear music, especially background music. Music is my job. Simply jukebox type music in a pub or shop can drive me out in seconds. I was gutted when the locals found out I was a DJ and asked me to play at their local club. In my head, I was like, *oh no, 'ere we go! holiday over!* So my eyebrows were fully raised at the prospect. "You have a club?" I asked. "Really? what's it called?"

"Bedrock", one answered.

I was flabbergasted. The place was so small and so far away, but even here, you couldn't get away from the omnipresent hand of the music biz. We were in the main bit of town for this conversation and I answered:

"Wow, so what? A franchise of Sasha and Digweed, is it? That is amazing. I'm very surprised. Really."

The dude just looked at me blankly, shrugged, and then pointed to a half-collapsed shack with a corrugated iron roof and a large graffiti of Barney Rubble on one side of the wall.

"Flintstones. BEDROCK, man!"

After we all stopped laughing, we had the party later (I protest a lot but never go anywhere without my CDs/USBs); it was off the hook. It didn't feel like a gig at all. It was a *proper* party. They were soca people and naturally, I had no soca or Caribbean music at all, but sort of got on a vibe somewhere near it with some very vocal house music. But they also loved it if you played a classic record from the past, but you know, it was Bedrock. So nothing *too* prehistoric.

THE INCIDENT

You don't forget your first paid booking out of town. To me, a 23-year-old house DJ back in 2003, the idea was mind-blowing: someone you don't know who lives hundreds of miles away from you has decided you have enough clout and skill to invest in and make a guest at their night, pay you a hundred quid and pay for your hotel? Wow. How cool was that?

Suffice to say when a booking to play at a small club in Oxford came in, well over 200 miles from my own little local scene, I took it very seriously and in the six weeks running up to it, I practiced like never before. I hunted down old records I'd wanted for years, I practised new blends, I told everyone I possibly could about it. This was huge for me. I felt it was a pinnacle moment; get this gig right and you've made it, you're on the national circuit. Fail and this dream is over. That's how much pressure I put on myself.

I'd actually got the gig through a forum. That's how a lot of us networked before social media. At the birth of the internet age, dedicated forums were like heaven to nerds like me. Prior to this, you'd pick up bits and bobs in magazines or from the people in the record stores, but the dance world seemed like a mystery waiting to be unravelled. But on forums, with every post, every discussion, every argument, I felt like I was learning.

From my small town on the English south coast, I suddenly felt connected with the wider world and found new like-minded friends across the country. There were forums dedicated to every genre and aspect of production, and my forum of choice was one hosted by a now-defunct magazine. They ran a monthly mix competition, so I dutifully entered every month. I would post the tracklist on the forum, offering to post a CD out to anyone who liked the look of it. I never once won the competition, but it's how I'd ended up with this booking and I really thought this could be a breakthrough: if I smash this gig, he'll post about it on the forum, others will book me and I'll be well away.

Finally, after what felt like an eternity, the night arrived. Me and my girlfriend drove down early and checked into the hotel, had a meal and a few drinks to warm up. The promoter came and picked us up at 10pm and everything was falling into place; I would play at 11pm, warming up for the main headliner who was just breaking through on Radio 1 at the time, and the club would most likely be pretty full by the time I started. True to form, it was packed by the time we arrived and true to my expectations and the pressures I put on myself, I played a set I could be proud of. No one left the dancefloor, I didn't trainwreck, the DJ after me let me play another tune and got everyone to give a little cheer before he started. It was a textbook gig; everyone was happy; I'd felt I'd smashed it, so went on to get pretty smashed myself.

By 2am me and my girlfriend – who is now my wife – decided it was time to take the celebrations back to the hotel room and again, it was a textbook celebration. Considering how much I'd drunk and the pinger I'd taken, I was on fire! Nothing could stop me. Besides sleep, which I'd missed out on a lot in the run-up to the show because I was so anxious about getting it right. Now, safe in the knowledge that I'd stepped up and delivered, I fell asleep with a very distant thought in my head that I should probably go to the toilet. But it was too distant to react to. I fell into a very satisfied slumber...

The next thing I know, I'm butt-naked in the hotel room corridor! What on earth am I doing here? I start to panic and thump the hotel room door. I'm calling my girlfriend's name but she's a deep sleeper at the best of times. I knew it was futile. So, in my hazy, wavey wisdom, I try the room next door, wondering if my friends were there. At other times, they would be – as clubbers, we'd travelled to various venues around the country and a few of the boys would usually share a room which would be the party room. I banged the hell out of the room next door and a girl answered, horrified and terrified. I cover my dignity as well as I can and explain that I'm locked out of my hotel room, I'm naked (although she could very much see this) and I thought maybe my friends might be in her room.

"They're not. Fuck off and take this."

She throws me a towel which I reach out to catch with both hands, completely exposing myself to her. Rest assured, I no longer feel like a champion in any way at all at this point. She slams the door in my face. I wrap the towel around me and begin the descent into the most mortifying hour of my life. Firstly, I had to go downstairs to the reception and explain the situation. They gave me a new card and I went back up to the room and woke up my girlfriend.

"I just woke up in the corridor naked. What's going on?"

"God knows, dear, you were probably just sleepwalking. Come back to bed."

Nah, sleep wasn't going to cut it at this hour. I'd just come to in a hotel corridor, naked. There has to be a reason. I sit down, open a beer and build a spliff. I need to sort my head out and work out what the hell is going on. I retrace every step of the night and keep coming back to the thought about going to the toilet. *I don't need to go now*, I think to myself. The penny drops… Did I just go to the loo in the hotel corridor? I put on some clothes to investigate and start realising the gravitas of the situation. There, in the doorway of a room opposite, was a not insubstantial number two. I have no recollection of doing it but it must have been me because I didn't need the loo anymore. My heart sank. This is not cool. This is an actual nightmare. My life is over. I stand there in the middle of the corridor for what feels like an eternity. My whole life shatters in my mind's eye. The hotel will tell the promoter, the promoter will have to pay damages and he'll tell the world on a forum and

I'll never DJ again in my life. I am ruined! I decided that honesty is the best policy and went down to the reception.

"Hello again, sir. You're dressed now, I see!"

The receptionist is far too jolly for the news I'm about to give him. "Er yeah, about that…"

I explain the situation and, in fairness to the receptionist, he plays a brilliant poker face. I have no idea if he's appalled, angered or amused about the situation. He just looks at me deadpan and takes in all the toe-curlingly embarrassing information I can give him.

"Okay, thank you for telling me. Let's get a porter to clean it up."

So we waited for a while for the porter to arrive with his cleaning equipment and I went up in the lift with him. I try to explain the situation to him but I get nothing. This isn't deadpan like the receptionist; this is pure, unadulterated stone-faced, I-am-definitely-judging-you, silence. The tension continues to rise as we walk around the corner and I point to the mess I'd made.

"There it is."

"Did your dog do this?" he asked me.

"No, it was me. I did this." With every monosyllabic word I say, I feel my soul crushing more and more. He sighs and goes to clean it up. Wanting to help him, I grabbed some paper rolls myself and went to pick up the remaining bits he hadn't got. I meant it with the best intentions. I wanted to help this man. I wanted the situation to be over as quickly as possible or, better still, a big hole to open up in the ground for me to fall in and be swallowed up whole. It was what I deserved. But, in the absence of a convenient vortex to another dimension, helping him was the best way to push this situation on and get it over with. Except it wasn't… Through adrenaline, anxiety and far too many intoxicants just hours before, I was shaking. As I picked up the final bit of excrement, my hand shook so much I smeared what I'd picked up on the wall.

"I'm so so sorry." I look the porter in the eye, devastated, completely and utterly rock bottom.

"Go. Just go."

"I was trying to help you!"

"Go back to your room and do not come out until you have to check out. Go."

Feeling about an inch tall. My dreams of ever being booked to play anywhere ever again completely dashed, I go to my hotel room. I reach for my card, yet another blow hits me as I find I've dropped it somewhere. I have no choice but to retrace my steps for the second time in an hour and I'll have to pass the porter. This time he didn't hold back.

"Listen, you disgusting man! I told you to go to your room!"

I explain how I've lost my card and he tuts at me in such a loud, disproving way it could almost snap my bones. Luckily the card was on the carpet by the lift door. I pick it up and walk past the porter for the final time that night. He looks at me with such a scowl I want to die there and then. I am scum. Drunken, out-of-town, corridor-pooing scum.

By now, it's 5.30am and there's no way my brain will let me sleep. Usually, a few spliffs in the toilet with the shower and extractor fan on would do the trick, but I was almost paralysed with fear of getting caught doing something again that I just lay there beside my girlfriend, afraid to move a muscle. Naturally, my thoughts got more and more paralysing as acute anxiety kicked in. I was doomed. There was no other way to look at the situation: the hotel would tell the promoter, the promoter was going to tell the world. I would never be booked again. I'd be the 'hotel poo guy' for the rest of my life. By the time my girlfriend stirred around 9am I was inside out with panic, lying there, crying, going over and over and over the only possible way this could play out.

It didn't matter how much she tried to calm me. I had worked myself up into such a panic that we just needed to check out, go home and wait for the worst to happen. After we packed up, I even asked her to check if the coast was clear. The last thing I wanted was to see our horrified neighbour who'd thrown me a towel. Thankfully the coast was clear and, even more thankfully, the receptionist was a different person who, unbeknownst of the troubles I'd caused just hours before, thanked me for staying and even had the gall to wish me a nice day. Have a nice day? I've just flushed my hopeful DJ career down the toilet. A poor analogy considering the situation.

And so began the plummet into despair. All the way home, my girlfriend somehow managed to smirk and laugh about it but also soothe my feelings in a way that only your number one can. She knew I was a mess but also found it hilarious at how I'd made such a mess after the night had been such a great success. "Don't worry, you smashed it, I'm sure it will be fine" was the overall headline. But I just couldn't see it. How on earth would the hotel not ring the promoter and tell him about it. He was probably on the phone to them right now, paying an excruciatingly steep cleaning bill. In a moment, he'd be posting on the forum about it and my name would be mud. This was long before we had internet on our phones, so I had no way of checking until we got home and I logged on.

"Why don't you text him?"

Now, this was a good idea. This could be the answer to my gut-curdling paranoia. If he replies with good vibes, then maybe it's all okay. If he doesn't reply, I know I'm doomed. Closure either way.

I put on a brave text face and gave him a "Gr8 night m8. Thanks for booking me! C U soon!" message. It was 2003; that's how we rolled on our Nokia phones. Then I waited. And waited. And drove all the way home, turning inside out with shame and fear while my girlfriend drove us home chuckling and giving me 'it's all going to be alright' looks. But I couldn't shake the feeling that it wasn't going to be alright at all. He hadn't replied. He'd told the world I was a hotel-pooer, I was going to have to move to Siberia and start a new life. Bye-bye, cruel world. After weeks of intense excitement had come this deep, fathomless shame. It was one of the lowest feelings I've ever had.

I get home, log on, and check the forum. Nothing. No updates or comments. Relieved but not feeling like I was out of the woods yet, I felt relaxed enough to fall asleep for a few hours. Then, mid-afternoon, I woke up to my girlfriend handing me my phone.

"You've had a text."

Behind the smirks and soothing gestures, I think she was just as keen for closure. The longer I remain in this unknowing feeling of doom, the harder I am to reason or live with. I sleepily check the reply.

"Buzzing m8! Thk U! C U soon."

And so begins the start of a wonderful anti-climax. Relieved even more, I started to think about the positive aspects of the night, how I'd played a great set and met some nice people. How we'd left the club at just the right time, so none of my new acquaintances saw how messy I was about to become. How I'd got that headliner's email and they said to keep them posted on my developments and send them tunes if I ever got to that stage in the studio. I still felt I wasn't out of the woods yet – perhaps the hotel might ring him first thing on Monday morning? Maybe they'll tell him next time he books a DJ in? He'll be blacklisted and he'll take it out on me.

But he didn't. The hotel didn't ring him. He remains none the wiser to this day. Now, having spent most of my career in them, I realise that hotels don't work like that. If I'd have caused billable damage, I'd have been charged there and then or when I checked out. Only if I'd refused to pay would they have had to contact the person paying my bill. There was no big inquiry about the hotel poo. There was no official complaint. The buck stopped at that poor porter and the receptionist and for that, I am eternally grateful and remain in their debt.

The following week the promoter posted about the night on the same forum and his enthusiasm about it got me two more new bookings. He also promised to book me again, which he did many times over the years. What's more, the headliner who'd just started on Radio 1 was the first DJ to play my music on national radio, which opened up a whole world of doors for me. And none of those doors would have opened had we not been booked for that same night.

In hindsight, all my pre-gig hopes were 100% spot on. If I do my first paid gig out of town right and smash it, it will take me to another level. Now, almost 20 years later and still very much enjoying my career as a DJ, I can safely say it really did. But alas, that's not how me or my wife remember that gig. I've lost count of how many times I've played in Oxford since, but I've always requested a different hotel.

BUSTED

We knew the police were coming for us. Well, I did. I've been doing illegal parties for a very long time. There are some basic rules, especially in Ibiza. You never go in a taxi. You always have a meeting point. It took me years to work out. I would put weeks and thousands into a party, hundreds would turn up in cabs and then the police would come within about an hour. Strangely there would be a neat queue of taxis always waiting outside.

Dawned on me, the taxis were calling the Policia as soon as they dropped off to get the return fare. Pretty obvious when you think about it. Even if the party is properly legal, they do it, as many ravers see the cops and just leg it out of guilty habit. Most of all, badly parked cars are kryptonite to an Ibiza promoter. The locals do not like it and the Policia especially. It's solid reasoning, though. If there is an accident or a fire, the emergency services can't get through. And no one parks more like a selfish idiot than a raver turning up at an afterparty.

This place we were doing was legit, and on a beach. It was fucking ideal man! Never had a better spot. Small family-run place: bar and restaurant. It was funny because the owner was an old Italian dude and it was a pretty sleepy spot. He was like, "Are you sure people will come at night? I don't want to open and it not be worth it." About two hours later, there were close to a thousand people crammed into it and spilt out all over the beach and he had to call every friend and relative he had to get more stock and help man the bars. He made more in one night than he usually did in a whole season.

Anyway, let me tell you something: money is not important in Ibiza. Money is everywhere. The only currency that really matters is noise. You can make as much money as you like and the mafia leave you alone, but make noise and they do not like it. Bring attention to yourself and it takes away from them in a way they very much do not approve of. Believe!

So we got the 'denuncia' which is the Spanish equivalent of 'cease and desist' but from the police. The clue is in the name and a hang-over from the fascist years. You are denounced. Grassed. A complaint is made. There were no neighbours at all and the owner was very con-fused. The sound system was inside, and I personally like clarity over volume every time. We were about half a mile from one of the big dogs, though, an established 'disco mafia' venue. I went to the police station, and lo and behold, there on the paper was their name. We were legal! 100% and I said as much to the Policia Local. But of course, there are three police forces in Spain. I was advised by someone very connected that this would not be the end of it. The Guarda Civil were coming. And they are not to be messed with. Paramilitary, gun-toting nutjobs.

I clocked it immediately when they came for a recce. They send in the Santa Squad. I call them that as you get them at festivals too, all over the world. They send in elderly cops, jolly fellows with beards and paunches who wander around the stalls smiling beatifically, admiring the beads, sniffing the joss sticks and letting mongs try their hats on. Doing selfies. Public relations squad. And you KNOW in the next field are vans full of attack dogs. Nasty, riot-loving skinhead bone specialists, gagging to break some limbs. Now don't get me wrong, I've dealt with police all my career and I am not knee-jerk against them one bit. It's complicated. Like any large group of people, they are good and bad, just like us. I've been on the good end and the bad end of it. I tell you this too, never met one who wouldn't rather be doing proper policing instead of breaking up parties. But that's another story.

So there we were, doing our thing and there's a couple of jolly Guarda and Nacional walking around the party being nice as pie, chatting, ask-ing questions and generally being very charming. Then as quickly as they appeared, they left. I turned to my partners in the events and they were like, "Phew! I thought that was the end of us, I guess that was a lucky escape!" and I replied, "Yeah, no chance. They will be here next week. Guarantee it. We are done".

As per they called me a doom merchant but I know what I'm on about. As the following week loomed, I got my records together and at the back of the box put a particular, special 12 inch. I hoped I was wrong, but I'd seen the name on the denuncia. They were a multi-million euro global operation. They weren't going to let us live. We were hype. The hot thing that year. And to be fair, having dealt with others like them, I understand why they call us 'Los Piratas'. Historically the Brits were pirates, robbing Spain blind.

To this very day, we arrive, fuck the place up and then get to go home and leave them to clean up. They make money, sure, and they like that money to stay on the island as both island revenue and island taxes. I get it. It's fair and righteous. But it has also led to the monopoly we see today. Just giant local mega clubs playing homogenous EDM, no variety, no soul. Just money, no art to it at all.

This season also saw some new powers for law enforcement. They couldn't just arrest you; they could take *everything*. Your sound system (rarely owned by you yourself), any money, your decks, booze, your records... the lot. This was why we were trying to go legal. It was a pain, not just for us; as I said, the police didn't want the hassle either. They'd rather be catching proper villains, but there was a politically-led clampdown that year that pretty much changed the face of Ibiza. This applied to villa parties too and clubs that didn't have the 'correct' license.

It was a purge led by the right-wing and the money behind the mega clubs. Within a couple of years, there was nothing left standing but the old guard. You could feel it too. This is why I was so certain of our demise. I read the news and tried my best to speak Spanish, poor as it was. I was hearing of clampdowns all over. It was blindingly obvious to me we had been targeted and were next. Then the following week nothing happened and the old Italian owner and my partners were all "Aaah! you were wrong! haha! We're safe!" and I just sort of shrugged and said "fingers crossed" but I kept my special record in the back of the box and right on-cue, the following week they came.

They do not fuck about do the Guarda. Mob-handed, they *steamed* in. Dogs and shooters too. They aimed straight at the booth or tried to. There were a lot of fucked-up people in the way. I always kept it very dark too, which added to the confusion. I employed a medic, an off-duty cop and someone to park the cars like an adult, but this wasn't enough. The car park kid knew the quick way to get to me on the decks via a gap in a fence around the back. So I got wind of the raid before I even saw a blue light or uniform. They came from all angles. Could see them in the distance on the beach too. Pushing and shoving.

It was time for my special record.

We were all about the newest, current music at our parties but this classic was very much needed. I pulled the needle off the one playing with a "GGRRRRRCHH" and dropped the other needle on KRS One's 'Sound of Da Police'. I soon discovered that a thousand nutters chanting "WOOP WOOP" into the faces of the cops did not endear me to the officers one bit. The place exploded with people jumping up and down, chanting and pointing at the faces of every cop. They eventually shouldered through to the booth, one of the officers who was clearly more senior gave me the evils, made a throat-cutting gesture and I wasn't stupid! I could claim innocence over the record at a pinch but no way could I risk disobeying the order to stop. So that was it. Busted.

It wasn't over. They took the lot. Two vans full and me included. The convoy took off with pretty much everything I owned, now freshly confiscated and me along with it. As we left, I could see rows of neatly parked cars in the car park, the kid earning his wage. Then as we left the gates and turned into the street, an endless stretch of jagged motors positioned by minds totally unaware of their actions. Some double-parked, stretching to the distance, a total mess. Our mess.

Funnily enough, the police don't respond very well to the traditional British method of communication, which is to shout in their face in English and get louder and slower the less response you get. Most of the upper end of any organisation in tourist zones can speak English, but it makes a positive impression if you try in Spanish, no matter how poor your grasp of it is. Nothing drastic happened back at the gig apart from my musical jape, which I was fairly sure they had endured the results of, but not clocked it was intentional.

Apart from the boss, that is. He made it quite clear with his looks in my direction that he knew exactly what was going on. I was hand-cuffed and pretty nervous, which is usually when I start making light of things as a defence mechanism. Not this time. It was deadly silent in the van and anyway, I've never once managed to make a local laugh unless it was to laugh at me, not with me.

When we got to the brutal-looking cop shop, a bunker on the edge of a dual carriageway, I feared the worst. They did not look happy at all having to hump the large amount of kit out of vans and into the foyer in the heat. Clear in the set of their shoulders was 'this isn't what I signed up for'. Then the boss had the bright idea of starting my punishment immediately by ordering the officers to stop and for me to bring it all in. Which was fine; I did it a couple of times a week all over the place. It was also an opportunity to check everything was there.

Once I got it all in the fairly spacious but bleak foyer, the atmosphere seemed to shift entirely. The various coppers started having cups of coffee and enjoyed the aircon. The previously irate and scary chief totally changed and became jovial and relaxed. He came over to me, a big fella with an old-school moustache, and slapped me on the back and said in perfect English: "So, DJ Man, what is this 'trance' thing? Trance, trance everywhere I go."

"Ah, well, you've come to the right place. I can help you there…"

Fast-forward an hour and there is an amp and monitor plugged in and one CDJ player.

"So this is electro, Juanito, not to be confused with the current 'Electro'. Yeah, I know, makes no sense at all…."

Eventually, the doors open another hour or so later and my partners come in to witness a scene like a painting. Several police are down to their vests. Juanito got me to plug the mixer and other CDJ and was attempting to DJ, the volume was fairly loud. A tiny breakfast police party. He cut the volume with a flourish and shouted at them: "Are you here for this one?" nodding in my direction.

They nodded meekly and he boomed with laughter.

"Get him out of here; he's making a mess of my lovely police station. This is the house of the law, not a disco!"

Turns out Juantio was the top sergeant and go-to guy when there was an illegal party to be dealt with. For the rest of that year, I did events nearly weekly and often, Juanito was the first on the scene, would see me, smile and roll his eyes theatrically. I'd learned my lesson and there were either no cars at all or very neatly managed and there were never any neighbours we hadn't avoided, paid off, invited or generally won over. The cars, he explained, were all he ever cared about. If it sounds and looks chaotic, it makes him look bad. If it was quiet and neat, he didn't care a bit. Paying some of his lads to moonlight as security didn't hurt either. It turned into a great final year of free parties.

Sadly they rotate the police frequently as an anti-corruption measure; you rarely get posted in the same bit of Spain as where you are from. This was a shame; I really got on with Juanito (not his real name, obviously). But this was pretty much my last year for free parties across the board, UK included. The new measures and the crackdown pretty much ended the Balearic free party scene to this day, and apart from a handful of newbies who find out the new regime the very hard way, it has stayed that way.

To be honest, though, I stopped not because the authorities made it difficult; it was never easy, really, just degrees of difficulty. No, the problem in the main with putting on a free rave is that absolutely no one who enjoys them walks around going, "Gosh, I bet this was costly and took loads of time and energy!" They are too busy trying to lick their own eyeballs and nick anything not nailed down. Eventually, you realise absolutely no one appreciates it. Not really. Not in any quantifiable way. I'm glad I got to do it for a few years, though. It was proper. It was loads of fun and it was *highly* educational.

SPRAY 'N' PRAY

Normally, playing the most famous club in Berlin was one of the highlights of the year. We had a good reputation and always had a crew of friends from the city and all over Europe. We'd usually play sometime on Sunday, midday or early afternoon, so we'd turn up shortly before playing, then sometimes get stuck in after. This time though, I'd started enjoying myself a little earlier than usual. It was about the tenth time we'd played the club and I was at ease with the surroundings, not over-awed as I had been at first.

Everything was going as normal for about an hour into our set, then the needle kept skipping. It happened a couple of times, so we changed the needle. This didn't help. In fact, it started getting worse, bouncing three or four times on each record. We asked the engineer to look at the tonearm and check out everything else. Still happening. We were desperate (we only had vinyl with us) that we even got him to change the turntable.

It got so bad you could see everyone clearing out from the dancefloor. The huge downer was somehow amplified by the fact I was high. I was mortified, it absolutely killed the dancefloor and we never got it back.

When it finally dawned on me what was happening, I felt even worse. I'd bought a new record cleaning spray, so as I was going along, I'd been spraying each record before I played it. Spray and play, spray and play. But I hadn't been wiping it off properly, so as it accumulated on the needle it was clogging up every time.

As much as our friends tried to make us feel better, I think that night I got doubly fucked to punish myself and was one of the last twenty people left in the club at midday on Monday. I'd seen the booker at the bar afterwards and tried to apologise, but I think he'd got there after we'd finished and was a bit distracted, so he gave me a hug and said it was fine. It really didn't feel fine. The next week my agency got an email from him saying, "What happened?" They'd had loads of reports of problems, so I just had to explain. I didn't mention the state I was in, just my liberal use of the spray.

Usually, we'd play there once or twice a year, but after that, there was noticeably a longer gap – maybe 18 months – before we got booked again. It was like being sent to DJ jail.

BAD BROMANCE

My first tour of the US was only a few years ago, so I guess my agent ran with what she could get. I'd had some amazing experiences: playing a Pride party at Good Room in New York, a hippie saloon where everyone was loved up. It all kind of made sense. Then I got to Miami. I already had doubts because the party I was playing was billed as 'The Warehouse Edition', but it looked more like an EDM event, and online, it said it was inspired by the 'underground scene'. That was a red flag.

Immediately after checking into the hotel, which was very glitz and glam with a rooftop pool with a muscular DJ playing, already feeling like a fish out of water, I had a dinner reservation with the promoter and another DJ from the UK. He was also playing and was from a major label, but I'd never heard of him, so there was a mismatch from the start.

Only the promoter was there when I arrived. Another red flag was that he was wearing an open Hawaiian shirt, but it got worse when he started talking at me about the habits of CEOs, neo-liberal indoctrination dressed up as positive-thinking, 'You can get what you want if you wake up early' etc. It was like hanging out with a Wall Street Wolf.

When the other DJ came in, it got worse. They started full-on bro-to-bro bragging, which was intense. They were talking about hanging out with models. One of them boasted he'd spent 900 euros on dinner. The other replied he'd spent the summer in New York because he hadn't made his usual pilgrimage to Ibiza and had been drinking 35 dollar smoothies. The parties I like to play are politicised, with people who are respectful and really fun, but at this point, it wasn't necessarily even offensive, just objectifying. They were talking about drugs too, which is when the promoter said: "What's the point of a line of coke if you're not doing it off a pair of titties?"

As a woman, it was so awkward, but I just kept eating my ceviché, which was the best thing about the meal. Afterwards, they wanted to hang out, but I made an excuse about needing to prepare and went back to the hotel.

The party was like something organised by a phone brand, a 'homage to the '90s dance music revolution'. It was in a club, although it did look a bit like a warehouse, and the interior was covered in UV decor. A woman they'd hired was dressed as a '90s raver handing out glowsticks. It was only half-full. Another woman, who looked like she was a desperate housewife from Beverly Hills, asked if I was from the 'Burner scene' and I had to tell her I had no idea what that was.

The DJ from dinner was before me and actually played a track of mine, which came as a big surprise. As the promoter was keeping me company, I said something along the lines of, "He's playing my track, that's nice." To which, he replied, "Go tell him; he's never heard of you."

I'm normally happy to adapt to a party, but I really didn't have what they wanted. People were kind of dancing and some of my friends were there, so I knew they were having an OK time. In the spirit of the evening, though, the promoter came up to me and said: "Can I give you a tip?"

"Sure."

"Play something *groovy*; it's Miami."

I didn't even know what he meant. I was playing ravey house, which was the theme of the event. And even talking to DJs I love, who I really see eye to eye with, we mean different things when we use the same terms. Words don't really cut it when it comes to music. The promoter hated *my* music so much he asked if the DJ after me could start 20 minutes earlier, which I was glad to let happen. He was a local who looked like something out of 'Jersey Shore'. Five minutes later, the police came in and stopped the party. They were really aggressive, so it actually worked out well for me.

The next day I had my first ever panic attack on the beach; it was like being in a k-hole. I felt so alone – my homesickness had peaked – and totally out of place in Miami. It was so glossy and flashy, totally different to where I'm from. For so long afterwards, I thought I hated it there. Later on, I realised something, though. It wasn't a Miami thing or a European vs USA thing. I now think maybe what I'd seen was 'EDM' in its purest form.

Not the front of house cake-throwing or super-commercial music, but a state of mind behind the scenes: careerist, materialistic, sexist. We're in a global scene now, and not everyone is in it for the same reasons or on the same mission. And a few months later, I got to play Floyd at Space in Miami, which was incredible. Very groovy, and not a wannabe CEO in sight.

TAKEN II

I'm not a household name; I've never been on the top of any bill or big festival line-up but, having been resident for a series of big global clubbing brands for almost 20 years, I've DJ'd every single working week of my life. It's an interesting life and has given me the widest range of vantage points a DJ can have. I've been booked to play somewhere as illustrious as Space Terrace, Ibiza, where I got to select sounds I really enjoy and that inspired me to DJ in the first place. Some situations will see me playing on a yacht for the launch of a sporting event or in the VIP room of a big corporate exhibition or art exhibition where I'm playing pop music and oldies. Other times it's an identikit mainstream commercial club in a random European city where the deepest I get to draw is David Guetta.

This isn't a complaint, by the way; it's just the way things have gone for me in my career. I enjoy the challenge and variety and whatever the gig is, I focus on one main job: making people dance. I'm not here to show off my deep knowledge of rarities, I'm here to keep spirits up, so I'm musically prepared for every single scenario and every single request.

Which became a problem at one show in Hamburg around the early 2010s. I can't remember the venue name, but it was a very typical commercial show. I was playing from midnight until 3am, and the DJ on before me was bashing out the 90 / 00s bangers like there was no tomorrow: Faithless, Eiffel 65, Spiller, Darude. You get the picture. It's a picture I've seen more times than I can remember in my career. I come on and follow suit and, as the night progresses, I take things into more of a hip-hop and r'n'b direction. This causes a bit of a stir and, as

I look over the crowd, I see one man in the middle of the dancefloor surrounded by incredibly glamorous looking women.

Grinning darkly, moving in slow motion like 'choose your character' stage on a video game, he's suited, he's booted and he has a look and air about him that instantly says 'organised crime'. I carry on dropping hip-hop tunes and everything I play gets some type of call or shout from him. We make eye contact and I give him a nod. Enough to pay respect to him but, I hope, not enough to encourage him to take our friendship further. Unfortunately, I have totally misjudged the situation. He sees my nod as an open invitation to come up into the booth.

"You've got the best music tonight!" he shouts in my ear. "Come to my club afterwards for the afterparty; you'll love it!"

I thank him but politely decline. My flight leaves at 9am; I wanted to get some sleep before an early start to the airport.

"No. Come to my club."

"Honestly, I'd love to, any other time I would. But I have another show tomorrow and I really can't. You know how it is. Maybe next time?" I pull out all the polite classics one would say in such a scenario, but they are falling on deaf ears.

"Come to my club. We'll have a real party. Not like this. Much better."

He seems pretty resolute, almost forceful, on this matter. The fact he's saying he owns his venue backs up my organised crime theory. I carry on playing to the gradually dwindling crowd and he loiters in the background sniffing coke, still proffering appreciative gestures when I play a tune he enjoys. At one point, two of his friends join him. Not the glamorous lady friends but two much bigger pals in dark suits. Henchmen. They, too, are nodding respectfully but not offering any type of cheer like their main man. I continue to focus on my set, but I'm increasingly aware of them lurking and talking behind me. At points, their conversation becomes a little heated... then it becomes all-too silent. I turn around and they've gone. Not so much of a goodbye or handshake; they'd just vanished. Relieved, I finish my set, say goodbye to the promoter and walk out of the venue… Only to be accosted by the two henchmen. One of them has me in a headlock; the other grabs my arms and pins them behind my back.

"Now we'll have a real party, yes?"

The main man appears from behind me. He's grinning but I don't see the funny side. I try to reason with him.

"Please, mate, I'd love to come and play for you, I can give you my card, but really I'm not comfortable in this situation. I have to fly at 9am." I try to sound as insistent and confident as possible but it's hard when you're being manhandled in such a way.

"Don't worry, we'll get you there in time, I promise. Come to my club; it's much better than this shithole."

As he's saying this, I'm being marched into the back of his car. At first, I resisted, but these men were strong. I'm six foot two and in no way a small person, but they were moving me around like a toddler. I'd been kidnapped, and my fate for the next few hours would be in their hands. I get in the car, wedged between the two men in monkey suits, and we drive to the venue. The main man is chatting away in the front, changing the radio and turning to me with a big grin on his face from time to time, like this is perfectly normal behaviour. After twenty of the most intense minutes of my life, we finally arrive.

"Welcome to my club! Let me get you a drink," he beams as we enter a shady looking establishment with literally no lights or branding, the type of private venue that you're only aware of on a need-to-know basis. Plush furnishings, big chandeliers, a water feature and shiny brass everywhere. Once again, the whole set-up screamed 'organised crime'. The number of henchmen in suits had risen by at least 20, too. I ask for a gin and tonic and I'm shown the decks.

"Let's see what you've got…"

My host takes one of my USBs, loads it into one of the decks and goes through the tracks. He knows his music, he loves his hip-hop and he even has a little mix himself as we go back to back. It's not the type of behaviour you'd expect from a kidnapper at all. He racks up a few lines and, worried I might insult him if I didn't accept, I take him up on the offer.

"Pure, uncut."

And he would know; it's his business. He opens up a little more and enlightens me on his credentials in the Turkish mafia. Even through the heavy cocaine buzz, this concerns me – but we're getting along pretty well and I remind him that I have to leave by 7am to get my bags and get to the airport in time for my flight. He nods, he hugs me tightly and he hits the dancefloor. I check the time; it's 4.30am. I reason with myself: *just keep this guy sweet for a few hours and I'll be fine.* Either that or I'll be dead. There's not going to be a happy medium here, unless they're sitting at a ouija board one posthumous evening.

6am arrives and the dancefloor is full of strange and suspicious-looking people. Most of them seem to be enjoying themselves, so I carry on playing and find they move to anything I drop. I play a bit of house, a bit of jungle and a whole load of heavy tracks that I wouldn't usually get to play. As far as gigs go, this was actually good fun… Good fun in that strange, tense, will-I-get-the-fuck-out-of-here-alive kinda way. I look around for my host and he's towards the back of the dancefloor, still whooping and hollering. One more hour to go and I'm home free. You can do this, I tell myself.

As the hour progresses, the dancefloor empties a little and I realise my host isn't looking as sharp as he did. His shirt is unbuttoned and untucked; he looks a little feral. I wonder if he'll remember our deal. I start to get strange looks from his henchmen. They're in a deep and distracted conversation and it's clear I'm the subject of their troubles. 'What's going on now?' I wonder to myself and I realise the main man is no longer on the dancefloor. Fuck, where is he? Can I just go now? I wonder how quickly I could run from the venue and find a cab. I play another tune and consider my options but before it runs out, my options are made up for me.

"Hey, bro!"

I feel a hand on my shoulder and turn around. It's him. My host. Now just standing there in his underwear looking pretty fucking dark. His eyes are bloodshot, he's covered in sweat and…. FUCK…. The dude's just bitten my arm! A deep, blood-drawing bite, too. This wasn't a cheeky nibble. I scream in pain and his henchmen appear out of nowhere, but this time, instead of grabbing me in a headlock, they grab him and take him away. Another man comes over to me and offers to clean up my arm and get me to the airport. He looks genuinely upset and concerned.

"We're so sorry. Usually, we get him home before he goes like this, but your music was too good. He didn't want to leave."

He presses a napkin down hard onto my arm to clean up the blood like it's something he's done before and hands me an envelope with five thousand euros in it "for my trouble". He keeps shaking my hand and apologising as he leads me to a car waiting outside. As we walk down the corridor towards the entrance, I see rays of light coming through the doorway and, besides the searing pain in my arm, I feel relief on levels I've never experienced before or since in my life. It's a new day; I have effectively survived a Mafia kidnapping and, what's more, it's exactly 7am. Just as they promised, I did get to the airport on time. To this day, it remains the most intense set I've ever done. And I've got the jagged, faintly circular scar to prove it.

THE REPRIEVE

We did some legendary parties at a beach bar in Ibiza in the early 2000s. It was a great time to be on the Island, there was a new underground scene growing up, the techno crowd from London and Berlin and Italy seemed to have rediscovered Ibiza, and the music was really exciting – but there wasn't so much hassle about noise limits or independent parties, or lots of Moet & Chandon branding everywhere yet. That came later.

One evening we had a gig there and I played the last set, just after Ricardo Villalobos. I remember being really annoyed when the venue pulled the plug on the soundsystem during my last track, which was Mathew Jonson's 'Marionette' I think. Such a special tune that summer.

At that time, the scene really revolved around the DJs. There were villa parties and barbecues that lasted for days, entourages of like-minded people that would travel with them, it was a scene within a scene and really exciting to be around. After this gig, though, one of my best friends had decided – out of the blue – that it was a good idea to invite Ricardo back to ours. In Ibiza, even in those days, Ricardo went everywhere with about 200 people. Like POTUS and his secret service, but with cooler sunglasses. Everywhere they went was an event. We could see all his crew getting excited by the idea of an afterparty.

The problem was that we were staying miles away in this rustic villa, really beautiful, with a pool, but nothing fancy. We didn't even have decks at the house. It definitely wasn't a party house. The owner lived on the bottom floor and had rented us the top. He was a sweet old man who had loads of cats. We were very worried what he – and the cats – would make of us turning up with a couple of hundred bug-eyed minimal ravers and DJs desperate for a crack on. We all knew it was a terrible idea, but my friend didn't want to go back on his invite and kill our cred with our hero. So we left in our car, with a convoy of at least 30 cars and several scooters following us.

We headed back down the coast, turned inland, the lights on the high walls of Dalt Vila twinkling in the distance, and headed deeper towards the countryside, filled with a sense of dread. Leading the convoy to a tiny villa with no music, no booze and no hope. The accidental Pied Pipers of crushing disappointment.

Then came divine intervention. We got to a T junction and our car just broke down. Ricardo came to talk to my friend, who told him what was going on, so he and the entire convoy backed up behind us just turned around and left. Thank fuck. That saved us from a situation that would have been really weird and embarrassing – for us, for Ricardo, and probably for the cats too.

WEEKENDERS

You know those cartoon snowballs, tumbling down a hill, picking up more and more snow and debris until they're practically an avalanche? Those used to be my weekends' DJing. With no manager, no real organisational skills and an inability to say no to anything that sounded like a party, it would never take long before things started tumbling out of control. I remember one particular weekend when it became painfully clear to me that this DJ life isn't anything much to do with normality, for better or for worse. It wasn't the most dramatic or anything, but as a slice of life at that time, it's pretty representative.

I was booked in to play three different festivals over one long weekend. Festival No.6 in Wales on Friday was up first. Saturday would see me at a new festival in Kent a mate was putting on, and Sunday would find me in Bournemouth for Bestival. Not a big thing to the big time DJ talent – indeed, I'd say it's more like a standard summer weekend for those guys – but this was a big deal for me at the time. You see, those big names would have a properly planned itinerary, have places to stay and travel all booked and probably even have a tour manager shepherding them along the way. I had a mate who'd agreed to do a bit of driving for me on the last stretch, as is often the case for most working DJs. I mean, it was going to be fine. They were all UK events anyway; it's not like we were going properly abroad or anything, right?

So we started our fantastic voyage on Friday and, immediately, that's when the wheels came off. I missed my train back from Wales – hands up, these things happen. But in the process, I did meet the drummer from Chic and even managed to hitch a ride back with him to London, which was pretty bloody handy. And the fact he turned out to be sound enough to not only get us back to town but also to throw in some guestlist for me and my dad to see them the next month was actually pretty amazing. You don't get that as a middle manager of a marketing company. But a middle manager for a marketing company probably wouldn't have found themselves back in London with zero money.

Somehow I blagged the train and was walking around the Kent countryside with a low-res image of a map, but I managed to find the next event. There are a lot of things you want to hear the promoter say to you when you are halfway through an epic weekend quest, but "Sorry, your set's been cancelled, and we can't afford to pay you" is not one of them.

Even the consolation prize of "but we got you a tent" didn't really do much for my mood at that point, I'll be honest.

So I did what you do when you're at a festival with your mates and you're not working… I got on it all night in some guy's van (classy, right?). Then I found my way to the local cash & carry and bought a shit ton of booze with borrowed money, thus becoming the hero of the festival in the process. Unfortunately, my heroic sheen – which existed, of course, only in my head and in the heads of some other spangled festival-goers – was rather wiped out when my until-now-surplus-to-requirements tent started blowing away. There's nothing like having to get your mate, who's about three degrees soberer than you, to help you secure your blowing-away fee-replacement shelter at a family-ish festival, just as everyone else is getting up, to confirm your fall from festival god to festival… well, I think 'idiot' covers it, for assuming that those guys would provide a decent tent in the first place.

Tents, though, weren't the end of these festival promoters' inabilities. If only. It turned out that the festival site was double-booked with a motocross event. So the planned 'jazz breakfast' was somewhat disrupted by the 200 Kent lads burning it up on their bikes nearby. I won't claim to really know what a jazz breakfast is supposed to entail, but I'm pretty sure that the sweet sound of Kawasaki wasn't one of the many variants they had in mind as a soundtrack.

So things weren't going swimmingly – but at least my mate had arrived to drive me away from this crime against festival promotion. Which was the plan until he locked his keys in the car. So we had to call and wait for the AA, just as a biblical storm broke out. We'd not even got to bloody Bestival yet.

Soon we were on the road. On the way there with another passenger, a Balearic-era DJ dude who can still party with the best of them. As he proved on the way there, in fact, as he spent the whole journey sampling (finishing) the 'supplies' while we stayed straight to navigate and drive, respectively. We actually got to the festival so late that we had to call someone already in to open the gates. But we made it – and my enduring memory of the Bestival gig has to be our Balearic Silverback mate wandering onto the stage while I was playing. He was brandishing a pack of M&S prawns, of all things, holding each one up the way Fatboy Slim would a John Paul Young record sleeve and had the whole crowd, thousands strong, chanting "Eat. The. Prawn! *Eat. The. Prawn!*"

THE TURNING POINT

I moved from West Michigan to Detroit in my late twenties, and I was really struggling. Not to find friends, not to find good music, not to be inspired, but to keep steady work.

I'd had a track featured on a friend's compilation, and that was what inspired me to move and try to make a go of it, try to be around a bit more of the culture. But my bills went up when I went into Detroit because, believe it or not, at that time, Detroit was a more expensive place to live than where I was from. My parents were like, "Why would you move to Detroit? What the hell's over there? This is the nicer side of the state."

I tried working construction and I couldn't take it. My dad had been really tough to work for, but he wasn't horrible to you. In Detroit, I ended up working for these freaks, these two brothers that were literally verbally abusing their current employee and each other and one of them was just huge, an enormous dude. I worked for two days and he kept it up for two days, so I quit.

I'd moved in with a girlfriend who had a car and the deal was like, "you keep your car, I'll get the place for us" then we broke up, and I was car-less. Detroit's not a walkable city, especially ten years ago; it was pretty desolate. You could hardly find groceries without a car. My ass wasn't downtown either. I was out off Jefferson in a slightly nicer neighbourhood, but it was right on the edge of the ghetto: lots of shootings and crazy shit. On the other hand, I'd met a few other DJs and promoters and I was going to a lot of great shows, and I felt like I most certainly wanted to stay there. I didn't want to have to go home with my tail between my legs.

Another positive was that I started going over to Berlin – and the very first time I went over there, a friend got me a gig at this club called VMF. It was a Wednesday night but it was not that quiet, actually a cool party. I came home super inspired and I started writing more music and going back to Berlin for longer stretches. I started meeting more people and got another couple of tracks released.

But things were really difficult in general. I was basically trying to piece together a career that made enough money. My rent in Detroit was only like $657. But then there were a pretty decent amount of bills on top of that too, because in Detroit, you have to pay a lot for heating and air conditioning because it gets hot and it gets cold. I was DJing quite a bit and even, travelling within the States, a few very small scale European 'tours', but I was a '$500 and a flight kind of DJ': no serious bookings. I think I played in New York, small parties in small clubs in Chicago. But really, nobody knew who I was.

I'd given myself an ultimatum: if I hadn't got my shit figured out by 30 and started making a career out of this then I was gonna consider trying to find some sort of normal employment again. And then, aged 29, I got an email from a friend, a more successful DJ who'd volunteered to act as a booking agent for me.

They wanted to book me at Fabric in London. They wanted to fly me over plus pay me £800. Not a lot, but that was back when the US dollar was half of a pound, so it was flight plus hotel and $1600 to go play at Fabric. And I was able to tell some of my close friends I'm booked at Fabric (I told my family too: they're like what's that? What's a fabric?). It was definitely a huge moment to be booked at one of dance music's meccas.

I was on cloud nine for the whole time leading up to that gig, and I worked tirelessly on my set because I was playing live. I worked day and night. I worked my ass off, and I was getting better. The set was getting better, despite not having a lot of money for great equipment to make music (a PC and the cheapest plugins) or travel with (just a pretty basic sound card and a cheap laptop) because I couldn't afford to buy anything. But I had everything set up and tested and rehearsed. I was ready.

Fabric felt like my big chance. I was playing room two, the biggest room I'd ever played. It was the most I'd ever been paid. And, obviously, I was super nervous. But I played well! I was in it and people were feeling it, and I had all my friends in the front row going crazy. The room was packed and the sound was awesome and it was going off without a hitch. I was somewhat crushing it, looking out at all these faces who were reacting to my music, my set. The work had paid off. Maybe this music thing was going to work out after all.

I played and I played and I played. And in the last five minutes of my set… 'splat'. The sound went out completely.

My cheap sound card had given out. I frantically tried to unplug and replug it. Back then, you had to reboot everything to get the computer to recognise the sound card, and it was horrendous. I couldn't get it back on in time. It felt like I was up there trying to get it turned back on for about an hour. Judy, the brilliant promotions manager from the club was over at the other booth (the DJ booth was about 30 feet from the live booth in room two) looking over at me, and I'm just looking at the computer, looking up at them and eventually I hold up my hands up in surrender. One of the legendary residents was already there too, getting ready to play after me, and thankfully with only five minutes left of my set he was ready to go. So he put a record on after that seemingly endless 'dead air', and that was it. The end.

I was just mortified. In Detroit, when something like that happens, people give you shit. I had played in Germany before, in small towns that aren't as like chill and artsy as Berlin and if your stuff fucks up on you during your set, the crowd and the promoter and everybody else will be like 'fucking amateur'. That's fucked, because it happens; it happens with live bands. It happens with everybody that plays music. Something can go wrong. I've seen it with some of the most expensive live acts from some of the most seasoned professionals on the planet.

It's not like I'm a bass player in a band and the guitar tech could just throw me another bass.

But I had been playing one of the better sets of my life. I'd built it up so much as a turning point in my career. I'd worked so hard to prepare. In my mind, I felt terror. Everybody was going to write me off as an artist. I just blew my chance of ever playing here ever again.

Five minutes afterwards, I was still drenched in sweat. It's a hot club, to begin with, but I was still bright red, adrenalin and shame coursing through me after that catastrophe. Mortified. Backstage, I'm packing up that bastard equipment, cursing it, feeling like the sky had fallen in, and Judy walks up to me. I start talking to her and I'm like, "You know, you flew me all the way from Detroit and I felt like everything was going so well. I'm just so sorry. I'm so sorry that I fucked it up and I'm sorry, I want to get a better sound card and a new computer. It's just this equipment is all I can afford."

But despite the fact I'm a sweaty mess, she puts her arm around my shoulder and tells me something I'll never forget.

"Darling," she says, "it's only a disco. There'll be another one."

It was the big turning point for me, that gig, but also that kindness. I felt like I was doing something right, which kicked me into high gear to stick it out. Less than a year later, everything had taken off. There were lots more gigs, at Fabric and everywhere else. It's not like I don't worry about money anymore because the music business is a bitch, but at least a year later, I could definitely tell people, you know, this is my fucking job. This is what I do, I make music and I DJ.

And also, I've seen the sound go out or the equipment fuck up at some of the world's biggest clubs and festivals. I've tried to remind younger artists that as long as they've prepared properly and they play their best, then not to worry about something that's not their fault. It's only a disco. There'll be another one.

THE HART OF THE MATTER

It was a very bright, sharp and brilliant summer morning. Been working a couple of nights and days straight through as usual. Some folks don't believe me when I tell them I've not slept on a weekend for something like 20 years. Even when not working. Can't sleep at weekends. Programmed. But yeah, it was a completely random house, as the afterparties usually are. Big city, but one of those Victorian ones that manage to be dirty and old but very green as well.

The Victorians were great. Even though they were sending kids down mines, they still couldn't even envisage making anything small and pokey like now. Even the poorest houses had big windows and high ceilings. This was a big old house with a huge garden full of students and freaks. Everyone was inside chatting shit, making no sense and having a pop at each other. Bang average afterparty. I was getting a bit tired of them by now. They were funny and adventurous and then they were standard and then one day they were boring. I was at this odd stage of being compelled to be there somehow but objecting to it simultaneously.

This would manifest as being there but always being on the edge of things. Not being part of the conversation. One foot out the door sort of thing. My party trick was disappearing. Get to a point where I'd had simply enough and just turn and walk out. No goodbyes. Sometimes say I was off for a piss and just walk out the door. Sometimes miles and miles from anywhere. No clue where I was. Would just walk for hours praying for a taxi. At 7am Sunday morning, there weren't many taxis.

Anyway. If the weather was good, I'd be outside. Club zombies don't like the sun the next day, but I always sat in it like a lizard. Like it kept me upright. Fed my cold blood. I was sitting in the middle of this house's big garden and although it was very green, it was bang in the middle of the city. Next to a big road. It was early and fairly quiet. Sun was already hot. I was in a deckchair sort of thing. Not easy to get in and out of, so it was an excuse to sit there for hours. Murdering time.

About 100 meters ahead, at the end of the garden, was a huge hedge amid trees. Like a sheer cliff-face of green. I was just losing the will to live and contemplating an attempt to get out of there when, and I'm not kidding, almost clearing the top of this barrier but more like crashing out of it, a fucking huge deer punched through it. I mean massive antlers, the lot. Big as a horse. Like I say. Middle of the city. It seemed twice as high as a man as it leapt through the bush. Leaves everywhere. It landed really heavily. It was huge. It then performed a sort of circle quite daintily. Very delicate for something that massive.

Then it saw me. It didn't seem alarmed. It was quite a calm look. As if I wasn't there. Then it briefly coiled like a spring and from a standing, stationary point just leapt clean over my head. Like a plane passing over. I was so exhausted I barely reacted. It was so *real*, though. As in absolutely not imaginary. In that fuzzy state, something hyperreal can properly sober you up. I mean to this day, I don't question it for a second. It happened. No one else was there. No one saw it but me. I don't know where it came from and didn't see where it went. I know it doesn't have a lot to do with DJing, but it's one of my most vivid memories.

I stopped wasting time after gigs not long after. Not because it was so odd and 'sobered me up' or anything. It was just such a very strange thing and it felt a bit like a message from reality. "Here I am. Where have you been?" it seemed to say. Maybe I was already finished with nonsense and just interpreted it as a 'sign'. But that was the day I stopped flushing my hours away. Sorry if that is a bit weird. But you did ask.

THE JOKER

Ibiza has this legendary rep in dance music, but the reality doesn't always live up to the ideal. Not for everyone, anyway. This happened about five years ago, just before I came back to the UK to live. It was a famous annual party at one of the most legendary clubs on the island. And I was DJing: following an internationally massive house DJ while a proper Balearic legend played the other room. So I'd gone on and there was a girl there who was one of the organisers of one of the Spanish parties at the venue. And it was a really good party that night, all good vibes and everything going swimmingly.

So this Spanish girl, very popular with everyone, is behind me. We'd previously got along well. I liked her, in fact. But tonight, she just started tugging at my sleeve whilst I was DJing. Now I don't like people behind me when I'm DJing at the best of times, so I turned around and asked, "What is it? What do you want?" and she said, "I want to tell you a joke, I want to tell you a joke." I said, "Can it wait? I'm actually DJing right now…." But she kept insisting, "No, no, I want to tell you a joke", and just kept tugging at my sleeve.

I ignored her, but she just kept saying, "I want to tell you a joke! I want to tell you a joke!" tugging away. So eventually, I just turned around and said, "Okay, tell it quickly because I'm playing records here." She says, 'Why don't Black people like the sound of chainsaws?" And I just thought: *this is completely off-key. What the fuck is this? Has someone set her up to do this?* Just a million things went through my head. All while trying to click back into my DJ set and decide what record I should play next? Mentally it's a question of: *do I react or do I keep playing?*

I thought *fuck this, it's just nonsense* and just turned around. But then she was tugging at my sleeve again, going, "I want to tell you the joke, I want to tell you the joke". And I told her, "Listen, that's not a joke!" But she was like, "Let me tell you the joke…" So I just thought, *let's let her tell the joke as she's just annoying me now*. So I say, "Go on, tell me the joke."

So she then says, "why don't Black people like the sound of chainsaws? So I just looked at her, eyes wide by now, replying through clenched teeth, "Why don't Black people like the sound of chainsaws?" And she looked at me, and it was actually a big Rumpelstiltskin moment; she was just hopping from foot to foot; she knows the punchline the way he knew his name.

"It's because it makes the sound 'r-r-r-r-r-r-r-r-r-r-r-r-r--run nigger run! R-u-n-n-n-n-n run nigger run!'"

So I just told her, "That's not a joke, that's not funny. Get the fuck out of the booth!" As she kept saying, "It's funny! But it's funny!" So I just pushed her – lightly – out of the booth.

Now you see the booth there doesn't really lock. So I was just looking around to make sure she wasn't going to come in again. Then I continued DJing. There was nobody around to tell what had happened. And it really rattled me for a few records, so the mixing went out and I just struggled to get back into it, to be honest.

By the end of the party, everyone's having a nice time and the host has brought some records in from his booth for a bit of a karaoke session after hours. Everyone's sitting in the bar and I was just telling people, "Do you know what? She's just told me this 'joke'…." Just telling them what happened.

And all sorts of people were saying, "Oh, you should have just stopped the music and given her the mic and made her tell the joke to everyone in the club". Yeah, but I'm not gonna do that. That's not going to go down very well with the organisers. And I just didn't feel like doing that. And people were telling me I should have punched her, that kind of thing. Easy to say to someone else after the fact!

But the main thing that people said was, "Why didn't you tell someone?"

But this is the thing: there was no one to tell – there was no security, there never is around there. There was nobody from the club to tell. And apart from that, she's one of their favourites anyway, they all really love her. So if I go telling tales, it's gonna be me that gets the shit, not her. Like I'm the one with the problem.

So everyone had all these ideas of what I should have done. But nobody actually said, "We should deal with this here." No one pulled her up for it. They all knew who she was. And it was all forgotten the next day. No one did anything. No one said anything. No one even asked me if I was alright. Not even the offer of a lift home. It was one of those awful moments for people of colour where you just have to suck it up. And you do suck it up. You walk away. And you get home and you think *I've just fucked myself over there*. Because by not saying anything, by not kicking off, the only person who felt this is me. And everyone else can carry on about their business. Can carry on enjoying this person's party like they're a lovely person. It's that whole thing of, how do you balance out reporting a racist joke? Is it just a joke? How do you balance that? How do you accept it as being just a joke? Because that's what I did, I accepted it as being just a joke. And I walked away.

But it made a massive difference as to whether I would continue living on the island. It became one of the reasons I decided that Ibiza wasn't for me. Black people always get pulled in for drugs there, but every drug dealer I know on that island is fucking white! There's a presumption of guilt for Black people in Ibiza. I mean, that's the case in the UK too, but even more so out there. I'm not Carl Cox; I'm not living in a million-dollar villa. I'm not playing at these huge budget events where I can command that kind of respect. I'm just a normal Black woman on an island that regards Black women like the shit on your shoe.

NEVER SAY BOUNCER AGAIN

We prefer 'security'. We never say 'bouncer'. It's easy to demonise us, but you'd be surprised how many times we help people. We don't beat anyone up unless they attack us. There are cameras everywhere these days; we'd never get away with it. And the way licences are now with all the responsibility on the venue instead of people's own behaviour? Well. The whole venue can get shut down if you put a foot wrong. I don't think people realise either that we do things like terrorism drills. I work at a major venue and we've been openly marked down on lists found by MI5 and the global secret services. When you are having fun at a country's capital, you are a prime target, especially one that is always open and predictable in its regularity. Look at what happened in Paris.

We train and train and the focus is on saving lives. That is our purpose. I wish people could put themselves in our shoes, but that seems to be a lost art lately. A mate of mine who is a police desk sergeant put it best for me. He said he clearly remembers a 'no drug' era compared to when they really arrived. You'd basically get terrible drunk behaviour but he said you could set your watch by when they all would pass out. Total silence between about midnight and 7am. Now he says he deals with people killing themselves by head-butting the doors and walls. Screaming like it's an asylum and they can go on for days. You really do not know what it is you are dealing with when you engage with someone on a night out. It's a game of Russian roulette and not only is my life at stake but everyone close by. Not long ago, a staffer asked someone to stop smoking due to COVID as much as the other rules. The guy didn't even look at him, just lobbed a bottle that went well wide and blinded a girl minding her own business. Totally random and uncalled-for.

I won't give you more horror stories; we'd be here all day and night. But this is why we sometimes have to put men down pretty hard and get them out of the place. We've no idea what we are dealing with these days. It's safer for everyone involved if we get a potential danger out ASAP. It's a cartoon the way we are perceived. Let me put it like this, you do not last long as a professional if you are unnecessary or corrupt. The gangster days of infiltrating our squads are over. I won't say we never have bad apples who get through the net, but they get found out and ejected from our company double sharpish. Maybe in some out-of-the-way places, the council or police turn a blind eye or maybe even have a finger in the pie but in the capital, we are pure professionals. There are guns, bombs, knives, biological threats... it's potentially hairy and we cannot mess about. Likewise, some nights are dull as you like! Which is fine by me. Dull is good. Dull is what I pray for.

A lot of it is about progress. Early days there was a lot of organised crime in the clubs themselves. The owners especially. It's a big washing machine for dirty money. Highly prized is a venue that throws a lot of cash over the tills. That has changed a bit, although one of the reasons I felt safe talking to Secret DJ is they were spot-on in his book where they say the crime lords just wear suits now. Venue rivalry used to be putting CS gas in the smoke machine and the odd drive-by or machete. Now it is all lawyers, accountants and the laundry is done offshore by some very big names. It's all a well-oiled machine. Of course, a lot of legit money is running through the clubs now too. Or, like a lot of things, it is owned by offshore interests. Look at it like football teams. The big ones have all sorts going on in the boardroom. I'm not really privy to any details or would not tell you anyway, but we've changed hands a few times.

I'm not here to talk out of school, that sort of thing that can get you hurt. I just wanted to say that we help more than we hinder. We pick people up who are down, we do first aid, rapid response to life-threatening issues, I've even helped deliver a baby. The clue is in the name. Security. We keep you secure so you can have a good time. In a sense having a slightly hardcore rep works for us. And we do not fuck about. Some of the lads I work with have worked private security all over the world. High level. We have solid female professionals too. We know how to put down serious issues. But it's not the only thing we do. Not by a long chalk. Try to use a bit of imagination. It's not easy dealing with people high as kites. We are stone-cold sober and some people not only are rude as hell, they just don't make any sense at all sometimes. It's difficult to negotiate that. We do our best, but maybe if you stop and think about what it is we actually do, we'd all get along and things would run a little smoother. There it is. Hopefully, you might bear that in mind next time you come to party. Said my piece. Thanks for listening.

EAST OF EDEN

It was quite a few years ago, and I'd literally just started DJing. Fresh and naive. I was scouted by this queer club night, who knew that I was a DJ and also a singer, so they asked me if I wanted to go on this tour with them, which would be in Asia and Australia. Of course I did! It would be my first time playing abroad. I was going with the promoter and two other DJs. I was the warm-up DJ and also singing a live PA.

Now, I didn't know any of the others. Hadn't met any of them; we'd just talked on the phone a couple of times. I was twenty-years-old, meeting these people for the first time and about to spend two weeks with them. But I was super excited, and it turned out they were lovely.

Taiwan was our first stop. We got there and the club was massive. Definitely the biggest place I'd ever played; two or three thousand capacity, maybe bigger. One room. Really high roof. Like Brixton Academy, if it was full of gay Taiwanese. Massive stage ten feet off the ground, with big video screens everywhere around it.

I did the warm-up DJ set and even when I went to the toilet, there were screens everywhere with my name in lights. It was incredible. I felt like I'd made it.

Then I came to do my live PA. Nobody really told me what was happening; they just gave me a microphone and I was on stage with the DJ. Next thing I know, all these gorgeous, scantily clad (literally just wearing thongs) little Taiwanese fellas jump on stage. They throw a pink feather boa over my head and push me onto this square in the middle of the stage and then two of them start grinding up against me.

So I'm singing away, and next thing I know, the podium, this three-foot square I'm standing on, starts to move, slowly lifting into the air with these two gorgeous little dancers.

The three of us are being hoisted about three metres above the stage. The only problem is that I'm a diagnosed acrophobic. Translation: I'm terrified of heights.

I'm still singing, trying desperately not to lose my shit. So scared. And as much as I should be having the time of my life, I can see myself on the twenty-foot video screen looking absolutely terrified. Slowly we start moving back down and when we get there, I decide rather than risk it again, I'll go and sing in the crowd. It's funny but the sheer terror of the previous minutes and then the warmth of being in the crowd probably made it one of the best shows I've ever done. I've never been on a rollercoaster (for obvious reasons), but that for me was the equivalent.

With bits of the tour falling through for whatever reason, our little crew spent a great week bonding in Taiwan – going to spas and waterfalls and exploring the island and just having an amazing time, before heading to Jakarta. Which would turn out to be a very, very different experience.

We got to this gig, another gorgeous queer night, lots of carnivalesque dancers and performers everywhere, no surprise hydraulic platforms on the stage, a lovely experience. We did our thing and then the people from the club asked if we wanted to go to the afterparty with them. Now our promoter hadn't been paid in advance for this gig, but he'd covered all the flights and everything and they'd agreed to pay from the cash they'd make on the night. So he asked for the fee. "Oh yeah yeah yeah," the club people said, "just come to the afterparty with us." I'm not complaining. I'm twenty-years-old. An afterparty in Indonesia after a great gig? Bring it on.

But then we get driven to this weird concrete basement, full of loads of really shifty looking people. Lots of young boys in the corner on tables smoking crack and meth. It was a complete drug den. There was dog shit all over the floor from this wild yapping dog that was running about. They were offering us drinks and all four of us were looking at each other, thinking *we do not want to be here in this crack den in Jakarta at this moment.* But we take the drinks to be polite. The first thing that's going through my head is *how do I know what's in this drink? What if it's spiked?* I was starting to get super paranoid. We all were. Our promoter's like, "we just need to get our money and then we can leave." Our flight was the next day. Not early, but early enough.

But the guy from the club was like, "the club is shut now, all the money is shut in there, you'll need to get it tomorrow before you leave." So we stayed in the crack den for just long enough to be polite, made an arrangement to go back to the club the next day and went back to our hotel, agreeing that the whole experience had been a bit weird.

The next day we were packed, dressed and ready to go. We waited for our car back to the hotel and no one showed up. Waiting, waiting. Our flight time is getting closer and closer. Eventually, this car comes and we go to the club. The club promoter is there and tells us: "we don't have the money here. Someone else has got it now. We'll just send it to you later."

Our promoter says no. They're like, "but we can't access the safe right now to get it; we'll send it to you later." Our promoter says no. Suddenly they say, "oh, actually, we have half the money." Still our promoter's not settling. Our flight is getting closer and closer. Time is ticking. But he's not walking away from our money. The big bouncers from the club are there in the middle of the day, these huge guys. It's kind of getting scary and intimidating. I'm the only girl and I'm feeling really nervous, especially after spending half of the last night in a crack den.

But we do indeed get the money. We wait them out, and miraculously, someone turns up with it. Our flight is in an hour and ten minutes, though, and the airport is an hour away. We haven't checked our bags, checked in, nothing. We're not gonna get this flight. But the club guys are now saying it'll be fine. They'll just call the airport. Having worked as a stewardess for a bit, I knew this was bullshit. But we get in a car anyway and start crawling towards the airport in heavy traffic, sweating and worried and stressed and wondering whether all the money from the tour will have to go on new flights home.

We get to the airport. We've missed the flight, of course. The next flight's not until the next day. We call the club promoters and ask them what he suggests. And they came through! They put us up in a hotel by the airport, paid for four new tickets, and the next day we made it home. I'll never understand it. If they hadn't fucked around for so long and dragged us to a crack den and pretended they couldn't pay, they would have saved a fortune on rearranging our travel. That's club promoters, though. In my experience, ever since that first tour, I've come to realise that logic is just a foreign concept, whether they're in Jakarta or Jersey. And it was also good to learn one of the rules of being a performing artist: 'never leave until you get the money'. Which is worth remembering, but never as useful as the best maxim of all: get the money in advance!

COOKIE MONSTER

This was during the smuggling years, the great smuggling years. Probably six or seven years ago. We were on tour in Asia. We were leaving from New York to Hong Kong and then from Hong Kong to Japan and Japan to Bali, the two of us travelling with one of our homies – who was also very excited by the idea of scoring ketamine in Hong Kong and taking it on with us to Japan. I had brought along a couple of marijuana edibles for the flight from New York.

We were flying first class.

I had these two chocolate cookies with me and I gave one to [my DJ partner] and he said, "I don't want it," and gave it back. Put it in my toilet bag and forgot all about it. I forgot that I had that cookie with me when I got to Hong Kong, had a killer show, had a crazy time and scored a bunch of ketamine. I forgot about that cookie when we turned the ketamine into liquid form by various methods and pushed on to Okinawa. Little did I know that Okinawa is a place where a lot of people smuggle gold from Asia into Japan. So they are strict over there when it comes to possible importing. They're super careful and on high alert for gold, and by extension, everything.

So we rolled up, three Americans: me and my DJ partner and our other homie. We're going through customs. My DJ partner is wearing a super flamboyant and colourful Adidas tracksuit, and we've got our typical DJ luggage in tow; Rimowa bags with stickers all over them or whatever. We think we look like fucking rockstars. We're coming through the fucking customs. They look at him and they're like, "Hmm, this guy – you come over here" and they give him a quick swab, and he sets off a fucking detector for cocaine. So they're like, "excuse me, sir, but we're going to need to talk to you – are you travelling with anyone?"

He points at me.

My stomach fucking absolutely dropped. Fuck no. Hell no. Like what? I gotta walk right through here man.

Nope. Stop right there. They were going to go through my bags. And in Japan, they go down to the microscope with everything. They start to take everything out, they start to check it and put it all in a methodical, immaculately organised row. So they're starting to lay all my shit out and they get into my toiletry bag where I have this piece of marijuana chocolate cookie – and as soon as they fucking find it, I start singing like a fucking canary.

"Oh you got me, in my country, this stuff is fucking decriminalised, I forgot that I had it, I was gonna eat it on the flight but I didn't have it that's mine that's marijuana I fucked up blah blah blah blah." But now they've got the rest of my toiletries to check.

They've got my shit laid out in front of me. And these are the smuggling days. And I'm smuggling 10 to 15 grams of K in liquid form in these various shampoo bottles and bottles of mouthwash or whatever. It is all spread out in front of me. And so, so I'm shitting my pants, but I'm trying to take some deep, deep hot yoga breaths. The guy brings the fucking testing thing, tests the chocolate – which obviously tests positive.

And he stops there.

That begins a 10-12 hour detainment period where I completely miss the gig and I end up signing some sort of confessional and paying a $2000 penalty.

The weird thing is that the whole time, these customs guys were so fucking friendly and cordial. They're asking me, "what kind of hip hop do you like?" and I'm like, "I like all types of stuff," and they're like, "so do you like Snoop Dogg?" and I'm like "yeah" and they're like "oh so, so how about NWA?" and I was like, "yeah, yeah, they're dope". They were so curious. They're like, "what does marijuana feel like? Does it feel good?" and I'm like, "yeah, yeah, yeah". We chatted for hours. Eventually, they pack up all my shit, neater than I'd ever packed it myself, I sign a document and I make it into Japan.

I had been extraordinarily certain that they would find the ketamine. That's obviously why I was drawing so much attention to the cookie. That cookie was my downfall and my saviour. I was extremely shaken up but kind of defiant too: I'd pulled off the smuggle and I partied. But then I got rid of all that shit because I did not want to bring it on to the next fucking country – and it occurred to me that if I'd been caught going into somewhere like Singapore I could have been locked up for life.

I'm now flagged and searched now whenever I fly, especially to Japan, which is a shame because it's my favourite country. My girlfriend hates it (the searches, not Japan). We've been together five years now and I've sworn off that nonsense, the smuggling years, travelling the world with bottles of ketamine, are over. The thing is, in retrospect, when we came into the industry, there were DJs we looked up to that seemed like superhuman and unstoppable, and they set this trend that the way to operate was just to be as fucked up as possible and invincible – and the reality is that shit is not sustainable.

When you stretch that across a career of playing events, hundreds of shows a year across a decade, *decades*, you know that kind of behaviour just turns you into a fucking substance abuse addict – and I think compounded with some of my own personal life instabilities, familial instabilities and a lack of having roots planted because I'm on the road all the time and and out of touch with myself and the real world – it's just a recipe for abuse.

My girlfriend basically, at some point, gave me an ultimatum: stop the fucking bullshit because you look and act like an asshole – or this, with us, does not happen. On your side, maybe it looks like you're fucking computing the secret of the fucking universe and figuring out what's actually going on and like between the fabric of space and time – but on the outside, you just look like a drooling asshole.

I live with her now, the two of us and our dog, and we live in a beautiful little lush tropical neighbourhood with a giant mango tree, beautiful backyard full of orchids and bamboos, gorgeous. I was just sitting out there under the mango tree, petting our dog and I was just looking around and I was like: I can't fucking lose this, you know? Time to clean up.

SING IT BACK

I was a lonely kid. I played the piano in school assembly and the organ in church. One of those kids. Maybe it's a thing with musicians and DJs? 'Always in the kitchen at parties' as the song goes? Maybe. When I grew up, the 'local crew' (the hired-in help to do touring band load-ins and outs) called me 'talkative'. It was kinda endearing. I guess. Deeply ironic, considering. I will come to that later. I mean, everyone had nicknames. Perv, Milky, Egg, Test Tube et al. I was always around the music scene in some way or another. I'd been in bands since school and specifically the technical rock world with a bit of progressive stirred-in. Not venturing to the electronic side until a cool kid with a moustache, who smelt of tobacco and could spit a rather long way, gave me a cassette of the Prodigy in '92 on the school bus home.

However, my band life continued along with a nascent synth collection until, having been thrown out of three groups for 'commitment issues' and seemingly never getting along with drummers, I realised I was far better suited to be a solo artist. With the absence of other players, I made electronic music, looping drum machines and synths. It was dancey, it was rocky, sometimes triumphant, yet mainly melancholic. It got signed to a big label after a bank loan took me and 100 CDs (which I'd burned in real-time, one at a time) to the Miami Music Conference without a clue what to do with them. I managed to pass out four, along with posing for a picture with Roger Sanchez in full Ali G mode. Luckily, they fell into the right hands.

So you've made an album! Cut a long story short, after then touring my own band, in various arrays flirting with success, playing pretty much every festival and main stage on the planet and after being promised the world, I ended up in significant debt. Then management piped up, "can you DJ?" I said yes. Of course, I couldn't at all. My hairdresser at the time had taught David Holmes to DJ, so he gave me a lesson. "Count to four," he said in a thick Belfast accent. "Make sure you start the next record on beat one, bring it in after a few bars and take the other one out." That was kind of it. I was a musician, so how hard could it be?

So the first gig up was The Egg, London. Armand Van Helden and Touché. (Two of the best DJs on the planet). And me: Johnny Newbie. I was woefully underprepared, a few tracks in and I stuck on 'A View to a Kill'. It jumped, then got stuck on the bridge. I melted and crumbled into a petrified pile. My set was cut short. I was completely crushed. Three gigs later and I was supporting Fatboy Slim in an arena. Crazy, right? It really is who you know in this industry.

Suffice to say, I learnt fast and my agent had industry power. I almost had the records required. I just about had the skills. I could smile, dance and wave my hands long before the EDM DJs. I was a musician, singer and a live performer so I could entertain, which was the way the industry was going. This was the early 2000s and there was money about. Residencies on hallowed grounds were offered. Suddenly I was 'a DJ'. Asia seemed to be an easy hit and I was flicking across oceans every weekend. CDJs came along and I could edit up my own tracks. This made more sense to me rather than playing somebody else's music. I never could see the point in flying around the world to DJ music someone else had made or had had made for them. A mantra I still have to this day. Vinyl became a thing to buy at car boot sales or get passed around at music conferences. It was clunky, gave me backache, was prone to mishaps and really just didn't work for me.

DJing is the most antisocial 'social' job ever. You are the only one in the club not really with anyone. Perversely I think that's why it appealed. You primarily turn up alone, pointing out to the doorman the poster of you as your passage of entry without saying a word, inside it's too loud to speak to anyone anyway; then you leave alone through a side door back to the hotel, entry via a magnetic keycard. I would often avoid the mandatory dinner, always preferring to prepare for the set and keep the stomach empty of carbs. So apart from the odd "cheers!" with the promoter, his gaggle of followers, or telling some random requester "no, I don't have that one" or waving to someone constantly in your eye-line rolling their eyes at you to 'fuck off'; generally you are a solitary beast. Stiffly you realise your only reliable 'friend' is the rider that you got through in record time and it isn't until after you go for a wee mid-set you realise you are way too drunk or high to be leading the dance tonight. Sure you can handle it? And the afterparty set? Also, more worryingly, do you have to go straight to the airport and onto another job?

I've partied hard. Significantly more than 1,500 international gigs. I didn't fuck about; there's a mannequin at home heavily weighed down with enough lanyards to make Mr T's neck ache and enough visa stamps to give Michael Palin a run for the border. I survived them all and these days, I'm a bit of a health freak. The ego died a long time ago. I got fit. Kept it simple: don't take anything too seriously. Life is precious, cherish it. I don't post motivational quotes on socials, though.

But I do have a story to tell – and it's about here I should drop on you the ailment I have and carry around with me constantly. It's the reason I like to travel alone and not speak to anyone. I've always called it a stutter. Which is not what you'd expect at all from a professional singer. Americans tend to use the term 'stammering'. However, medically it is referred to as 'speech disfluency'. What most people don't realise is that you only see the physical manifestation from the outside. The' symptom' if you like. In the same way that say, perhaps a cough is a symptom of what could be almost anything internal. The core issue of the external stutter goes much, much deeper within. Apart from the anxiety drawn up from it, the fundamental physical problem is you trying to speak whilst inhaling, which, if you try to do yourself, is pretty much impossible. Amazingly, no one really knows what it really is or what causes it, but in my experience, it is both a brain disorder and a learned physical affliction working together in brutal tandem. The physical manifestation that people see is actually a coping mechanism like a facial tic to try to avoid the stutter in the first place. These tics then become a hard-wired habit and all present themselves ahead of the actual inner problem. It is a very complex and challenging situation that we stutterers present ourselves.

I guess in extremis, you could call it a disability, although I wouldn't. At its worst, I can't speak at all sometimes. Harsh, right? I've never really talked about it before, ironically considering the issue, but people understanding and being educated about it always brings a measure of compassion and serves the greater good. Films like 'The King's Speech' did a lot for awareness, albeit in a rather soppy 'we can beat this' Hollywood way. However, there are people like Daniel Kitson and Scroobius Pip who have taken it to a completely different level with their divine brilliance.

Looking back, I'm not really sure as to when it manifested; more likely, it's always been there. I'm sure I remember not having it until I was aged five or six. I can remember being exempt from reading out loud in a classroom. Mainly as I flatly refused to. There really is no trauma to be found, though. In my teenage years, a lot of therapists tried to regress me to 'that moment', but there is really nothing to find. I came from a very strong and stable background but there is a history of stuttering in my family and it tends to skip a generation. My grandad on my father's side had one and one of my cousins has one on my mother's side too. So I guess the odds were stacked in favour of it developing in me. Also, being male and left-handed apparently increases the odds dramatically. It's more unusual to carry it into adult life as I have, but to ease that journey, music always seemed to be an ideal path. I really always fancied acting and being a Broadway dolly, but we all want to do things we aren't necessarily well suited for. In my early years, I avoided jobs that relied on sales or 'people skills' as I clearly didn't have the fluency for it, but I found myself at one time having to call existing clients on the phone, which was hellish. The trick to this affliction is to remain as zen and as calm as you possibly can. Music can speak for itself, and for me, but you still have to do the business side of the game, and if you're to produce tunes with other people, you need comms skills. Fortunately, in a comfortable studio environment, none of this has ever been a problem.

When the internet and smartphones came along, it was an unbelievable game changer. The phone went from a thing of absolute terror to a beacon of communication. The internet blew all the rules out of the window. I made a firm choice to stop using the telephone to make calls around ten years ago and have survived and indeed very much thrived without it. Relics like the bank and mobile phone companies were the last to let you do everything online, but sometimes calls that should have taken two minutes took me 20 minutes or more as I struggled to rattle off long numbers to prove an identity, and they just wouldn't let anyone speak on my behalf.

As painful for me as for the recipient. The phone has always been brutal for a stutterer. 75% of people would just hang up on you even if you explained the situation; they just didn't have the patience to take the call. Yeah. Really is brutal. Not the worst part, though. People's face-to-face reactions can be tough. Most people laugh at you. Which is pretty weird, really. I'm not sure if they actually find it funny or if it's a gut reaction to the unknown. Maybe a defence mechanism? I have grown such a thick skin that it is all water off a duck's back to me now. I mean, everyone has something they have to endure. The weird thing is; when they realise you actually have a stutter, they never apologise for laughing at you. I guess it turns into embarrassment. Although inwardly, I kinda enjoy seeing them squirm these days.

Then in order, this is typically what comes next…

"Are you okay!?"

"Oh my God! You're so smashed."

"I'll have some of what you're on mate!" etc., etc.

Next up, unbelievable, I know, but very often, people imitate my stutter as a response to it. Pretty strange, huh? I can get a lot of clarity from this, an instant insight into their character, or lack of, and excise them from my life when that happens. Would you walk up to a deaf person and imitate them? Would you mimic a quadriplegic? Insane, really, that people think it would be okay to do that. Oh wait, isn't that what Donald Trump did once? Ironic. The weird thing is it's one of the last afflictions considered 'fair game', much like Tourette's Syndrome. A lot of people like to have a laugh at it without taking into consideration any feelings the sufferer has or the mental turmoil going on inside their head. "Oh, the Tourettes bloke said bollocks, isn't that funny?" Have a think about what he actually wanted to say at that moment for a minute and heaven forbid, try to put yourself in their shoes as he's shouting 'bomb' while in a public space. So here's some advice; it's not a lot to ask for a drop of patience and respect. If a stutterer is clearly having trouble with a word and you clearly know it, gently slip it into the conversation. That's fine. You aren't interrupting but moving the conversation along as anyone would in normal verse. Often the first thing anyone says to me is, "should I finish your sentences for you?" I reply, "if it helps the flow, go for it. If it's a wild guess that has nothing to do with anything, best keep your mouth shut."

The spectrum of it swings from the sublime to the ridiculous. For example, I can speak to a crowd on the mic with no problem. Performing live, you kinda transcend the impediment as you get into a trance in a Jim Morrison way. We've all seen classic concert footage where the singer is in another realm. Well, that's the goal here. Singing is a rhythmic and often repetitive form. You know the words already. So a mind isn't reaching for them or stumbling over to form fresh sentences. I can indeed sing like an angel. To which people always say, "why don't you sing all the time?"

Yeah, thanks for that Einstein, mental malware doesn't quite work like that! On the days where nothing comes out at all, often combined with drink and drugs, it gets way worse. 'Computer says no' and no sound emerges at all. Not a pleasant method of communication and often a deeply misunderstood situation. I once got thrown out of a festival I was playing at when two security guards thought I was refusing to answer their questions about what I was doing backstage with no wristband on. All I was trying to say was, "I'm DJing next", but the mild gurn and silence from me said otherwise to them. I got slung out. I had to scale the fence to get back into my own show. In fact, almost every day, there is some adventure due to it.

My advice for anyone else working with this? Much the same as any affliction. If you want the best for your fluency, look after your body and mind and soul, keep yourself fit and active. Everything in moderation, cut out caffeine, casual drinking, processed foods, preservatives and sugar. Eat healthily, keep your mind trained and focus on breathwork. It is primarily fed by anxiety, so anything that triggers that is best avoided. There's no cure, but management treatments will give you the tools to incorporate skills into your life, such as breathing through your diaphragm, much as athletes and opera singers do. Once again, breath control is pretty much key, alongside resilient mental strength.

You could argue that the stutter drove me to become a master of what I do. Did it shape me as a person? Difficult to tell how I would have turned out otherwise. I'd probably have had a huge ego in my younger years without it and ended up living in LA and wearing Zorro hats at Burning Man; Jesus! Be thankful for small mercies, huh? Would not having it have made me more successful in this business? Certainly. But how do you judge true success? It is what it is, grasshopper. It is what it is.

PRECIOUS CARGO

Thinking back to these times for you has been very emotional, much more than I thought it would be. These events were sometimes joyous and often challenging, but they did not embitter. Now that I'm through the other side, I realise the experience made me a stronger, deeper person and a better DJ.

I started DJing as a teen on high school radio and college radio. Like many DJs, I worked in record shops, first in America and then over to the UK. After moving to Europe, my DJ career started to peak, but by 'peak' let's just say doing well enough to earn a living. I had an agent and DJ'd internationally. Of course, all that stuff is relative; you only discover later what your peak really is, and it has little to do with money. And just as that summit was reached, I had the crazy idea of getting pregnant.

Even though I had just started a new weekly residency, I was in the middle of my 30s (twilight time for conception) and felt maybe it was now or never in terms of having a baby. The first trimester is very important as it's the easiest time to miscarry. So, like many working mothers, I hid it as I didn't want to sabotage my career. This included props like 'dummy cocktails' of alcohol-free fizz so nobody would ask questions. I had to be careful with my body and maintain my drastically fluctuating energy levels. I was creating a new life inside me while attempting these late night-time marathons. I was pretty healthy, but the strain from the hours was intense and hiding it started to crack. This goes for new mothers across the board, not just in our biz, but there are a certain set of obstacles in our path. Or you could call them choices. And this was during a time when the DJ world was truly a boys club (thankfully less so nowadays). The pregnant DJ was a rarity.

Naturally, I had a lot of support from men as they were in a position to help me along the way, but this 'man's world' wasn't always easy to navigate. Male colleagues had children as well, but during this era, most were not the primary caregivers. If anything, with a kid in the picture, they had to work more. They had to. For me, on the other hand, it was immediately apparent that there would be points in the near future in which I wouldn't be able to work at all. I had a plan that by six months, by the end of the second trimester, I would stop DJing altogether with little idea as to when or even if I would DJ again. It wasn't just the lifestyle and the travel, but I strongly sensed the sonic environment could influence through to the womb. Who knows what effect sub-bass frequencies could have on a developing baby?

I was still active in the first trimester, travelling and working and hiding it. Then in the second trimester, I was 'showing', so I had to tell people. But the spectre of insecurity was looming. No maternity leave. No employer. No real picture of the future. Would I be able to keep up with new music and the scene? Would I have the windows of availability to gig? Would anybody even want to hear me play?

At one point, an Eastern European promoter who had booked me for a festival found out I was pregnant and told me outright that I could not play. They cancelled my set because I was going to have a baby. I knew it was early enough in my pregnancy and safe to travel and DJ, but this man thought he could tell me what to do. At another point, I was DJing (barefoot and pregnant) on the beach overlooking the sea and the promoters had been mistakenly told I was eight months gone and had an ambulance arranged by the side of the stage, which was hilarious. We had a good laugh and had a great party. When I was five months into my term, I DJed in Malaysia, where once again, I was treated as a sort of liability. My larger caucasian stature gave them the impression I was some sort of unexploded 'Momb'. Kid gloves and panic abound!

Eventually, it got to a point where my arms were getting short, which is to say my belly was pressing against the decks. Perhaps a curved table would've been useful. I had never seen a pregnant DJ and the whole thing was a leap into the unknown. Who could I look to? Where was the precedent? I'm sure there have been others, but I didn't feel I had anyone to talk to who could relate.

Thankfully, I was still able to do my radio shows, but things were starting to change for me, not just physically, but internally. Fundamental changes. Something about pregnancy makes you highly introspective and reflective and I began turning inward, which is a very good thing. I started to tap into different sounds. I dug deep into my record collection, remembering who I was and what I represent musically. I went back to my roots and it completely changed how I play.

Then I gave birth and I definitely could not work. I was very lucky that my husband was able to financially support us; not every woman has that choice and the financial security to be able to spend time with their kid. My daughter grew up with me, and from day one, she was exposed to (in my opinion) a varied palette of great music, sitting in the studio while I'm doing dance mixes for Japanese radio, strapped into the baby carrier at the festivals. These were joyous occasions. She even came on the road with me, international gigs and all. But breastfeeding on the road ain't easy, so my husband came along and stayed with her in the hotel while I worked for a few stolen moments, back and forth at all hours. Yes, I was the DJ who had to breastfeed at 3am in a hotel room as an after-show. It was sometimes fun, sometimes very tough.

And then my agent dropped me. It was an upset, not least because I'd stayed with her when she had her baby. I can't tell you 100% she dropped me because of my 'family way'… who knows? Business is business. But then I get a reality sandwich when shopping around for new management and am told, "we already have a female DJ on our roster". I didn't realise there was a quota of one allocated per agency. It becomes claustrophobic like you are being set against each other, and I try to live by the mantra of women sticking together. After I had our daughter, the gigs went from weekly to once a month, if I was lucky. Things were drying up and it seemed like people had forgotten about me.

Surprisingly this amnesia seemed to ring true even with people with whom I was already working. Before I got pregnant, I was co-hosting an event and thought my partners would understand that I would need to take some maternity leave. Especially as one of them was a dad. Then I found out they had tried to consolidate it as a new business, cutting me out completely. I don't think they are terrible people; I just don't think they stopped and thought about it. I've faced 'normal' discrimination quite a lot as a woman; there is a pretty steady baseline of sexist behaviour: being told I don't know much about music or sound, giving credit to any of my perceived successes to a male who may have helped me along, ass-pinching, physical threats, having to carefully monitor my own intoxication levels and going home straight after the gig to mitigate potential sexual assault, and back in the good ole days rarely getting booked if there was already another female on the bill (unless it was 'Ladies Night', of course). Once I was even told I wasn't who I said I was (my DJ name isn't gender-specific) and not allowed into my own gig. That sort of thing is par for the course. But it is the more subtle stuff that gets to you and really messes with your head; the not being taken seriously, being overlooked and having to quietly endure a steady stream of male entitlement. The people who appear like nice middle-class liberal types who do the dirty and it is along the lines of; *would they have done that if I was a man*? There is no use asking, as they would vehemently deny it, but you have that niggling feeling all the same that you would not have been treated that way if you were male.

Some of my friends put on another party with some of the kit I had helped purchase and never asked me to DJ or even hang. This is a part of it, too. When you are pregnant or are looking after a toddler, you are no longer 'on the scene' and being on the scene is crucial. They don't see you around anymore so it really adds to the invisibility factor. It's a Catch 22 scenario. You get excluded. Way over and above the usual baseline sexism, your musical compatriots begin to fade away. I'd invite colleagues to guest on my radio show, and very, very few would invite me anywhere in return. The reciprocity simply starts to fall away. I found that many men were happy for me to help them along and open doors but once they were through, there was often no backwards glance at all. Big entitlement scenes. Then again, you do get the few who reach out and support and I always remember and am forever grateful.

The positive side of all of this was it drove me back into the recording studio. I built a pre-production recording studio at home, recorded an album and did a lot of remixes. When my daughter was a toddler and taking long afternoon naps, it was a golden opportunity to get a sitter and slide off to my friend's proper recording studio nearby and get some real work done. Being away from 'The Road' and having to work with limited time made it a rich and creative time.

However, I did feel professionally isolated by 'Mom Life'. Playgroups and coffee mornings ended up replacing discos and afterparties. And I constantly wondered and worried if it was (or ever would be) relevant. Someone actually told me point blank to my face: "nobody wants to hear a 40-year-old female DJ." And that really hurts. Then those dreadful internet forums start to take hold and suddenly you are called "a MILF", the decades of your hard work and dedication to your musical vocation are casually dismissed and reduced to some guy's sexual fantasy for other guys to laugh at. It may sound crazy, but I found forums frightening. The public bullying gets into your head. One particular guy seemed to enjoy harassing women so much that one of my female DJ comrades gave him his comeuppance with a physical punch. Bless her.

At the time it was tough watching the male DJs I came up with go on to make the big time, but my journey was just different. One of them told me he knew some influential so-and-so at such-and-such trendy magazine and if I needed anything, just ask. He was part of a big feature about DJs who were people I consider peers, so for the first time, I advocated for myself (as many men usually do) and asked if he would have a word with the journalist about including me. The response? "Nah, it's about dudes and their record collections".

Eventually, I got a tour in Japan as I have a very long and deep relationship with that country. But now that I had a kid, long term childcare had to be arranged and the lengths I had to go to were astounding. My husband was running his own business in an office with many employees and we never had a full-time nanny. Instead, I had to take all my DJ kit and everything you'd imagine that goes along with a two-year-old back to the States so my family could watch her before heading off to Japan. Once I was there, it was like having my old life back. Aside from the work commitments, long days stretched ahead of me in which I only had to look after myself. I could go record shopping for hours at a time. Imagine that! But talk about exhausting. The time zones, the late nights again, the gigs, the travel. Then back via The States to pick her up from my family and through a good old-fashioned New England blizzard to the airport only to get trapped on the runway and have to call my Mom to get us with more baggage than an Arabian camel train. The next day back it was to the airport to fly to Canada to connect to London. My toddler and I arrive in Canada and then THAT flight gets cancelled and we get stuck in a hotel. And then the next morning the hotel bus to the airport breaks down. Then I do.

Verdict: solo international travel with a toddler within three time zones, all for a spot of babysitting: not advisable.

Naturally, I wouldn't change anything for the world. Everything happened for a reason and I love my daughter more than life itself. Professionally, I became much more deeply involved in making music rather than just playing it and a better DJ with a wider repertoire. And now my daughter is grown, it's gone full circle – and when I'm playing in a field in Croatia for a thousand people, the only opinion I care about is hers. Naturally, she is very much into music and even goes to my gigs with her friends. She is studying music tech at 'A' Level (one of the only two females in her class) and even sings on my records.

Personally, I've never been happier and looking back, I can see how my career has been a slow and steady organic build which, in my view, is better anyways. Everything that happened needed to happen for me to be here. Here is good. To have a child is a blessing and having a great relationship with her is amazing. I wouldn't change a thing.

MEMENTO MORI

Can I name names? I'd like my bit to be a sort of memorial for my friend Howard Marks. Younger readers may need to do a quick Google, but he was famously one of the world's biggest weed dealers and had books and films about him. He was very much a part of the club thing. Very. I mean, he DJ'd, after a fashion. More of a Jamaican-style selector, but he had more gigs than I did. He was booked a lot in clubs and clubs are where I would always see him. And airports. He was a bit of a fixture in the discos of the late 90s. A part of what we do. He became a travelling folk hero of sorts. It wasn't just about drugs; he became a bit of a lightning rod, especially pre-internet, a totem for anti-establishment people to gather around. I can't say I knew him best. Many knew him much longer and way better, but I was part of his renaissance and was a friend from the week he was released from maximum security to the week he died.

The thing I would say that defined Howard (if there could be such a thing) is that he really *listened* to people. I don't know if it was inherent or something that developed in prison, but he was almost unique in that he would absolutely listen to what you were saying, digest, then observe and comment in a way that was really astounding. He made you feel special because he didn't just wait his turn to speak (and god knows he had things to say) but spent that time taking things in, then moved the conversation along and elevated it. That was the immediate impression I got from him in a kitchen at a party in the mid-90s. I had no idea who he was, and indeed he wasn't famous then. Or rather, he'd not yet reconnected to his 1970s notoriety. His book wasn't out, and he only recently was. Of all the people there, and it was a GQ Magazine party and chock-full of characters, he quietly made the biggest impression on me by a long way.

All I wanted to do was record that voice! You couldn't help but love Howard. It was his superpower. Like I say, he wasn't famous at this point, not to my generation at all. He was the oldest person in the room by some margin and would continue to be wherever we met. He stayed like that for the rest of his life, always a patriarchal figure. Always involved in what was new and fresh but in an effortless way. Some older types in younger crowds can be a bit sad, desperate, and maybe even a bit pervy. Not at all with 'H'. He was very at ease and made others feel easy, like The Fonz from 'Happy Days' (who, when you think about it, was totally a massive dealer too).

H was also usually twice if not three times more intelligent than anyone around him, if not merely by dint of age and experience than certainly by his Physics degree from Oxford. Way smarter, but he never once wielded it like a weapon. Quite the contrary, really. He'd listen to total dimwits like me patiently. Rarely using his superior abilities to aggrandise or elevate himself, which he could have done with great ease. He was just genuinely humble and happy to be around energy and freedom. Even if I couldn't have put it into words at the time, I got that vibe from him. He had a sort of Zen-like calm to aspire to. He was always surrounded by acolytes a bit later but never had that cultish swami vibe some famous people have when boxed-in by followers. If anything, he always seemed a bit embarrassed by it all.

I made a recording with him at one point, again really just about capturing that voice. I am a huge fan of Richard Burton and Howard was easily the closest living example of that timbre and resonance. He could read a telephone directory and it would mesmerise. I got to record a spoken word thing. When it was finished, I went to meet him along with Shaun Ryder in a London hotel. The only place I could play the tape was in my car nearby. Sitting in the vehicle, I soon realised I was with two of the heaviest smokers on the planet. The stuff they were passing to me was FIERCE. I played it to them and after it finished, Howard said in those immortal tones,

"Ah yes, I like that. Very much. It's really rilly GROOVY."

I was exceedingly high and just spluttered and went, "Groovy?? GROOVY? who says 'groovy' anymore, H? where have you been for the last… oh!"

Next thing I remember was being significantly late for my DJ residency, which literally never happened before or since. As I arrived, the owner was at the door looking highly displeased. I explained simply: "So sorry I'm late! I was smoking weed with Shaun Ryder and Howard Marks."

The boss took one look at my face (a light shade of green) and shrugged.

"Guess we're lucky you made it here alive then." It was possibly the best and most immediately understandable sicknote you could ever have at a disco.

Not long after that, under the umbrella of the same project, I was directing a video with Howard in it. This was a man who'd never acted in anything in his life and spent, what was it? *Seven years* inside maximum security? He actually went on to appear in quite a few films but this was the first. I told him:

"H, have you seen 'Grease'? You are Frankie Valli in 'Beauty School Dropout'. Basically, you are god descending from heaven."

"Oh righto then," he replied.

…and totally got it, first take. Wallop! There were professionals involved that took days to do some parts. Took him about five minutes. He just had this ease about him. He really did radiate calm.

In private, Howard never used his voice or skills as a raconteur or to dominate. He was full of stories and could easily bewitch a crowd, but you'd more likely see him in a corner, smiling beatifically. Highly stoned naturally and very much the air of Santa Claus about him. A jolly old fellow sat in his grotto. This belied the steel trap of a brain he had. I mean, you don't elude the FBI and con MI6 for decades if you are dim do you? Incarceration and age did not dull him at all. For every smokey, droopy and jolly after-hours session with him, I'd be jetting about touring the planet and I would constantly bump into him. Usually in Zurich airport. It wasn't an accident, apparently. I asked him on one occasion: "H, how come I always see you here in Switzerland? I honestly didn't know you toured that much!"

"Oh well, you know, just keeping an eye on a few plants. Growing is legal here, you see. Selling? Not so much. Got to be careful, though, haven't I? Always watching, they are."

"Watching you? Still? Come on! Has to be ten years since you were inside?"

He just shrugged and nodded toward a set of bolted-down airport chairs, where a man was sitting holding a newspaper.

"Yoohoo! Hello! How are you doing there, George? Got everything you need for the day?"

H could make his big voice really carry if he wanted to, like an actor. To my surprise, the newspaper was dropped and the bloke stood up and almost ran away. I would call it a scuttle. A textbook scuttling was performed.

"See. Always watching they are."

This wasn't the only time he performed his party piece in front of me. Several times he'd call out a seemingly innocuous bystander and they'd leap up and leg-it when busted.

When I first met him, we'd spend a lot of time chatting and hanging out, but as he got more famous and we both worked harder and harder, the great pleasure of his company became rarer. I see him in clubs and he'd be surrounded. However, I'll never forget the time I got to hang with him for a sizable chunk during his peak. Once again, I bumped into him on a long journey, but this time we were both going to the same place for once. A gig at the big solar eclipse that was best seen in

Cornwall. Radio One had turned it into a mini-festival and it turned out we were getting the same train. Naturally, being the UK, the train was filthy, overcrowded and expensive. Packed with people off to stare at the sun like lunatic cavemen. Howard took one look at the cattle truck and said: "come with me…."

We walked into the totally empty first-class carriage. I know people think DJs go everywhere like this but not at all. I mean, at this point in my life, I'd literally never even set foot past the hallowed buffet car. Never been in first class on any form of transport. We sat down in the impossible luxury and he immediately got his little tin out and started purposefully building this massive parsnip of doom. So I figure, *OK, it's for later. Hope no one sees us.* Then he finishes it and sparks it up. I mean, I was a pretty green kid and was really shocked.

"Howard, man! What are you doing? You can't even smoke a normal cig on a train, never mind that… monster root crop!"

He fixed me with that gaze that never faded or clouded and calmly replied.

"What are they going to do? Arrest me and send me to the highest security prison in America?"

And after I finished laughing, we spoke for hours. He laid out his encyclopaedic knowledge of law and liberty and made a very strong case for everything, as was his wont. Bear in mind how refreshing this was; I mean, hey, I'm a DJ, so I speak to a lot of idiots, myself included. It was very interesting to hear the legal issues too. He touched on these things frequently in his live shows, but due to also being a touring act, I never got a chance to see any of them. That is until the very last one.

We drifted apart somewhat over the following years. I took to social media fairly well for someone my age, but it wasn't for Howard at all, so that kind of takes over a little. You stay in touch with people online but lose touch somewhat with those who don't use it. I think social media stopped me from using the phone to speak to friends for some time. He wasn't the only one I lost touch with. Some time passed. Then I heard he was seriously ill. I tried to get in touch with old managers and agents, but all had fallen by the wayside. I was sad, but by now, H was a superstar. A film about his life was in the pipeline. Mega stuff. My star had waned; I was a nobody. I also figured there was something a bit naff about trying to reach someone you'd not spoken to for years about their sickness. Kind of 'oo hello, not spoken for years but here I am now you have cancer'. I dunno… didn't feel right at all.

Eventually, one of his old managers got me a couple of passes for his live show. Apparently, H needed the cash, which was unfair, I thought. Someone ill should not be forced to work. Seemed very off. So I went to see it. I wish I hadn't. Backstage was full of 'characters' all trying to out-knobhead each other. It was the final London show (and his last ever, it transpired), so consequently, it attracted all the wrong people. I couldn't bear it, so I didn't even try to see him personally. Couldn't get past all the wreckheads anyway. Went out to meet my date.

Went in to watch the show with her and I could see straight away, as soon as he came on, I was the wrong person in the wrong place. The crowd was a sausage party of male dope fiends, chanting and honking and generally a bit sort of hooligan-y. Lots of people openly smoking, as you tended to get wherever Howard went. A one-man protest movement he was. There was a roar from his acolytes when he came on, but I just saw my old friend, wasted, thin and straining. He shouldn't have been there. He stumbled through lines he must have said a thousand times and the crowd didn't encourage him; they howled and booed like monkeys. They didn't know or didn't care how weak and ill he clearly was. I began hating everyone and every moment of being there. My date couldn't understand why I wanted to leave and never spoke to me again after we left early. She didn't see me crying as she walked away furiously. Not tears for her! But for what I had just witnessed. A truly grim spectacle. If I had known I'd never see him again, I might have tried harder to see him. I think maybe I knew then that I wouldn't.

I was actually happy to hear he passed surrounded by his beloved family. Delighted, if that is possible for such a tragedy. That news made up for that show completely. But to be so separated from my old friend, a mentor of sorts, really. Stood in a crowd while his wasting frame was cruelly and starkly lit on a stage. It was a lonely feeling, but I can only imagine what it was like for him. It's a strange life this, the life on the road. Very odd indeed sometimes. I'm also kind of glad at least I got to see him that once, even in such strange circumstances. It really was an honour to have known him. He elevated our scene in a way, gave it a sneaky gravitas. Reminded me, perhaps if no one else, that we are a protest movement at heart.

He wasn't a totem for hedonism like that braying, honking crowd held him to be, not at all. He was a serious student and subsequently a great teacher of *liberty* in the purest sense. He used what voice he had to speak of being free of puritanical shackles. I can imagine what he would make of cannabis being legal now in most of America after they hounded him so. If I knew him at all, he would shrug and say it just made perfect sense. 'Beneficial herbs', he called them. I mean, I wasn't even much of a smoker! For me, I followed him for his words. Delivered in heavenly tones. He wasn't perfect by any means and was the first to admit it, but he stood up, man! Stood tall. For that alone, he deserves every plaudit laden on him. As far as I'm concerned, he was everything a DJ or a person should aspire to be.

May his name live on. Howard Marks. One of the best of us. I won't ever forget him. This DJ life means you can get to meet some of the most amazing people you can imagine. The scene is a lightning rod for the world's oddest and most special. It's a privilege to have spent a lifetime in it. Now some of our stars are starting to fade, proving that it has been around for entire lifetimes. You can be born into dance music and die in it. That gives me strange comfort somehow.

Viva acid house. Long may it reign.

GLOSSARY

AAA – Arrogant Arseholes All

Acid – The burble, the beat, the botheration.

Acid house – A domestic edifice that has all the acid in it.

Advice from elderly DJs – The lowest coinage you can possibly spend, anywhere.

Afterhours/Afterparty – Seriously. Just GO HOME.

Alcohol – Society-endorsed mind-altering narcotic not to be confused with other, non-taxable – and therefore evil and dangerous – mind-altering narcotics.

Ambient – Music for libraries.

Album – Electronic music's ultimate vanity project

Artist liaison – A backstage childminder for adult toddlers in a club or festival scenario. A lanyard and day-glo bangle tree.

Arsehole – It's not now, or ever has been, 'Asshole', asshole.

B2B/back-to-back – An embarrassment of riches.

Bass – How, in fact, low *can* you go?

Berlin – Where all the fun went and got lost.

Bouncer – A word you'd better not use… OR ELSE.

Booker – A professional bluffer.

Brixton Academy – Neo-classical concert/rave-up venue in London's finest manor.

Cash and carry – Bling and buy sale.

Chicago – A hard habit to break.

Cocaine/coke/pure – The grout that holds absolutely nothing together.

Controller – Phat.

Crack – A drug that makes you want more crack/(US) a CIA-funded urban destabilisation project.

Dancing – An archaic athletic pastime once widespread, now used to fill the occasional spare moment between selfies, queuing for a smoke, smoking, queuing for a cubicle, doing drugs, and staring at the DJ like a total mooncalf.

Darude – A very nice, polite boy, despite the name.

Day-glo – A safety device for children and tradesmen using the brightest of colours to denote whom to very much avoid.

Doughnuts – No, YOU'RE a doughnut, you *doughnut*.

DJ – A human excess of product.

DTI – Professional fun killers.

Edible – Making it into a cake doesn't stop it being drugs, mate.

EDM – The commodification of something beautiful by late-stage capitalism. What all electronic music would sound like if we only did this for the money.

Electro – Not to be confused with electro.

Entourage – Hangers-on, a troupe of the talentless inadvertently amplifying the inadequacies of the equally untalented by the sheer presence of their numbers.

Fabric – If you know where to look, there is a Secret DJ-shaped groove in a particular corner of the floor from over 11 consecutive years of bi-weekly attendance.

Face, A – A known and aspirational quantity in a person. Someone you might like to be just as long as you never actually get to know them properly.

Female DJ – A DJ.

Fee/DJ fee – Blood from a stone. A stone that properly hates you.

Festival – Taking a highly questionable and chaotic animal and then releasing it blinking into the wild, a wild it has never even seen. An alfresco chaos vortex.

Fisting – Somewhat extreme puppetry. Oh, Sooty, what have you done?

Forum/online forum – Where people used to gather before social media to swap DJ tips, discuss the issues, hurl abuse and and tell each other your set at the weekend was shite and your shoes are nasty.

Frank Sidebottom – Hands-down Timperley's finest and quite possibly only export.

Free party – The greatest threat to public order since the repeal of the Corn Laws, apparently.

FYRE festival – The world very, *very* briefly showing justice to the very worst of us.

Gabba – Silly fast bollocks.

Glory hole – Wrong golf.

Gypsies – Along with fatties, gingers, shortarses and the lanky, the last people, it's totally fine for wankers to be openly horrible about for their sad kicks.

Hackney Wick – The latest transient hip hole.

Heaven – No actual celestial paradises available.

Henchmen – Now known as henchpeople. Presumably, some hench is a qualification.

Howard Marks – They just don't make them like that any more. And for some international authorities, that is probably just as well.

Ibiza – Still. Yeah.

Imposter Syndrome – See, 'DJ'.

Jungle – O mi GOSH!

Kebab – Something akin to an elephant's leg.

Ketamine – Urrrrrrrrrrr.

K-Hole – Extreme dissociative state brought on by ill-judged use of ketamine, a drug pioneered for battlefield surgery. I'll take a trip to another dimension; pay close attention. OK. Not great for paying attention, now I think about it.

K-Pop – Korean pop music, a form of audio SARS. On schedule to take over the planet by 2025.

Las Malvinas – Best not get this one wrong in the wrong place at the wrong time.

Lighting rig – Where one may frig.

Live PA – A needless elaboration.

Maxi Jazz – Famous spontaneous voguer and ageless sleep dodger.

Minefield – Easy now.

Magic mushrooms – Caution, may not contain actual magic.

Manager – Honestly? No idea.

Minimal – Proof positive that sometimes the cure is far worse than the disease.

Mix – Yeah, you are supposed to mix, you know. It's kind of THE JOB.

Old Bill – Nee Naw (…and repeat).

Ouija board – Social Media is basically a vast ouija board, innit? Millions of little sweaty fingers subconsciously pushing the cursor around to spell out their fear. And a few quite consciously pushing harder than the rest for a laugh to form petrifying sentences.

Pantomime – Oh yes, he did.

Pirate radio – Just like radio, only more beards.

Podium – A dancer's stage, a performer's kingdom, a narcissist's playground.

Policia – the praetorian guard of Ibiza's disco emperors.

Promoter – The main reason you need an agent.

Punter – A unit of punt. The coins that make up the entire value of the event and, as such, are by far the most important.

Rapture, The – Not the band, div.

Raval El – "If you do down to the woods today, you're sure of a big surprise…."

Ravemuck – Shin cack.

Record shop – An offline geographical IRL nexus where you could purchase and download tracks in physical form while being sneered at by someone in an obscure record label T-shirt.

Resident – Yeah. If you know, you know.

Ricardo Villalobos – The human eye at the centre of the wobblecane vortex.

Rider – Liquid tribute to the entourage.

Sequins – Stick-on personality. The cocaine of garments.

Scuttling – One of my favourite words, forgive me if I keep putting it in there.

Showing out – Getting fresh at the weekend, obviously

Shit – The other thing apart from music that comes out of DJs quite a lot

Sick – Quite good, apparently.

Socials/social media – Digital bile duct. A release valve of effluvia into a brown river of liquid evil.

Sound technician/sound man – Possibly the most important person there, and no one but him knows it. A rare human confluence of self-importance and arcane technical knowledge, asleep on a flight case

Soundcheck – Pre-gig technical run-through that's like a gym membership in February: often aspired to, rarely accomplished.

SoundCloud – A digital highwayman who doesn't even have the decency to dress like a dandy.

Spectrum – Bang on it, mate. In all senses.

Stickler – Keep it tidy.

Sybaritiques – French for massive pervs.

Techno – Yeah yeah yeah.

Threads – Ultra-realistic nuclear attack TV series from a time when an atom bomb was genuinely likely to drop on you, which was one of the many reasons we decided to start raving instead. Dancing was definitely more appealing than being evaporated in a vast fireball.

Tiesto – Very expensive Spanish gardening equipment.

Tour – If you pick up your landline one morning at home and expect someone nonexistent on the other end to do stuff for you, *then* you've been on tour.

Tour Manager – see books one and two

TUMBLEWEED – The physical inevitably of mediocrity.

T.W.O.C – Taken without consent.

Uncut – Oh, shut up. It's *always* cut.

USB – Actually had to fire someone once who pronounced USB as "OOsubb" with great relish, very often. Just for that and nothing else. Sounds awful? THAT is how annoying it was.

Venue – The space in which we tumble through the stars.

Vibes – Just like a glockenspiel, only made of metal.

Vinyl – Still? Christ almighty.

Villa party – Like a proper party, only it's outside, the booze runs midway through the first set and finding a taxi home is a nine-hour ordeal.

VIP – Vacuous ignorant parasite.

Wavey – Bit like a wave.

Wronghole – If you enter it, it will become immediately apparent.

X – A nameless DJ.

Yellow Pages – When you used to be able to hold the internet in your hands and if you were really strong, rip it in half.

Zammo – Bad boy/loser character from 80s BBC TV show Grange Hill who remains a hero to a generation. He comprehensively failed to just say no.

ACKNOWLEDGEMENTS
& AFTERWORD

And I died, of course. Not metaphorically, but I actually lost my life functions for five minutes in a coma from COVID, which is another book entirely. Then we found out a COVID-induced coma doesn't just disappear your muscles, but the integrity of your bones can go too. So I'm writing this from a hospital with a shattered leg and a year of wheelchair touring ahead. COVID is not 'over'. Not for millions of people. Readers of the other books may enjoy the very large circular irony going on here. The first book started in a life-ending vortex and the pattern doesn't seem to be stopping any time soon. If this shows anything, it is that life just never stops coming at you. On the plus side, I can report that you get better at dealing with it all.

Duly, I'd like to thank those who helped me get through it. As a citizen of nowhere, I had absolutely ZERO financial assistance or indeed help of any kind except from my family and friends. Hey! You really learn who your mates are in extremis. Absolutely shocking amounts of money came from a couple of people to help me, and if I only knew who you were, I'd name you in lights right here and now.

Without my Mum and Dad, I'd never have come out of this alive, and they would have known nothing of my unconscious predicaments were it not for the ever-trusty Brian Beezwax, defacto King of Ibiza. My excellent cousin/brother Paul also leapt to the rescue, flying in immediately from his home in Vienna. Then many of you named in this book contributed to a fund that kept the wolf from the door, helped me heal, and I truly wish I could thank you all personally. One day I hope to somehow.

The ambulance service of Ibiza took me to Can Misses hospital, then helicopter to Son Espases in Majorca, all of whom contributed to saving my life. Later the staff of Policlinica Rosario in Ibiza followed up by scraping me off the pavement and putting me back together not a couple of weeks later. The amazing Mr Sherman Harris got me almost back into shape with his excellent physiotherapy. It's been a ride.

Most of this book was done and dusted before these disasters. The delay was my being conscious enough to help Duncan put them all together. Duncan has been the rock behind this project since day dot, the voice of reason and the Jiminy Cricket on my shoulder, curtailing my obsessions and recklessness. I'd be nowhere without his constant glacial patience and even-handedness.

There is a note of serenity that follows in your wake wherever you go after a great personal crisis. I wouldn't change anything. I look back on my own story and now also those of others in here and see that it could not only never have been any other way, but was completely necessary to get to this point. And then you wake up and realise just how important this point really is, and absolutely every single one that follows.

I think the previous books thanks most mentors and friends. For this one, however, particular mention goes to our tour booker Liam Monahan and all the UK venues who flexed with me when everything had to be postponed, jiggled or cancelled. James at Sheaf St. Leeds was particularly patient and helpful, as were my friends at Golden Lion in Todmorden. I can't wait until it is really, properly safe for us to meet again. I will be there, the wheelchair is bought and the plans are in play.

My good friend and universally loved amigo John 'Johnno' Burgess was a brick as ever.

Mark Devaney, always.

Skiddle has been great.

Colin Steven at Velocity Press: thanks for all your patience and support.

Graham Sahara, prince of Pacha.

Foz. Just Foz innit. What a bloke.

Russel Brown.
Rainer Weichhold.
Nikki Gordon.
Thomas Gandey.
Jon Carter.
Mr. C.
Andy Kayll.
Simon Mu.
Alfredo Fiorito.
Colleen 'Cosmo' Murphy.
Roger Quilliam.
Private Eye.

Chukuma Charles Ojorojo Ijomanta. A lifetime of him.

My good mates in the Eivissa Barrio. Paradise Lost crew and all who sail with her. My mates down at Bodega, especially Tommy. Vanessa and Lorcan.

To my excellent neighbour in Dalt Vila, Don Julio; gracias con mi corazon estimado vecino.

Shout out to my old Gladiator School, the Faith Mob and Boys Own. Particularly Duncan Brown, Chris Sweet, Simon Ewins, Howler, Terry Farley, Will Nicol, Adam Porter, Dan Poole and all that mob who brutalised me into shape over many years.
Ben Santiago's Memory Stick.
Jon Dasilva and Josh Posthuman.
Mik Quinlan.
Ambrose Bierce.
The Royal Literary Fund, thanks, Eileen.
Society of Authors Union.

National Union of Journalists.

Clanger. King of capes.

Martin Lefteri and Jessica Banks.

Bozak and Pioneer.

Dazzla and Grayson.

This book is dedicated to the memory of Jean-Louis Santoro. Merci, mon ami.

SPECIAL THANKS TO EVERYONE WHO
BOUGHT THE BOOK ON PRE-SALE

Nicholas Adams, Michael Ainley, Alistair Aitken, George Ankrett, Benjamin Annis, Richard Austin, Neil Bailey, Ian Bainbridge, Jonathan Ballard, David Barlow, Martin Barraclough, David Barton, Ryan Battles, Gemma Baughan, Tim Belcher, Joanne Bennett, Pardip Benning, Lee Berry, Mark Blee, Van Bolle, Keeley Boon, Mark Bowers, Chris Bradley, Alex Brady, Jayne Brayley, Keith Brosnan, Mitch Brown, Russell Brown, Christian Broyd, Markus Buhmann, Elliott Buss, Rob Calcutt, Ewan Cameron, Niall Carroll, Jeremy Case, Josh Castles, Alexandra Chadwick, Steven Clarke, Mike Cliffe, Mark Clowes, Travis Collins, David Cooke, Alistair Cooper, Rob Cooper, Ed Cotton, Samantha Craven, Thought Criminal - Fierce Collective, Andrew Darling, Jon Dasilva, Marc Dean, Marc Deeley, Carlo Delgaudio, Mark Devaney, Paul Dillon, Bob's Disco, David Dombrosky, Andrea Done, David Doughty, Alan Dunlop, Richard Dyer, Paul Eastburn, Michael Eckert, Graham Edwards, Iain Farrell, Lynn Fergusson, Jonny Fieldhouse, Barry Firth, Robyn Fletcher, Gavin Ford, Karen Ford, Tom Forrest, Tim Forrester, Joel Fowler, Mike Foy, Paul Francombe, Mary Freer, P & J Gallagher Chimney Sweeps, Mark Gillam, Dave Glennon, Max Forbes Gower, Rob Gray, Chris Greenfield, Sean Griffin, Paul Growns, Austin Hackett, Martin Hanna, Rob Hardy, Craig Harrop, Barney Harsent, Tara Katherine Hawes, Ryan Haxton, David Hazell, Matt Head, Jonny Henfrey, Kai Hepworth, Steven Hicks, Laura Higgins, Gaynor Higginson, Keith Hill, Neil Hill, Lynsey Hoskins, Thomas Hnatiw, Mark Holmes, David Howie, Andy Huckle, Marc Jackson, Steve Jackson, Adam James, Michael Jardine, Anurag Jha, Lorie Johnson, Shane Johnston, Danny Joseph, Matt Keighley, Dan Kelleway, Ross Kemp, Si Kemp, John Kirkham, Steffen Korthals, Inara Kreica, Catriona Lang, Claire Lanigan, Rosie LeBall, Adrian Lightly, Ian Lloyd, Gary Lockerby, Grigory Loginov, Neil Lumsden, David Lynam, Mario Macari, Ali Mackay, Scott Maclennan, Ed Mahon, Chris Marsden, Ben Marsh, James Masters, Alex Martin, David Martin-Jewell, Adrian Matheson-Bruce, Nichola Mayer, Paul Macdonald, Liz McAulay, Ian McGee, Alan McGregor, Kevin McLaughlin, Kay McMahon, Andy McManus, Gregor Mcpake, Gareth Mellor, Mundia Miles, Griff Miller, Daniel Mouse Moore, Lee Monaghan, Wayne Morgan, Christopher Murphy, Tim Murray, Patrick Neary, Doug Newman, Paul Nichols, Gareth Noyce, Matthew Parsons, Steve Parsons, Shane Perkins, Michelle Pettitt, Paul Pickering, Paul Pinder, Scott Pirie, Gerald Powell, Carl Puttnam, James Puttock, Tom Ralph, Mark Ratcliff, Damien Ratcliffe, Craig Reid, Stuart Ridley, Terry Riley, Cyrille Rivallan, Craig Robinson, David Round, Ben Russell, Marc Samuel, Rob Sanders, Hannah Saunders, Robert Schon, Konstantin Semionov, Marc Seven, Jes Sewerin, Lee Seymour, Ann-Elizabeth Shapera, Ian Shelley, Paul Shirley, Claire Shrimpton, Robert Sillitoe, Mark Simpson, Sean Sinclair, Jon Slade, Gregory Smith, Martin Smith, Jon Smith, Pablo Smet, Jason Stapleton, Jacob Stone, Leigh Strydom, Chris Sweet, Michael Taylor, Rebecca Thompson, Danny Toft, Carly Tonkin, Daniel Torres, Rowan Triffitt, Edward Tully, Paul Twomey, Tim Underwood, Simon Uren, Jenny Veitch, Mark Walker, Matthew Ward, Roland Warren, Andrew Wedgwood, Hugh Wernham, Simon Westfield, Alex Woodhall, Dominik Zapadka